DISCOVERY

The title page of Gerard and Cornelis de Jode's atlas, Speculum Orbis Terrae, *1597, was elaborately decorated with the picture of a strange long-necked marsupial with twins in its pouch. Decades before Europeans set foot on the Australian mainland, was this the imagined form of a kangaroo?*

DISCOVERY

THE
QUEST
FOR THE
GREAT SOUTH LAND

MIRIAM ESTENSEN

ST. MARTIN'S PRESS
NEW YORK

Title page: Title page to *Speculum Orbis Terrae*, Cornelis de Jode, 1593
(Mitchell Library, State Library of New South Wales, Sydney)

St. Martin's Scholarly and Reference Division
175 Fifth Ave, New York, New York 10010

First published in Australia in 1998 by Allen & Unwin.
First published in the United States in 1999 by St. Martin's Press.

ISBN: 0-312-21756-0

Cataloguing-in-Publication: data entered with the Library of C

Set in 10/14 Caslon 224 Book by Bookhouse Digital, Sydney
Printed and bound in Australia by Griffin Press

First edition: January 1999

10 9 8 7 6 5 4 3 2 1

For Arvid Karl, who also sailed

Contents

Acknowledgements

In following the trail of the Great South Land, I acquired debts of gratitude to many people and institutions. To the staff of the Mitchell Library of the State Library of New South Wales, I owe much for time, advice and sources, and for sheer inspiration in being shown some of the library's historical treasures. My special appreciation goes to Paul Brunton, Cheryl Evans, Jennifer Broomhead and Elizabeth Ellis. My thanks also to Natalie Camaleri of the Queensland Museum, to Peter Gesner of the Maritime Archaeology Section of the Queensland Museum, and to Dr Patrick Quilty of the Australian Antarctic Division, Hobart; to Dr Mickey Dewar, Museum and Art Gallery of the Northern Territory, and Claire Roberts and Paul Donnelly of the Powerhouse Museum, Sydney—all of whom provided information on some otherwise obscure historical and archaeological questions. Another archeological puzzle was generously addressed by Dr John Stanley of the Geophysical Research Institute of the University of New England, as were my questions on New Zealand finds by Dr Robin Watt of Wellington, New Zealand.

My debt to the Western Australian Maritime Museum and the Western Australian Museum is considerable—to Jeremy Green and Myra Stanbury, who bore with many queries and provided a range of information, and to C. E. Dortch.

Thanks are due also to David Nutley and Tim Smith of the Heritage Branch of the New South Wales Department of Urban Affairs and Planning, to Denis Gojack, Historical Archaeologist of the New South Wales Parks and Wildlife Service, John Sharpels of Museum Victory, Melbourne, to the staff of the Institute of Marine Science, Townsville, Queensland, and to Margaret Lawrie of the John Oxley Library of the State Library of Queensland, whose enthusiasm for early Australian history did much to stir my own.

My appreciation also to Elizabeth Feizkhah, for her valuable help in shaping the final manuscript, and especially, to John Iremonger, Academic Publishing Director, Allen & Unwin, whose interest allowed this book to be. To my family I owe a very special debt for their unfailing help and encouragement in every possible way.

1.

A Time Before Time

Out of the dark ocean that sheeted the earth four billion years ago a ragged outcrop of rock erupted into a lifeless world. It was a segment of the land that was to become the tawny continent of Australia, and tiny zircon crystals which came to rest in it are the oldest known fragments of earth's crust. In time the warm waters around this rocky shelf shared the earth's strange, rich marine life of algae, molluscs and echinoderms, sponge-like organisms, trilobites and countless other creatures.

In the 200 million years or so that followed, the future Australia became part of Pangaea, the solitary megacontinent in an ocean that covered more than two-thirds of the earth. Plant life proliferated into dense, primitive forests. Amphibians flourished and reptiles evolved, among them the dinosaurs.

Some time after 245 million years ago monumental rifts opened a seaway across Pangaea, creating Laurasia to the north and, to the south, Gondwana, a supercontinent which in turn would break apart to become South America, Africa, India, Antarctica and Australia. The magnetic poles shifted, land masses moved, the earth's crust heaved and

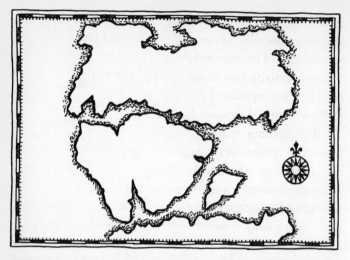

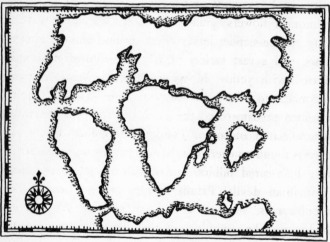

Some 180 million years ago the earth's single landmass, Pangaea, was breaking up into the supercontinents of Laurasia and Gondwana (top). A hundred million years later (bottom) these supercontinents had separated into continents that began to resemble those of today. Australia was still attached to Antarctica.

folded. Ice ages came and went, and for millions of years at a time Australia lay under the flint-hard bonds of colossal glaciers. The sea inundated vast areas and withdrew. Volcanic activity laid down the great stretches of igneous rock that are exposed as dramatic granite hills and boulders in New South Wales and Queensland.

The rending apart of Gondwana was a long process. About 53 million years ago the last land bridge between Australia and another continent sank into the sea. Antarctica moved south. Australia drifted north.

Australia bore with it plants and animals once shared with other young continents, but in thousands of millennia of isolation these took their own evolutionary paths. There arose banksias with cone-like seed pods and colourful, cylindrical flowers; grass trees with their green tufts of long, needle-slender leaves; furry red and yellow kangaroo paws; and a vast variety of tall, spare eucalypts; wattles dusted with yellow blossoms; scented, brown-flowered boronias and others. Sea-encompassed, Australia acquired no alien predators and the marsupial life that was nearly exterminated on other continents evolved freely into species found nowhere else, among them kangaroos, koalas, tiny long-eared bilbies, and ferocious little black-furred Tasmanian devils. Primitive egg-laying mammals, the monotremes, survived as the duck-billed platypus and hedgehog-like echidna. Another survivor was the Queensland lungfish, one of the few species of fish able to breath air. Alone, Australia developed a largely unique flora and fauna that millions of years later its European discoverers would regard almost with disbelief.

About 70,000 years ago the world entered another ice

age. Much of the its water was locked into vast, deep ice sheets, and sea levels were 100 metres or more lower than they are today. During this time human beings probably migrated into Australia. Most likely coming from Southeast Asia, they crossed many of the present seaways on dry land, including Torres Strait, which now separates Australia and New Guinea. Between Indonesia and northern Australia there were, however, channels up to 100 kilometres wide, which people would have had to cross, possibly on rafts.

Giant marsupials—great wombats and kangaroos, bull-sized diprotodonts, marsupial lions—and huge flightless birds roamed Australia when its first human occupiers arrived. Middens, hearths and stone tools show how they spread throughout the continent over the next 30,000 years or so. During a time of glaciation they wandered across a dry channel into Tasmania, to become separated from the mainland by rising sea levels some 14,000 to 15,000 years ago.[1] These rising seas also flooded Australia's northern land bridges, and isolated, unknown to the outside world, the continent's inhabitants pursued their hunter-gatherer way of life undisturbed.

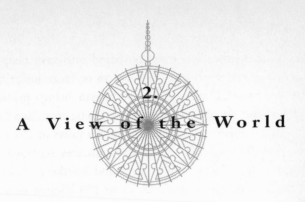

A View of the World

Over five centuries before the birth of Christ, in the Greek colony of Croton in southern Italy, the philosopher Pythagoras and his followers arrived at a reasoned conclusion that the earth was round. The sun and the moon were obviously spherical; it was only logical to assume the earth was too. This view eventually gained general acceptance among classical Greek thinkers, including Aristotle. Later scientist-philosophers, most importantly Erathosthenes, calculated the circumference of the earth. The precise length of their units of measurement, *stadia*, is not certain, but some results came to about 45,000 kilometres, just 11 per cent beyond the true circumference. From their studies there developed a belief that was to shape Western man's view of the globe for centuries: that the earth's land mass of Europe, Asia and north Africa must be balanced by a large continent dominating the southern half of the planet.

This view was most cogently articulated by the Greek astronomer and geographer Ptolemy, working in Alexandria, Egypt, in about A.D. 140. His *Geographia* presented a description of the earth that thirteen centuries later, after the long intellectual inertia of the Middle Ages, was revived in a new age of aggressive curiosity about the world. Maps then drawn in accordance with Ptolemy's instructions and information showed Mediterranean lands in considerable and largely correct detail. Northern Europe, Asia and the rest of Africa sprawled away amid many inaccuracies. The Americas did not exist, nor did Australia. Instead, across the bottom of the globe and extending through most of the southern hemisphere to join with Africa and Asia was a vast, irregularly shaped region that European map-makers from at least the fourteenth century labelled Terra Incognita, 'unknown land'. They looked upon it as undis-covered but, due to its connection with Africa and Asia, not entirely inaccessible, and the awakening intellectual energies of the age began to grapple with the puzzles of its existence. Logic required that it be there to keep an otherwise unbalanced planet from tumbling into space. Analogy suggested that it largely duplicated the geograph-ical zones of the northern hemisphere. The Spanish scholar Juan Luis Arias de Loyola wrote to King Philip III, 'this part of the earth is as fertile and habitable as the northern hemisphere, for the south has of necessity the same distri-bution of zones as the north.'[1]

Renaissance princes, scholars and adventurers gazed at this geographical mystery and imagined cities of incredible size and wealth, peaceful, welcoming populations and end-less sources of gold. The concept of Terra Australis would possess men's imagination for centuries but prove to be an elusive goal that steadily receded before the widening arcs of maritime exploration. It would be another 300 years before it finally surrendered its secrets.

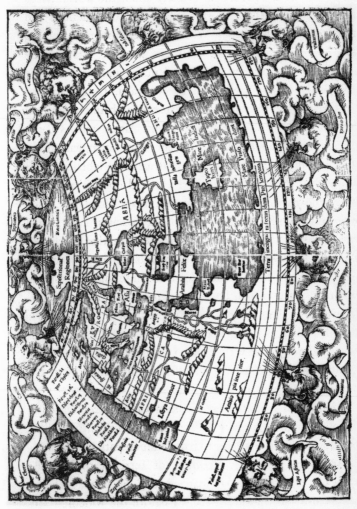

The Ptolemaic world map of 1482 displays the continent that was believed to span the entire southern hemisphere and to connect with both Africa and Asia.

(Mitchell Library, State Library of New South Wales, Sydney)

THE NEW VIEW

The belief that Terra Australis extended south from Africa and Asia was dispelled in the late fifteenth and early sixteenth centuries by the discoveries of the Portuguese navigators Bartolomeu Díaz, Vasco Da Gama and their successors. Columbus and the Spanish, French and English explorers who followed gave the mapmakers of Europe partial outlines of the eastern coasts and islands of the Americas. In 1520 Ferdinand Magellan rounded South America by sailing through the strait that soon bore his name. Magellan reasoned that the land he saw to the south, which he named Tierra del Fuego, that is, Land of Fire, for the campfires he saw, was part of the southern continent. It would be another century before Tierra del Fuego was understood to be an island. Thus when in 1538 the great Flemish cartographer Gerardus Mercator published his map of the world, he incorporated Magellan's speculation and on the large southern land mass inscribed the legend, 'That land lies here is certain but its size and extent are unknown.'[2] It was a very confident statement that firmed further the challenge of an undiscovered continent capping the lower reaches of the planet.

Mercator's successors followed his lead. Abraham Ortelius's world map of 1570 also depicted the southern land, amending its name from Terra Incognita to an assured Terra Australis Nondum Cognita, 'Southern Land Not Yet Known'. On his map of 1587 Rumold Mercator, Gerardus's son, abbreviated this to a simple Terra Australis. On both maps the land mass encircles the entire southern hemisphere, extending north in large promontories to above the Tropic of Capricorn near New Guinea and Indonesia and dropping back to the south below Africa and South America. Place names were inserted along the coast in what is the approximate location of Australia—regions designated Maletur, Lucach and Beach. These names derived from faulty transcriptions and outright misunderstandings of Marco Polo's descriptions of today's Malaysia and Indochina, and on the expanse of Terra Australis both Ortelius and Rumold Mercator stated, 'That vast countries exist there follows from the records of the Venetian Marco Polo.'[3] Magellan's term Tierra del Fuego remained on an area separated from South America by a narrow seaway. Such names gave even greater solidity to the idea of a southern continent.

How did Europeans visualise this gigantic unknown? To Maletur, Lucach and Beach, Ortelius and Mercator added the legends *provincia aurifera*—'gold-producing land'—and *scatans aromatibus*, or 'overflowing with spices', again borrowing from Marco Polo. A strikingly definite but otherwise unsupported statement appeared on the reverse of a 1593 map of New Guinea by Cornelius de Jode:

> On the south of this region [New Guinea] is the great tract of the Austral land, which when explored may form the fifth part of the world, so wide and vast is it thought to be.[4]

Four years later Cornelius Wytfliet wrote in the text of his atlas, 'The Terra Australis begins at two or three degrees below the equator'.[5]

Shortly after, the Duke of Sesa y de Vaena, Spanish ambassador to the Vatican, discussed Terra Australis in a letter to his king:

> from what has been seen so far in both the old provinces of the world and in those newly discovered [the Americas], ... there cannot fail to be found in that region land which is very good, very rich and temperate.[6]

Several books on travels in the East were now circulating in Europe, stirring the imagination of their readers—and those who merely heard of them—with accounts of treasure and wonders in little-known parts of the world. In the early 1500s the Italian adventurer Lodovico Varthema described the splendours of Vijayanagar in India, and Pegu, the capital of Myanmar, while towards the end of the century the Dutch Jan Huyghen van Linschoten recounted his six years in India, as well as the experiences of other travellers, in two widely read books. He also discussed Java, which he did not visit, speculating on whether or not it was an island. 'Some thinke it to be firme land, [and parcel] of the countrie called Terra Incognita,'[7] he wrote.

Earlier an unidentified writer had produced under the name of Sir John Mandeville a volume of travel adventures which he claimed to be his, but which were in fact taken from previous works, stories which he retold with many embellishments. A marvellous array of incredible events, strange customs and fabulous creatures made his *Travels* immensely popular reading throughout Europe for some 300 years. Westerners were, in fact, prepared to believe in marvels almost anywhere beyond Europe.

These accounts also received serious attention. Christopher Columbus read Mandeville's *Travels*. Mapmakers studied the travellers' descriptions. On his world map of 1569 Mercator noted that while Mandeville was a teller of tales, his opinion on the location of Java was not to be overlooked.[8] In his atlas of 1572 Ortelius cited as authorities 'M. Paulus Venetus, Lodouicus Vartomannus, et Ioannes Mandeuilius'[9] that is, M. Polo the Venetian, Lodovico Varthema, and John Mandeville. He added, however, that Mandeville's work also contained many fabulous stories. The Bible itself lent weight to the likelihood of a forgotten source of riches across the sea.

> King Solomon also built ships at Ezion Geber . . . And Hiram sent his men—sailors who knew the sea—to serve in the fleet with Solomon's men. They sailed to Ophir and brought back 420 talents of gold, which they delivered to Solomon.[10]

By the sixteenth century Ophir was believed by many to be somewhere in the South Pacific.

Actual discoveries also reinforced belief in a Great South Land. The Spanish navigators Alvaro de Mendaña de Neira and Pedro Fernández de Quirós were convinced that the South Pacific islands they came upon were part of this continent. Quirós wrote to Philip III of Spain on 'The greatness of the land newly discovered . . . Its length is as much as all Europe and Asia Minor as far as the Caspian and Persia.'[11]

In 1616 the expedition of Willem Schouten and Jacob Lemaire sailed from the Netherlands to 'discover new and unknowne Countries'.[12] In the far South Atlantic the explorers fleetingly saw ice-bound cliffs, which were soon taken for part of the southern continent, but in rounding Tierra del Fuego they saw only ocean to the south. The land thought by Magellan to be part of Terra Australis was obviously an island. On maps the southern continent retreated a little below South America, but otherwise it remained Terra Australis, sometimes with the added name of Magallanica and always, to the men who studied its mysterious outlines, vast and enigmatic.

Was the South Land inhabited? Opinions differed. Church authorities generally upheld the view of St Augustine, who centuries before had declared that the 'fable that there are Antipodes . . . men who walk with their feet opposite ours . . . is on no ground credible.'[13]

Whoever wrote as Sir John Mandeville disagreed. Those in the 'Antartyk' are 'feet ayen [against] feet' of those dwelling in the Arctic, and those dwelling under us are 'feet ayenst feet' with us, he wrote.[14] In *Imago Mundi*, his great work of 1410, the French theologian Cardinal Pierre d'Ailly maintained that entire earth might be inhabited. By 1602 the Duke of Sesa y de Vaena was assuring King Philip III of Spain that the South Land was 'very densely inhabited'.[15]

The inhabitants of Terra Australis were visualised in diverse ways. Maps were drawn depicting exotic Asiatic populations. Quirós assumed that the people would be 'numerous' and, like those he had seen in the Pacific islands, 'simple heathens, divided into tribes',[16] while the Dutch, hoping for the kind of contacts they had made in India and Indonesia, instructed their explorers to investigate the people's 'method of building houses . . . dress, arms, manners, diet, means of livelihood, religion, mode of government, wars'.[17]

Over the centuries the vision of the Great South Land hovered like a mirage, elusive and changing until voyage by voyage its mystery was peeled away to finally reveal the reality of the planet's fifth continent.

THE IMPETUS FOR DISCOVERY

In the fourteenth and fifteenth centuries the geographical and intellectual borders of the mediaeval world expanded as the multiplicity of petty fiefdoms coalesced into kingdoms with growing reach and power. The Crusades had taken thousands of Europeans from their native fields and strongholds, broadening their knowledge of the world and sharpening their appetite for change. An awakening desire to observe, to experience and to question was pushing aside some of the past centuries' acceptance of precedent and dogma. The focus moved from God and future salvation to man and present concerns. Admiration for man's achievement displaced superstitious fears of the past as people looked with new eyes on the magnificent ruins of Greece and Rome. When in 1453 Constantinople fell to the forces of Mehmet II, Ottoman sultan of Turkey, European scholars found themselves sharing the classical documents, largely forgotten in the West, that Byzantine refugees brought with them into Italy. Among them were the works of the geographer-astronomer Claudius Ptolemy.

As trade and commerce, backed by developing banking systems, gathered pace, the general standard of living rose. As countries grew, national armies increased in size and number. To provide for these, there was a surging demand for gold and silver, for gems, for silk and for the spices important in preserving food and making it more palatable. The source of these commodities was the East, from where they came overland, but on the new maps drawn from Ptolemy's data, there was also a strange, wide land of unknown possibilities in the far south.

Certain technical advances coincided with these events. One was the invention of the printing press, which made it possible to spread information quickly and cheaply. In 1477 some 500 copies of Ptolemy's *Geographia* were printed in Bologna, and other editions followed elsewhere in Italy and in Germany.[18] Less than 40 years later there were printed seacharts designed for shipboard use. There were advances in shipbuilding and navigation. New types of ships, on which square and lateen sails were combined to suit wind conditions, could undertake ocean voyages with a reasonable degree of safety. The marine compass had become a commonplace addition to navigation by sun and stars, winds and currents, and other navigational devices followed—the cross-staff, back-staff, quadrant and astrolabe, all designed to measure the angle between the horizon and a celestial body, usually the sun at zenith by day or the North Star by night. With readings from these instruments together with astronomical tables, mariners could determine their latitude with some accuracy. Another invention was the portolan chart, a map on which a network of lines represented compass bearings, and which a pilot could use to work out the heading he needed to get where he wanted to go. Early charts, however, disregarded the earth's curvature, and their north–south meridians, drawn running parallel, gave false readings of distances. Of vital significance, too, was the development of guns, which gave both real and psychological power to mariners venturing into unknown parts of the world.

None of these improvements changed the essentially cruel conditions of life on board. The small wooden ships were never entirely still upon the water and in rough weather were flung about, along with everything and everyone in them. Yet wet and plunging decks had to be crossed, tillers held steady and sails adjusted at frightening heights despite buffeting winds and sometimes icy conditions. Below deck, quarters were dark, rat-infested and fetid, crowded with wet clothing and unwashed bodies, at times bitterly cold or stiflingly hot. Injury, illness and death were never far away. Men lost their footing and fell or were struck by the violent lashing about of a taut cable suddenly released or a spar breaking in a storm. In 1676 a single wave swept 36 men off the deck of a Spanish galleon. Infection was commonplace, care rough and rudimentary. Disease spread quickly, whether dysentery, typhus or tuberculosis. Scurvy, with its acute pain, bleeding, loss of teeth and eventual death, could decimate a ship's company. And there were other ways to die. Always dependent on the wind, ships could be becalmed or driven off course, delayed for weeks or even months while food and water ran out and men perished from thirst and starvation. Antonio Pigafetta, the young Italian adventurer who accompanied Magellan, wrote of their Pacific crossing,

we ate only old biscuit turned to powder, all full of worms and stinking of the urine which the rats had made on it ... And we drank water impure and yellow. We also ate ox hides ... And of the rats ... [we] could not get enough. ... twenty-nine of us died ... twenty-five or thirty fell sick.[19]

In 1657 a Spanish ship which had left the Philippines more than a year before was sighted off the Mexican coast. She was headed south, with everyone on board dead.

Ships and men also simply vanished in storms or were destroyed in the most terrifying of all disasters at sea— fire. In timber vessels, wood-burning cookstoves, lighted lanterns, torches, gunpowder, even lightning, were constant dangers. The galleon *Santo Cristo de Burgos* was two years overdue in her voyage across the Pacific before those awaiting her gave up hope. Eventually pieces of her charred planking were cast up in the Mariana Islands.

Violence could erupt when hard, angry, desperate or avaricious men fought each other, and there were perilous encounters with enemy ships in war, with pirates, or with native warriors. Of the Dutch ship *Duyfken*, returning to Indonesia from what was probably the first European coasting of southern New Guinea and Australia, an English observer recorded, 'there were nine of them killed by the Heathens,'[20] This would have been about half the crew, and many such incidents occurred over the years. Even on the later well-organised ships plying between the Netherlands and the East, an estimated 15 per cent to 20 per cent of those on board died during the months-long journey.[21] And there was fear, the indescribable terrors of ignorant and superstitious men in whom mediaeval beliefs still lingered —that at the equator the ocean boiled, that the biblical

Leviathan waited for them with flames pouring from its mouth, that on a strange sea even the familiar would fail. Columbus's *Journal* records, 'The pilots took a bearing on the Pole Star, and they found that the compass needle declined a full point northwest; and the sailors took fright.'[22] In this instance Columbus could explain what had happened, but captains could not always do so. And yet these men went to sea.

Why? The Portuguese historian Gómes Eanes de Zurara listed the desire to discover the unknown as first among the reasons for the explorations sponsored by Prince Henry of Portugal between 1425 and 1434. With the restless curiosity of the Renaissance, men wanted to know what lay beyond the rim of the ocean and, impelled by a peculiarly Western urge to conquer the unknown, they were ready to face fearsome dangers. In some, like Columbus and Magellan, there was a single-minded drive to prove something in which they believed. For those whose lives were not much more than bare subsistence— the majority of Europeans—voyages of exploration also held the lure of becoming rich on a share of a returning cargo of spices or gold. For captains there was the likelihood of high administrative positions in new colonies and dazzling honours from a grateful king. Columbus demanded and was promised one-tenth of all riches to be found in the Indies he discovered, a noble title and the rank of Admiral of the Ocean and Viceroy and Governor of the Indies. Often there was a religious motive, a conviction that Christianity must be brought to the rest of the world. A letter from one of his diplomats to Philip III of Spain urged that no time be lost in discovering that Austral Region, so far unknown, so that those peoples may have a knowledge of the Gospel and be brought into the spiritual obedience of the Holy See, and the temporal obedience of your Majesty.[23]

This view was expressed many times in correspondence and memorials, and Spanish and Portuguese explorers who claimed new territories for the king were invariably accompanied by friars charged with converting the heathen.

Some time around 1570 Portugal's great poet, Luis Vaz de Camões, described his sea-going countrymen:

spirited as lions and brave as bulls, exposing themselves to privations and vigils, to fire and sword, to arrows and cannon-balls, to burning heat and devastating cold, to the blows of idolaters and Moslems, to shipwreck and the denizens of the deep, to all the uncharted perils of the universe.[24]

It was a colourful description of the terrors of the sea, but a statement too of courage, will and an aspiration to adventure. Coupled with the belief that great, elusive territories lay beyond the horizon, these ideals contributed a powerful impulse to the discoveries that in time led to the unveiling of the Australian continent.

Into a Wider World

The nation of Portugal came into existence during the Middle Ages, expanding southward from a small region in the northwest of the Iberian peninsula until by the mid-1200s the little kingdom extended all the way to the southern coast.

With its shoreline facing the Atlantic Ocean to the west and to the south, the Portuguese had a long tradition of seafaring as fishermen and traders. Southward across some 200km of ocean lay North Africa and the Muslim states that had previously ruled Portugal for centuries. To the Portuguese, Africa remained dangerous, intriguing and mysterious.

AN OCEAN LANE TO THE EAST

In 1415 an army under King João I attacked and captured the Moroccan city of Ceuta. Henry, the king's third son, aged 21, distinguished himself in the battle and received the governorship of the city. Serving his father in North Africa in war and peace, the young prince became increasingly interested in the world to the south and southeast of

Europe, where camel caravans crossed deserts and mountains to carry textiles, salt, spices, copper, gold and slaves from Asia and the depths of Africa to Mediterranean ports. Watching this commerce, Henry saw immense opportunities for Portuguese trade and the propagation of Christianity. Yet the overland routes to the east and into the African interior were jealously barred to outsiders by Muslim merchants and local rulers.

Henry was a soldier in the profoundly religious, dedicated mould of the crusaders of centuries before. He was also a Renaissance man, with a restless mind and a passion for factual knowledge. His birth as a prince gave him wealth and authority, but behind this there was an unbending will. In a contemporary portrait we see a long, lean face and a thick fringe of dark hair cut bowl-like under a large, draped black hat. The dark eyes are steady, the mouth full but firm, the expression hard.

Henry saw before him a problem of enormous interest and challenge. What, he asked himself, if the wealth of Africa and the East could be reached by sea? This would enable Portuguese traders to circumvent the monopolies held by the great block of hostile Muslim lands in North Africa and the Middle East as well as to bypass the hold of Venice and Genoa on trade with the Far East. It would establish an uncontested route to India and beyond, to the gems, silks and spices that Europeans coveted and, even more importantly, to the human souls which Henry, as a devout Christian, believed lay in dire need of salvation. On Henry's maps Africa's southernmost reaches were joined to the the Great South Land. That in itself—with or without a seaway through to the East—promised incredible discoveries.

The imponderables were many—the dangers of uncharted seas and equatorial climates, the very size and shape of Africa and whatever lay to its south. These, however, were problems Henry was singularly well equipped to tackle, both as an individual and as a prince of Portugal. In 1419 he left his father's court to become governor of Portugal's southern province, the Algarve, and established his own small court on the Sagres peninsula, the southwesternmost tip of Europe, where the sea winds sweep about the precipice that drops sheer into the Atlantic.

To Henry's court came naval architects, mapmakers, sea captains, travellers, and a diversity of scholars, who under his patronage worked on problems of geography, shipbuilding and navigation. As well, the prince dispatched sea-going expeditions into the Atlantic. He contributed to the exploration and settlement of the Madeiras, and later the Azores, but far more significant to him were the ships that year after year he sent south along the little-known, desert-edged west coast of Africa. Here the limit of previous exploration was Cape Bojador, possibly not the more southerly cape today known by that name but Cape Juby, east of the Canary Islands and some 1200km southwest of Portugal. Terrifying tales of whirlpools, water spouts, tempestuous winds and fiery equatorial heat, and of a giant magnet that would draw every iron bolt and nail out of a passing ship, as well as the actual hazards of reefs and difficult currents, surrounded the area. There were probably few sailors who had not heard of the Genoese Vivaldi brothers, who about a century before had set off down that coast and never returned. Henry sent at least fifteen expeditions to round the cape. All failed. Even one of his own courtiers, Gil Eannes, returned with failure and excuses. Henry reprimanded him harshly and sent him out again. In 1434, Eannes turned Cape Bojador.

Thus, slowly, with countless failures and many disasters, the coastline of west Africa crept southward on Portuguese charts, until, by the time of Prince Henry's death in 1460, his captains had reached the shores of modern Sierra Leone. The powerful impetus to exploration that Henry had provided did not die with him. Between wars and other crises, the kings of Portugal continued to send out their ships, and Portuguese navigators mapped new headlands and rivers, set up their *padrões*, the 2m stone pillars carved with the arms of Portugal, and established fortified trading posts to acquire gold, slaves and pepper.

Probably in 1484, King João II was approached by an intense young Genoese mariner with a plan to reach Cipangu, or Japan, and other parts of the East by sailing west. Cristovão Colom based his proposal on the accounts of Marco Polo, the biblical Apocrypha, the geographical work *Imago Mundi* by Cardinal Pierre d'Ailly, and the maps of Ptolemy and the Florentine cosmographer Paolo Toscanelli. Just how Columbus, as we know him, presented his theory to the Portuguese court is not known, but it appears that it did receive the attention of a learned commission. The idea was not new. The existence of islands to the west of Europe was part of the sea lore of the time. More importantly, educated people knew very well that the world was a sphere; it was only logical to conclude that the East could be reached by sailing west.

The Portuguese commission, however, rejected Columbus's proposal. Among their reasons seems to have been skepticism about his estimates of the distance westward between Europe and the East, but it was also a fact that Portugal had committed decades of time and money, and probably her immediately available ships, to the search for a way to the East around Africa. Columbus left Portugal to seek royal patrons in Spain. Four years later, in 1488, Bartolomeu Días successfully doubled the Cape of Good Hope and Portugal's way to India lay open. Africa was shown not to be joined to Terra Australis. The Great South Land was yet to be found.

After Columbus's voyage of 1492 and the territorial claims he made for the Spanish monarchy, both Spain and Portugal became acutely concerned for their respective rights in what they regarded as newly opened parts of the earth. In 1493 Pope Alexander VI decreed a line of demarcation running from pole to pole 100 leagues—about 600km—west of the Cape Verde Islands. Spain would henceforth have exclusive rights to all lands and seas west of the line and Portugal would retain her rights to Africa and the ocean routes to the East. Neither country was to occupy any territory already held by a Christian ruler. King João of Portugal, however, was not satisfied and opened direct negotiations with Spain. At a meeting of Spanish and Portuguese ambassadors the following year at Tordesillas in Spain, the line was moved to 370 leagues, about 2000km, west of the Cape Verde Islands. There was no agreement on where these two hemispheres of power would meet on the opposite side of the globe. At the time, with no accurate means of establishing longitude, no one really knew where the continuation, or counter-meridian, of the Tordesillas line would fall.

INDIA AND BEYOND

Portugal pressed on with her sea route to the East. In July 1497 four ships and 170 men under Vasco da Gama sailed from Lisbon with orders to reach India. Rounding the Cape of Good Hope, they steered north along Africa's east coast. They were now intruding upon the southern edge of the Arab world and met with open hostility from Muslim rulers and merchants in their thriving African ports. On 24 April 1498 Da Gama sailed east from Malindi in Kenya, and after an easy 4000km run across the Arabian Sea, dropped anchor on 20 May off the port of Calicut.

In Calicut Da Gama found a wealthy city with a busy harbour, ruled by a Hindu prince. Commerce, however, particularly in gems and spices, was firmly controlled by Muslim traders, who sent these luxuries by sea to ports on the Persian Gulf and the Red Sea, then overland by caravan to the Mediterranean and into the hands of Venetian and Genoese merchants. This hugely lucrative, mainly Arab monopoly now seemed threatened by the arrival of an armed fleet that, despite the sea-worn appearance of the men and ships and the contemptibly cheap trade goods they offered, was clearly the agent of an organised and menacing nation. Da Gama left Calicut at the end of August with a token cargo of spices and jewels and five or six Hindus who were to enlighten the Portuguese king on the customs of India. The journey home was harrowing, a struggle against contrary winds, starvation, scurvy and storms. The survivors, two ships and 57 men, reached Lisbon in the summer of 1499.

Da Gama's voyage was a triumph for him, for King Manuel I and for Portugal, and the follow-up was rapid. On 9 March 1500, less than six months after Da Gama's return, thirteen ships and 1200 men sailed for India under Pedro Alvarez Cabral. Early in 1502 Da Gama himself commanded a third expedition. Three years later the experienced soldier Francisco de Almeida was made viceroy of Portuguese territory in India, and sailed with a grand fleet of 21 ships to establish a lengthening chain of fortified trading posts on the Indian coast. His son Lourenço led expeditions to the Maldives and Sri Lanka, seeking alliances and commercial connections. This intrusion into their trading sphere brought retaliation from the sultanate of Egypt and other Muslim states. In 1508 young Almeida's ships were trapped by an Egyptian fleet off Chaul on India's central western coast. His legs crushed by a cannon ball, he sat against the mainmast and continued to direct his ship and the battle until he died. His enraged father destroyed an Egyptian fleet and its local allies in a battle off Diu in northwestern India. Only then and under pressure did he surrender his authority to Afonso de Albuquerque, who had come to replace him as governor of India. On the journey home Almeida's ship stopped at Table Bay, the site of today's Cape Town, to take on fresh water. A shore party landed on the plain below the flat-topped bulk of Table Mountain, and in a brief skirmish with natives some Portuguese were wounded. Prevailed upon to lead a retaliatory group ashore, Almeida died with 64 of his men under a hail of spears.

The pattern of Portuguese expansion into the East had been established. The goal was a monopoly on the valuable merchandise of Asia, and maintaining it required ships and secure commercial centres with good harbours. Thus fortified trading posts multiplied along the coasts of Africa, the southern Arabian peninsula, India and eventually Southeast Asia. The Portuguese were not interested in conquest, but expanded their mercantile power by alliances and good relations where possible, and by violent and ruthless confrontation where necessary. A small nation with a population of less than one and a half million, Portugal had limited manpower and few other resources, and its captains had to operate thousands of kilometres and many months away from home base instructions or support. Their opponents used both firearms and cannon, but the Portuguese had more and better weapons, a stubborn willingness to fight, superior ships, skilled and vigorous seamanship and well-built fortifications ashore. Although they were frequently outnumbered in skirmishes, they only occasionally faced alliances of any size and could generally overcome one community at a time, in many cases using local enmities to their advantage. Native princes frequently saw benefits in treaties with the Portuguese. That the interlopers were satisfied with coastal bases did not necessarily make them welcome, but they did not seize large territories or try to unseat established rulers. Their recurring cruelty did not endear them to local people, but cruelty was endemic in all sixteenth century warfare and accepted in many social systems as well. Portugal's mercantile empire grew, but remained precarious with its dangerously extended lines of communication, sporadic local uprisings,

The nao, *a small but sturdy ship, carried sixteenth-century Portuguese explorers to Africa and Asia. Typically broad-beamed and three-masted, they were built to accommodate valuable cargoes from the East.*

calls to assist one local ruler against another and, in the century to come, the armed incursions of other European powers. The rewards for these risks were high. And India, however rich, also served as a way station, a stepping-off point for further expansion. Eastward lay the Spice Islands and, somewhere beyond, the Great South Land.

The principal organiser of Portuguese naval and commercial hegemony in the East was Afonso de Albuquerque, who succeeded Francisco de Almeida as governor of India in 1509. The soldier-diplomat descendant of a noble family which for generations had served Portuguese kings, he had spent over ten years fighting the Muslim Moors in North Africa and several years more in exploration, raids and fortress-building on the coasts of east Africa, Arabia, Persia and India. Albuquerque was 55 years old, a lean, wiry man of medium height, with a high forehead and a massive triangle of a nose. After losing his fort at Goa in May 1510, he is said to have vowed not to cut his beard until he recaptured it. Apparently he did not do so even then, for in a drawing done some years later he has a very long grey beard. Fearless, fiery-tempered, brilliant and autocratic, he dedicated himself to his task with the passion of a crusader and almost no interest in personal gain.

As governor, Albuquerque began an energetic campaign to win for Portugal full control of all the main maritime trade routes of Southeast Asia. His method was to extend the system of strongholds and to back them with settled populations and sound trade connections. After retaking Goa in late 1510 and putting its Muslim defenders to the sword, Albuquerque set his sights on seizing Malacca on the strait between Sumatra and the Malay peninsula that served as the main sea lane to the Far East.

Albuquerque's thinking encompassed every aspect of his governorship: Portugal's maritime dominance, finance—he constantly pushed his trade officials to seek out new profitable products—and administration, in every part of which he involved himself. Each morning at Goa he rode out, carrying a stick and wearing a straw hat, followed by four clerks with pens, ink and paper. As he dictated, his orders were written down. Then he checked and signed them. Throughout the day his door was kept open for anyone who needed to see him, except during his midday hour of rest. In war his participation was no less personal. He lived among his men, shared their meals of curry with his spear propped beside him, worked with them in repairing Goa's fortifications after its recapture, and at Calicut in January 1510 was carried severely wounded out of the heaviest fighting, one arm permanently lamed.

Albuquerque's ideas for conquest were soaringly imaginative. To split the formidable concentration of Muslim power in the Middle East, he proposed to set Persia against the Turkish Ottoman Empire, and in other schemes suggested diverting the Nile River in order to starve Egypt into submission, capturing Alexandria and Suez, and attacking and burning Mecca and taking Jerusalem. As Albuquerque leaned over his maps, his eyes must have fixed at times upon the empty space south of Indonesia. His charts would have shown mainly distorted shapes representing Sumatra, Java and a few other islands, but he would have had, or seen, world maps that displayed a Great South Land. What a triumph for Portugal possession of that new world would be. Albuquerque, however, was fully occupied with laying down the strategic and economic foundations of Portugal's Eastern empire.

Goa rapidly developed into a naval base and the principal port of western India as well as the seat of Portuguese dominion. After taking the city, Albuquerque married some of his men to the widows of the defenders they had slain, and afterwards continued to encourage such mixed marriages to establish a stable, friendly population with connections to the hinterland on which the city depended for supplies. Innovatively for the time, he left the management of local affairs in native hands and asked for teachers to educate Hindu clerks in Portuguese procedures.

In 1511 Albuquerque attacked Malacca, now Melaka in Malaysia, and seized it from its ruling sultan. The town of timber and palm-thatch houses stretched along a low, jungle-backed shoreline, its wharves and bazaars humming with the activity of merchants from all over Asia as well as from Europe. Long a sailors' stopping place for fresh food and water, as well as a market centre straddling divergent trade routes, Malacca overlooked and potentially controlled shipping in the narrow strait, no more than 64km wide at one point, that separates it from Sumatra. Linking the Indian Ocean with the South China Sea, the Strait of Malacca is the shortest sea route from India to China. Its importance to the Portuguese was therefore immense.

Albuquerque's attention now focused on the Spice Islands or Moluccas, today's Maluku, in Indonesia. Pepper, cinnamon and a number of other spices were grown in India and other places, but cloves, nutmeg, and mace, the dried covering of the nutmeg seed, came only from the tiny islands of Ternate, Tidore and Banda in the Moluccas. Direct dealings with these islands could give Portugal an invaluable monopoly.

Obtaining intelligence was essential to Albuquerque's eastward push, and in April 1512 he wrote with obvious satisfaction to King Manuel that he was sending a section of a Javanese pilot's map secured for him by one Francisco Rodrígues. Late in the previous year Rodrígues had been appointed pilot to a fleet of three ships and 120 men sent by Albuquerque to explore the eastern Indies under the command of Antonio de Abreu. Their purpose was twofold: to reach and claim the Moluccas and secure the spice trade before Spanish competitors arrived, and to form some opinion as to whether the islands lay on the Portuguese or the Spanish side of the counter-meridian of the Tordesillas line. A claim that Ferdinand Magellan accompanied the fleet is very doubtful, but the fleet's second-in-command, Francisco Serrão, was evidently a personal friend of that Portuguese officer, who would later sail for Spain: Magellan had apparently saved Serrão's life while they both served with the Portuguese fleet in India.

The expedition had a curious degree of success. As the fleet followed the Indonesian islands eastward, Serrão's old ship caught fire and was destroyed. The remaining vessels, with Serrão, reached Banda, and here the determined captain bought a local junk, loaded it with spices and began the return journey. A few days out, the junk was hit by a storm and wrecked on a reef. Serrão and nine men survived and, perhaps as captives of pirates, seem to have reached Mindanao in the southern Philippines. Evidently from there Serrão was summoned south to Ternate by the island's sultan, travelling as either the pirates' prisoner or their colleague. Whatever the case, Serrão established Portuguese claims on the island and settled down to trade in cloves. He married a Javanese woman, had a son and daughter and was appointed by the sultan to command his forces in recurring wars with the neighbouring island of Tidore. Serrão steadfastly refused to return to Portugal or to a main Portuguese base, which raised concern, even suspicion, among his European masters. Some ten years after coming to Ternate he died, apparently poisoned by the enemy king while leading troops against Tidore. Serrão's letters to Magellan probably provided his friend with considerable information on the Spice Islands, particularly 'what was necessary for the discovery of, and the navigation to those islands', as the Spanish official Antonio de Morga wrote almost a century later.[1] Were Portuguese agents instructed to end this correspondence? We do not know.

The pilot Rodrígues, meanwhile, had returned to Malacca with new intelligence on the Indonesian islands. His work survives in a book of navigational rules and tables, rutters or sailing directions, 26 charts of coastlines from Europe to China and 69 panoramic drawings that show the northern coasts of the Indonesian islands Rodrígues passed on the way from Banda back to Malacca. Rodrígues made no mention of any islands south of the main chain of the Indonesian archipelago, nor of any region that could be construed to be Australia. His work was intended for pilots and included no speculations.

4.

Visitors from Asia?

Afonso de Albuquerque pored over the charts and drawings of Francisco Rodrígues. Here were marked out the farthest limits of Portuguese expansion, encompassing a storehouse of riches for Portugal's king. But just what lay beyond those carefully drawn lines? To the south, as world maps showed, a vast continent waited, unknown, undiscovered. But was it undiscovered? Could other outsiders have already reached it?

THE INDONESIANS

The Indonesian archipelago stretches almost 5000km, at its northwestern extremity almost touching the mainland of Asia and in the southeast coming within 400km of Australia. Contacts of many kinds between the island chain and the Asian mainland go back thousands of years. Court annals from China's Han Dynasty (206 B.C.–A.D. 220) record what the Chinese looked upon as tribute-bearing missions from parts of the archipelago, and Han pottery has been found at Indonesian sites. Contacts with India brought the people of the islands even more extensive trade and to some areas a Hindu-Buddhist religion, whose most impressive surviving expression is the monumental temple of Borobudur in central Java, built around 800. Arab traders reached Sumatra at some unrecorded date, and by the fifteenth century the Islamic faith was firmly ensconced in coastal settlements as far east as the Moluccas.

The Indonesian islands were politically fragmented into myriad local communities, some coalescing into minor principalities, others at times into substantial kingdoms. The ambitions of rulers and the demands of an extravagant court life often led to wars and piracy, but also to expanding trade. Princes and nobles desired the textiles, perfumes, precious metals and jewels of India, and the silk and porcelain of China.

Seafaring was essential to all these activities, and Indonesian sailors long ago learned the ways of winds and currents. Small craft plied the waters between islands, carrying foodstuffs, timber, resins, ivory, camphor, slaves and spices, much of this reaching markets in Java, Sumatra and Malacca, and eventually Europe, India and China.

Given their generations of sailing experience and their light yet seaworthy vessels, it is not surprising that at some point Indonesian sailors should have happened on Australia's coasts. Between the south coast of Sumatra or Java and a western Australian landfall lies an ocean world of thousands of square kilometres, empty except for the small, steep-sided fleck of Christmas Island. Much shorter, however, is a direct line from a southeastern island like Timor to Australia's Melville Island or the Darwin area. On either of these routes monsoonal winds would have carried a vessel to the south or southeast and, after the necessary wait while the winds turned, back again.

Just how or when Indonesian seafarers—particularly groups from Macassar, now Makasar, in Sulawesi—first reached the continent's northern coast is not known, but they did, and in the shallow, sunlit water around reefs and shoals they found huge numbers of trepang—bêches-de-mer or sea cucumbers. Dried and sailed back to Macassar, these were sold to merchants arriving annually in junks from China, where they were prized as a medicine and aphrodisiac. In many places across the north coast of Australia there are the remains of the pits and stone fire-places used in the preparation of trepang, and groves of the tamarind trees the fishermen introduced perhaps with the discarded seeds of the fruit they brought with them.

Establishing the antiquity of the trepang industry is difficult. The archaeological evidence is generally recent: earthenware similar to modern types, Dutch coins, and glass from Dutch-manufactured gin bottles, none—with the exception of a single coin from 1680—dated earlier than 1700.[1] Radiocarbon analyses of charcoal from trepang fireplaces have produced estimated ages of 400 to 800 years, but the reliability of these results is under question. Tests on mangrove wood like that used in the fires also seem to produce older-than-reasonable dates.[2]

One hint as to when the trepang industry began can be found in a sixteenth century Chinese treatise on medicinal substances which contains the earliest known mention of the sea cucumber. A century later there are numerous Chinese references, even in poems, to trepang. In 1615 the Englishman George Cockayne wrote to the English East

India Company from Macassar that a Chinese junk had in that year arrived there for the first time. It seems reasonable to assume that as demand grew and Indonesian trepang fishers depleted local stocks, they would have sailed farther and farther afield, eventually reaching the warm reef waters of northern Australia. Another factor was probably the expansion of Dutch control over other trade in eastern Indonesia in the later seventeenth century, which may have forced Macassans to look elsewhere for a profitable product in which the Dutch had little interest. Some 130 years later Europeans encountered trepangers on the northern Australian coast.

In the context of the trepang industry, then, the first Indonesians probably arrived in Australia less than 400 years ago, although small, unheralded groups of fishermen could have come before that, even if inadvertently. Did certain Indonesians, then, have some knowledge or tradition of land to the south, which they might have passed on to the Portuguese? Portuguese navigators are known to have had Indonesian informants, and informal exchanges between European pilots and local captains must have occurred many times. There is, however, no specific record of any early voyage to the South Land by either group.

THE CHINESE

In the seventh to twelfth centuries under the Tang and Song dynasties, China developed an extensive maritime trade. Some of this was conducted by Chinese merchants aboard sea-going junks, but numerous foreign traders— Arabs, Persians and Southeast Asians, as well as a few

Europeans—were also involved, drawn to the ports of southern China by the hugely attractive and valuable merchandise available there.

In the latter part of the twelfth century an inspector of foreign trade in China's southeastern province of Fujian compiled a geographical work, *Zhu fan zhi* or 'A Description of Barbarous Peoples'. The inspector, Zhao Rugoa, was a man of some status, distantly related to the ruling Southern Song dynasty. Zhao Rugoa's position put him in contact with the foreigners who frequented the ports under his jurisdiction, most notably Quanzhou, then a large, crowded city on today's Taiwan Strait. The outside world, except for its commerce, was generally of little concern to contemporary Chinese, but Zhao Rugoa's personal interest in foreign countries, peoples and products was keen and lively. He talked at length with Arab sailors, Indian captains, Persian merchants and others, asking questions and listening attentively, and later in his study took up his brush and meticulously recorded the facts he gathered. These he combined with some information from earlier Chinese sources, but the account as a whole remained straightforward and factual, free of the fanciful tales typical of other Chinese writers of his time.

The book's descriptions of foreign lands and their products are wide-ranging, with short references to places in India, Africa, and the Middle East, as well as Sicily and the southern coast of Spain, which became known to the Arabs, and longer, more detailed notes on Southeast Asian lands, including today's Indonesia. Nutmegs, Zhao Rugoa says, come from 'foreign tribes in the depths of the islands'[3] described as dependencies of Java, probably

Maluku, the Moluccas. Timor, which he lists among places where the people are fierce and primitive, is the southernmost point in Asia that he mentions.

Zhao Rugoa's countrymen took scant interest his work, which remained virtually unknown until it was uncovered by a Chinese scholar in 1783. Before that the only extant reference to the *Zhu fan zhi* is a single brief comment in a thirteenth century work.

A century after Zhao Rugoa, between 1311 and 1320, Zhu Siben, a mapmaker during the Mongol Yuan dynasty, produced in the form of an atlas a large map of the Indian Ocean and China Sea which again makes it evident that the Chinese knew of virtually the entire Indonesian island chain, from Sumatra to Maluku, but nothing of the lands beyond, especially to the east and south. Other works referred to the unknown as a region of barbarian countries bound by a world-encircling ocean. Here facts ended and imagination took over.

The zenith of Chinese sea voyaging was reached in the early fifteenth century during the Ming dynasty, about the time when, across the world, Portugal's Prince Henry was sending out his explorer-captains. The energetic third Ming emperor, Zhu Di, not only began rebuilding Beijing as his capital, with the fabulous Forbidden City at its centre, but also turned his attention to great ocean-going trade and diplomatic ventures. In 1405 he sent out a fleet of 63 large, five-masted junks and over 100 smaller ships, manned by a reputed 30 000 to 40 000 men and commanded by Zheng He, a Muslim Mongolian and an influential member of the imperial court.

Zeng He was the son of a noble who was also a *hajji*,

a Muslim who had made the pilgrimage to Mecca. At about the age of ten he was captured when Yunnan, the last Mongol stronghold in China, was reconquered by Chinese armies. The boy was castrated and sent into the army as an orderly. Clever, brave, a skilful officer and negotiator, he distinguished himself in the field and won important friends at court at a time when the emperor, Zhu Di, was extending trust and power to a cadre of loyal eunuchs who had supported his accession to the throne. It was Zeng He, then about 34 years old, whom he chose as admiral of his flotilla and as his diplomatic emissary throughout the East.

The fleet sailed to Southeast Asian ports, India and Sri Lanka, and in the succeeding years six additional expeditions of similar size, all commanded by Zeng He, visited numerous ports along the northern rim of the Indian Ocean and parts of Indonesia. As a statement of the naval power and diplomatic influence of the Chinese emperor, the expeditions would have been spectacular, and Zheng He commanded them forcefully. Encountering treachery from the king of Sri Lanka, he defeated the monarch in battle and took him as a prisoner to China. He returned from another voyage bringing the envoys of more than 30 Southeast Asian kingdoms to pay homage to the emperor, and sailed them back to their homelands on a subsequent trip. Clearly the voyages extended China's political influence across the maritime countries of Asia, bringing home tribute, intelligence and perhaps some commercial advantage. Exploration, however, was not one of their aims.

The embassies were suspended by Zhu Di's successor in 1424 and ceased entirely after a final voyage in 1431–33, probably as a result of new influences at court. Zeng He disbanded his crews and became garrison commander at Nanjing, where he reputedly lived in a 72-room mansion until his death in 1435.

There is no evidence that any of Zheng He's fleets came to Australia. The journeys are well documented and the regions they visited—the coasts of India, Vietnam, Thailand, Malaysia, Indonesia, Arabia and Africa—are known. This, of course, does not preclude the possibility that individual, unofficial vessels touched upon the north coast of Australia; Chinese merchants did visit even far-flung Indonesian islands. There is documentary evidence of Chinese trade goods in western New Guinea, today's Irian Jaya, in the late sixteenth or early seventeenth century. In October 1606 the Spanish navigator Luis Baéz de Torres sailed from east to west through Torres Strait, becoming the first European to traverse this passage. For weeks the Spaniards did not know where they were until, going ashore on an island now identified as one of the Pisang group off Irian Jaya's MacCluer Gulf,[4] they made a joyful discovery. As Torres later wrote to King Philip III of Spain, 'It was here in this land that I found the first iron and bells from China, and other things from there, by which we understood more surely that we were near the Moluccas.'[5]

Diego de Prado y Tovar, an adventurer accompanying the expedition, elaborated:

In the village we found an iron harpoon, such as the Chinese use, and hooks and lines from China, . . . and pieces of dishes of china clay, which was a good indication to us to give up the idea that we were lost, as we thought, and a sign that we were near where the Chinese trade.[6]

Such trade goods, of course, could have passed through many hands before reaching the Pisang Islands. However, a few days later Torres and Prado met a local Muslim chief and an Italian-speaking Moor, once the prisoner of Europeans, who told them that 'Chinese ships used to come in those parts to barter gold but they had not come for three years, and they also traded for black pepper.'[7] From some of these locations a venturesome captain might well have been tempted to look for markets to the south.

In 1751 the commander of the Dutch outpost in Timor reported to his superiors in Batavia that a Chinese trader from the island had, after seven days of sailing and drifting, come upon a coast to the south. Here he encountered people who sound very much like Aborigines. While the trader believed he had landed on an island, the Dutch official was certain that it was the coast of what was by this time known to the Dutch as New Holland. There are also other, earlier accounts of vessels being blown off course from Timor and finding land.

There is no reliable archaeological evidence of early Chinese landings in Australia. A Chinese soapstone figurine uncovered in Darwin in 1879 has been shown to be of relatively recent date, not a Ming dynasty product as was once speculated. Similarly, a shard of porcelain found on Winchelsea Island in the Gulf of Carpentaria off Arnhem Land dates only to the nineteenth century.

THE ARABS

Among the great sea-goers of the eighth and ninth centuries were the Arabs. In pursuit of trade they seem at an early date to have adapted the nomadic life of the desert to a similarly wandering existence on the oceans. The advent of Islam in the seventh century did nothing to alter this, and with its emphasis on proselytising and on a personal relationship with God, it may have been particularly suited to the traveller.

The Arabs followed ancient sea trade routes, the tall triangular sails of their dhows filling with monsoonal winds as they crossed the top of the Indian Ocean to reach India, Sri Lanka, and eventually Sumatra. Substantial evidence of their presence in the Indonesian islands begins to appear in the thirteenth century, and by the fifteenth century island and coastal kingdoms had converted to Islam at least as far east as Ternate and Tidore. Torres, leaving Irian Jaya in 1606 and proceeding west towards Ternate, noted that the people on the intervening islands were Muslim.

Early in the ninth century Arab scholars began working with Byzantine maps, and the Caliph al-Ma'mun (786–833) sent Syrian translators to Byzantium to buy other Greek manuscripts. The Arabs acquired copies of Ptolemy's works and would have been aware of the large continent he posited in the southern hemisphere. There are, however, no recorded voyages in search of it.

In 1944 a member of an Australian radar unit found five Islamic copper coins from Kilwa, in Tanzania, on a beach at remote Marchinbar Island in the Wessel Islands off Australia's Northern Territory. None of the coins bear

Carried by monsoonal winds, Arab traders in their dhows crossed the Indian Ocean to reach India, Sri Lanka and eventually the islands of Indonesia. Did they reach the northern coast of the Great South Land?

dates, but from the inscriptions, two may be from the tenth century and three from the early fourteenth. Strangely, Kilwa coins seem not to have been circulated much beyond East Africa. The puzzle is further compounded by the fact that three small Dutch coins and one from Liège in Belgium, dated from 1680 to 1784, were found in the sand in the same place.[8] Experts assume that all the coins reached Marchinbar by ship—but what ship? Or were they left there on two separate occasions, over 400 years apart? Arab traders, a Dutch or Portuguese shipwreck, or

Indonesian trepang fishers are among the possibilities. The site has never been excavated, and any answers may still lie deep in the sand.

Like the Chinese, Arab merchants probably found enough trade commodities in the Indonesian islands to satisfy their interests and no tales or evidence of spices, gold or other merchandise sufficiently convincing to entice them farther south. That an Arab trader might have been driven southward by storms and currents is, of course, possible, but no such sailor is known to have left a trace upon the Australian coast—unless perhaps the Marchinbar coins— or returned to tell his story.

Afonso de Albuquerque died in 1515, as he returned ill to Goa after the conquest of Hormuz, at the mouth of the Persian Gulf. He dictated a last letter to his king, had himself dressed in the velvet garb of a commander of the Order of Santiago, put on spurs and sword, and with a final effort stood to watch as his ship approached the stronghold he had created. He died shortly before dawn as the ship came to anchor. Despite sometimes daunting obstacles and furious opposition, Albuquerque had forged a mercantile empire in the East that was to endure for centuries. The Great South Land, however, had remained beyond his reach, and he never knew if others had found it before Portugal could do so.

5.
Beyond the Indies?

From the perspective of local Asian peoples at the time, the Portuguese were essentially sea-going merchants, better armed and bolder, perhaps, but otherwise not unlike other foreign traders who for centuries had done business on the margins of India and Indonesia.

In their aggressive curiosity, did the Portuguese ever go farther than their predecessors and penetrate the uncharted seas south of the Indonesian archipelago? Surviving maps and documents show that they had only limited information on the southern coasts of the Indonesian islands and less on the seldom-sailed waters beyond. In the sixteenth century, however, there were certainly rumours of land to the south, and their strongest lure was a spellbinding vision of gold.

ISLANDS OF GOLD

In 1512 there arrived in Malacca Tomé Pires, formerly an apothecary of the Portuguese court, whose reputation for diligence and honesty, and apparently his knowledge of the medicinal properties of spices, had brought him an appointment by Albuquerque as a secretary and accountant and 'controller of the drugs',[1] referring to the popular use at the time of spices as medication. In the course of his duties Pires travelled to Java and other islands, and eventually wrote *Suma Oriental*, a report to King Manuel on economic and geographical features of the East, from Egypt to Irian Jaya. Pires never visited the far eastern Indonesian islands, but he nevertheless assembled considerable information on the archipelago's people, the spice industry and trade in general. He seems to have combined persistent curiosity with objectivity and discretion, and to have been not only a loyal and industrious public servant but an interesting, intelligent man. He reported on what he heard in short, informative passages tempered with his own reasoned judgment. His interest was mainly commercial. The Aru Islands, less than 500km from Australia, were the source of the brilliantly hued *nore* parrots: 'which are prized more than any others'.[2] Timor, under 600km from the Australian mainland, was

> where the sandalwoods are ... The Malay merchants say that God made Timor for sandalwood ... I asked and enquired very diligently whether they had this merchandise anywhere else and everyone said not.[3]

Pires recorded frequently that goods in various islands were paid for in small quantities of gold. Sumatra, he said, 'has gold in great quantities',[4] produced at two principal mines in the island's central interior. Only three kings, he wrote, 'can collect from one mine and the other, which is the law of the land'.[5] The port of Baros or Barus, in the west coast kingdom of the same name—also known by the Malay and Arab names Panchur or Fansur—was an outlet for the wealth of the interior. 'This kingdom is at the head of the trade in these things in all the island of Sumatra, because this is the port of call through which the gold goes.'[6] To Barus and two other coastal communities, people from the Indian state of Gujarat came 'every year and do a great trade. One, two and three ships come every year.'[7] And Java, Pires added, 'has a goodly quantity of gold'.[8]

Pires's enthusiasm for travel, shrewd eye for business and ability to report in accurate detail were not lost upon his superiors. Eventually he headed Portugal's first diplomatic mission to the imperial court in China, where, after years of mistreatment and imprisonment, he died. His *Suma Oriental* was virtually forgotten until 1937.

On the subject of gold, rumour was far wilder than Pires's judicious comments suggest. João de Barros, Portugal's great sixteenth century colonial historian, wrote that in India there was widespread talk of an 'island of gold' southeast of Sumatra, and that the governor of Portuguese India, Diogo Lópes de Sequeira, was sufficiently intrigued by the rumours to dispatch an experienced navigator, Diogo Pacheco, to find the island. In the sixteenth century such an assignment was not remarkable. Gold, found in unbelievable quantities by the Spanish conquerors of Mexico and Peru, had fired Europeans with a consuming passion. By underwriting the economic growth and early industrialisation of Europe, gold became a source of national prosperity and power. Spaniards, Germans, Portuguese and even Sir Walter Raleigh for England were obsessively searching the jungles and deserts of the

Americas for gilded kings and golden cities. Europeans steeped for generations in travellers' tales of treasure in the East were more than willing to believe in Marco Polo's description of Lucach, which cartographers were now placing in the Great South Land: 'Gold is so plentiful that no one who did not see it could believe it.'[9]

The north coast of New Guinea had been sighted in 1526, and in 1528 the Spanish captain Alvaro de Saavedra Cerón, seeking an eastward route across the Pacific, followed it for some 500 leagues—roughly 3000km. His imagination roused by the island's huge size, he called it the Island of Gold. Headwinds forced Saavedra back to the Moluccas, and the following year he died at sea. Difficult winds, sightings of only very primitive people, and no further reports of treasure discouraged landings by later navigators. Saavedra's Island of Gold was not explored.

Diogo Pacheco, however, was certainly captivated by a vision of gold to be had for the taking. He made two trips from Malacca to Barus, where, on interrogating local people, he was told that the isle of gold was far to the southeast among shoals and reefs. Low-lying and fringed with palms, it was inhabited by black people who, though fierce, were willing to exchange quantities of gold for cloth. The trip was said to be long and hazardous, and many had been lost en route. Pacheco, accepting the story, sailed to the southeast and was lost with his ship, although some of his Malay crew apparently survived to bring the news of the disaster back to Malacca.

How much truth was there in the account given to Pacheco? The natives he quizzed might have been trying to protect their own local sources of gold with an alluring story designed to lead the Portuguese meddler astray. Perhaps they simply exaggerated tales they had heard from others. Or were they in all honesty recounting a local tradition that contained some kernel of fact? Could the island of gold they described to Pacheco have been the west coast of Australia?

Between Barus and Australia's North West Cape lie some 3200km of open sea. However, a ship bearing south from Timor would run between reefs and small, low islands, among them the Ashmore and Cartier Islands at the edge of the Australian continental shelf. This compares interestingly with the approach to the 'island of gold' described to Pacheco. The early seventeenth century Portuguese historian Manoel Godinho de Erédia, himself part Macassan, referred to sources, probably Asian, which said there had been commerce between Indonesia and a rich southern land which was broken off centuries before. The evidence he offered, however, was vague and confused. In 1838 the explorer George Grey discovered Aboriginal cave paintings in the northwest of Western Australia which he believed showed clothed human figures, possibly of Asian origin. The paint has now deteriorated so badly that it is impossible to see the paintings as Grey saw them, but they are known to be depictions, common in the region, of the mythical spirit beings called Wandjina.

Such false trails, however, do not preclude the possibility of foreign visitors to Australia's northern coasts, even Portuguese journeys for which no record survives. Portuguese commerce was a royal monopoly, entrusted to officers of the crown and subject to fairly strict accounting, but over the centuries there certainly was private trading as well.

The likelihood of Portuguese voyages would be all the greater if Indonesian sailors were aware of the land mass to the south. Francisco Rodrígues obtained a portion of a Javanese pilot's map, and other European seamen would certainly have acquired or seen such maps. Independent traders would have dealt closely with their Indonesian counterparts, in partnerships, with pilots and crews, and sometimes through marriage into local families. It seems reasonable that the acquisitive and adventurous Portuguese would have seized upon—and perhaps acted upon—any knowledge of commercial value that came their way, especially if it concerned a source of gold.

An archaeological find in Western Australia in 1916 led to considerable discussion of a possible Portuguese landing. In July of that year HMAS *Encounter* entered Napier Broome Bay on the far northwestern coast and sent a landing party onto tiny Carronade Island. Some 25 paces from the water's edge the men discovered two small bronze cannons of a type called swivel guns, partially sunk upright into the ground about 2m apart. One is an unadorned gun just over 1m long, identified as a Southeast Asian *lantaka*. The second, of about the same length, is emblazoned on the barrel with decorative emblems, including a crown, that led a number of historians to argue for a European casting. Some suggested that the guns were put on the island as navigational leading marks by the Portuguese.

This notion was largely put to rest by Jeremy Green of the Western Australian Maritime Museum in Fremantle, who in 1982 concluded from x-ray and chemical analyses that the gun with the crown marking was also of Southeast Asian manufacture. Lack of corrosion in iron parts in contact with bronze—a normal reaction when these metals have been in sea water together for any length of time—makes it unlikely that the gun came from a shipwreck.[10] There is no evidence that the particular crown emblem was known or used in Portugal or Spain. In addition, there is a gun said to have come from the harbour in Surabaya, Java, that is very similar to the decorated cannon.[11] However, there is no way of determining a precise date of manufacture for any of these guns.

Some researchers argue that Portuguese mariners may have left the guns on the island even if they were not of Iberian manufacture. In the vicissitudes of life at sea, pieces of ships' ordnance were often lost or irreparably damaged, and a ship months away from home would have sought local replacements. The positioning of the guns, buried perpendicularly in the ground, also remains a puzzle. Markers protruding no more than about two-thirds of a metre above ground would have been scarcely visible from the sea, particularly from a vessel that was itself only a few metres above sea level. Another question is whether they could have remained in this position during four or five centuries of tides and cyclones. It is now generally thought most likely that the guns were left by later Macassan trepang fishers, who did carry small cannon which they sometimes used in skirmishes with Aborigines.

THE SECRET QUEST

By 1529 both Spain and Portugal had recognised the impossibility of determining exactly where the counter-meridian of the Tordesillas line would run on the largely unknown opposite side of the world. In any case, neither country had the means of policing such a remote and arbitrary border. A compromise was reached. For 350 000 ducats from Portugal, Spain would withdraw her claims to the Moluccas and agree to a demarcation line 297.5 leagues east of those islands. As negotiations proceeded towards this new agreement, the Portuguese might have thought it important to investigate further the vast area under discussion. What if rich lands lay in the unexplored region that would go to Spain? Yet while it would be desirable to find out, no voyage of investigation could be taken that might antagonise Spain and thereby damage Portugal's bargaining position. Any exploration would have to be carried out in secret.

Certain events may have flowed from these considerations. In 1525 the governor of the Moluccas sent out from the island of Ternate an expedition led by Diogo de Rocha and the pilot Gómes de Sequeira. Its purpose has been given variously as exploration or a search for gold, but the voyage is scantily recorded by Portuguese chroniclers, and it may in fact have been a reconnaissance mission into what was at the time a diplomatically sensitive area. Driven by strong winds, Rocha and Sequeira appear to have reached one of the western Caroline Islands before returning to Ternate. Sequeira sailed again, this time south into the Arafura Sea. Reputedly blown hundreds of leagues off course, he discovered two islands, which were marked with his name on later maps. In recent times they have been variously identified as Bathurst, Melville and Croker Islands, the Coburg Peninsula and the Wessel and Prince of Wales Islands. Thus Sequeira may have coasted and perhaps charted the Australian northern seaboard. If so, he was the first European discoverer of Australia. Since no one could then calculate longitudinal distances correctly it would have been impossible to determine just how far east Sequeira had gone; in any case the Portuguese government did not publicise news of his discoveries. Aside from not wishing to antagonise Spain by possibly having trespassed into its territory, Portugal might not have wanted the Spanish to know of the extent of new lands to which they would be surrendering future claims. Such is the theory, and whether Sequeira and his masters believed that he had touched upon the Great South Land remains an unanswered question. Hard evidence that Gómes de Sequeira discovered Australia is simply lacking, and as a result he figures only briefly, if at all, in most histories of the country. There is, however, another possible discoverer of Australia for whom more support has been raised.

The principal mention of Cristovão de Mendonça comes in *Da Asia*, a history of Portuguese expansion by the chronicler João de Barros. Mendonça, Barros relates, was a captain in a fleet of fourteen ships that sailed from Lisbon for the East in mid-1519. Two years later he was placed in command of three ships that left Malacca on a voyage south from the west coast of Sumatra. It is clear that Mendonça returned from this journey with at least one ship, because Barros mentions that he travelled to Goa and that later he was appointed governor of the island of Hormuz. Of the voyage south from Malacca and Sumatra there is no record whatsoever.

Where did Mendonça go and why? There are several possible answers. Reports of the 'isles of gold' beyond Sumatra were clearly considered plausible at the highest levels of government. In 1520 the Portuguese governor at Goa received a royal order to discover these islands, and Mendonça's commission in 1521 might have been to find them. The contemporary expedition of Magellan and the later journeys of Drake, Jansz and any number of others eventually became common knowledge, and their charts and log books added to Europe's store of information about the world. Some of these still exist. Thus, the almost complete lack of surviving records for this particular voyage suggests that someone ordered its strict concealment. Yet if the islands in question lay south of Java and Sumatra, they were indisputably within Portuguese territory and there would be no need to hide the fact that an expedition had been sent to find them. Historians, therefore, have advanced other possible motives.

In 1519 Ferdinand Magellan sailed from Spain on his voyage around the world. This was an aggressive move by Spain, which would take Magellan's fleet directly through the Portuguese hemisphere. By March 1521 Magellan had crossed the Pacific and reached the Philippines. One suggestion, then, is that the real mission of Mendonça's three ships was to intercept the Spanish fleet. However, Magellan left Spain with five well-armed vessels, and it is doubtful that the Portuguese in Goa or Malacca knew that he had already lost two of the five. Not knowing, they would have

GERARDI MERCATORIS RVPELMVNDANI EFFIGIEM ANNOR·
DVORVM ET SEX — AGINTA, SVI ERGA IPSVM STVDII
CAVSA DEPINGI CVRABAT FRANC. HOG. CIƆ. IƆ. LXXIV.

Gerardus Mercator, the great Flemish cartographer. His imaginative depiction of the vast continent of Terra Australis spurred on the quest for the Great South Land. (Gerardus Mercator, Atlas, Duisburg, 1585, I, f.2v. Brussels, Royal Library, VH 14.348 C RP)

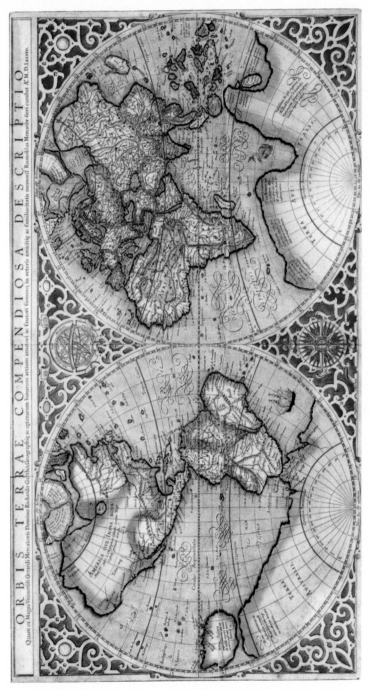

Gerardus Mercator's world map, Orbis Terrae Compendiosa Descripto, from his atlas of 1587, shows the great continental landmass of Terra Australis. A narrow seaway between Terra Australis and South America reflects Magellan's passage in 1520 through the strait now bearing his name. (Mitchell Library, State Library of New South Wales, Sydney)

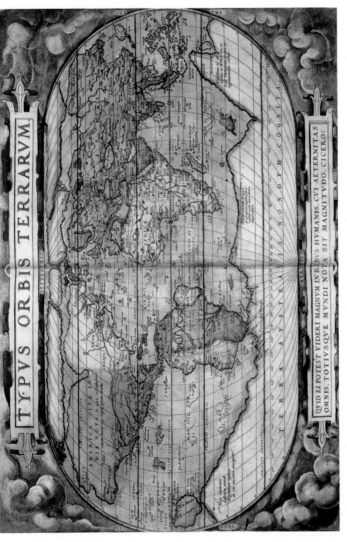

Abraham Ortelius's world map of 1570, Typus Orbis Terrarum, shows Terra Australis Nodum Cognita (the great 'not-yet-known' southern continent) which was believed to reach northwards towards the equator approximately where Australia is located. At the southern-most tip of South America, Tierra del Fuego, not yet understood to be an island, is part of the landmass. (Mitchell Library, State Library of New South Wales, Sydney)

Afonso de Albuquerque, governor of Portuguese possessions in India and at Melaka in Malaysia. To ensure Portuguese control of the maritime trade routes to the East, he began establishing a line of fortresses stretching eastward, and in 1511 sent an expedition to gather information and chart Indonesian waters as far as the Spice Islands, on the northern threshold of the imagined southern continent. (Instituto dos Arquivos Nacionais/Torre do Tombo, Lisbon)

believed that Mendonça's squadron would be outnumbered and outgunned. Furthermore, Magellan's route could only be surmised by the Portuguese. And a confrontation with Magellan, if it occurred in Spanish ocean territory, would have been extremely detrimental to Portugal's diplomatic position. On the whole, it seems questionable that the Portuguese would have despatched Mendonça to oppose Magellan.

An alternative explanation for Mendonça's undercover voyage is that he was instructed to explore and chart unknown regions to the southeast, amassing information that Portugal could use to her advantage in future negotiations with Spain. To be effective at the right time, perhaps to get concessions from Spain that she would not otherwise make, the reconnaisance would have to be concealed, all the more so if the exploration was carried into what might be Spanish space. Weight is added to this possibility by the fact that the eventual agreement between Spain and Portugal stipulated that if the exact position of the Tordesillas counter-meridian was eventually established, the agreement could be cancelled. Although a boundary line would later be set at 297.5 leagues east of the Moluccas, the Tordesillas counter-meridian, which could not be correctly determined without an accurate means of measuring longitude, remained a serious, unresolved issue between Spain and Portugal. For two centuries to come experts would position and reposition the meridian in some grossly mistaken locations. Thus in 1521, before Spain and Portugal had reached any agreement as to a demarcation line, the Portuguese might have felt it important to know more about the territory involved. The sailing of three ships from Malacca could not be disguised, but their purpose could, and seeking islands of gold within Portuguese territory would have been an acceptable cover story. However, like the intercept-Magellan theory, this scenario is pure conjecture.

Some researchers, however, believe that there is archaeological evidence that Mendonça's ships reached Australia. In 1836 a boat carrying three sealers capsized in Armstrong Bay between Port Fairy and Warrnambool in Victoria. Two men reached the deserted beach and came upon the hull of a wrecked vessel among the sand dunes. Some 40 subsequent sightings of the wreck were reported up to 1880, when it seems to have disappeared permanently under the sand.

The colour and density of the vessel's timbers and its unfamiliar construction led those who saw it to describe an 'antique' 'mahogany ship'. Speculations on its identity have ranged from a ship of Mendonça to a convict-built escape craft or a more recent whale boat.

Several serious attempts were made to locate the wreck, but without result. Then in 1992 the Geophysical Research Institute of the University of New England, in Armidale, New South Wales, selected two possible sites for high-definition magnetic mapping. European ships of the sixteenth and seventeenth centuries were routinely armed with bronze and iron guns using both stone and iron shot.[12] In addition, they carried such large iron objects as anchors—several, to provide for emergencies—and stoves, as well as iron tools, cooking equipment, and all the hardware—nails, bolts, pintels, hinges and much else—used in a vessel's construction, together with spare parts. Remote sensing equipment can find such objects, even if they are buried many metres underground.

At each site the GRI team systematically examined a seven-hectare area with high-performance magnetometers and used ground-probing radar to home in on magnetic anomalies of particular interest. Buried at one site was a wire fence, and at the second a long metal rod, almost certainly an auger lost in 1974. There was no wreckage of a vessel with any kind of iron equipment.[13]

In 1847 a workman digging a pit for a lime kiln near Corio Bay, Victoria, found a set of five keys. A short time later Charles LaTrobe, then superintendent of the area and an amateur geologist, was examining the strata in the pit when the find was mentioned. Two of the keys were already lost, but LaTrobe was given the remaining three. They had been found, he was told, in a layer of shells 4.5m down in the pit, which was about 12m back from the bay's high-water mark. Latrobe concluded that the shelly stratum in the pit had once been the beach itself, and that the keys, encrusted with calcareous matter but only a little rusted, had been dropped there at that time. They appeared to him to be quite ordinary and no more than 100 or 150 years old.

Some have linked the keys to a landing by Mendonça in 1522, but this is ruled out by recent carbon dating, which has established that the shelly layer is over 2300 years old. As the pit was dug, the keys were most likely dislodged from somewhere higher up and fell into the shell layer. Yet the debate continues, for unfortunately, LaTrobe entrusted the keys to others, and they have since been lost, making the simplest age test, an analysis of the keys, impossible.

A related argument centres upon whether Mendonça found and entered Victoria's Port Phillip Bay. This large bay has been matched with one named Gouffre, which appears on certain sixteenth century maps, but Gouffre has also been identified with George Bay in Tasmania. If these maps were based on Mendonça's exploration, as some believe, then he may have reached Tasmania, not Victoria.

Another site sometimes associated with Mendonça is Bittangabee Creek, which empties into a coastal inlet about 400km south of Sydney. A short distance upstream stand the ruins of an unfinished rectangular stone-and-mortar structure, approximately 20.5m by 10m, which some suggest was built by Mendonça and his men. If so, its purpose is unclear. Stone walls suggest a long, planned stay, unlikely for explorers. Even in the event of some catastrophe, the surrounding forest offers ample timber for quicker, easier construction of a sort that a ship's carpenter and a few crewmen could handle. The structure's building materials and techniques are, in fact, similar to those used in the area by much later agriculturalists and stock-raisers. Some people claim to see a date of 15 4 on one stone, but this appears to be just an imaginative interpretation of some of the pick marks that cover the ruin.[14]

On the whole, then, there seems no reason to believe that these particular finds survive from a voyage by Mendonça. Still, the departure of his fleet from Malacca and his own return are documented. No journal of his voyage has ever surfaced, and no chart of the journey has ever come to light. Yet fifteen years after his expedition the first of an extraordinary series of maps appeared. Commonly referred to as the Dieppe maps, they are in the view of some scholars the earliest cartographic representations of Australia.

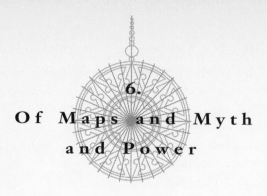

6.
Of Maps and Myth
and Power

To the Europeans of the sixteenth and seventeenth centuries much of the earth was a great unknown. Yet they believed that in its remotest reaches slumbered the possibility of immeasurable riches, to be won by trade or conquest. Charts and navigators' reports that revealed or were thought to reveal these unexplored territories were thus extremely valuable. For nations vying for maritime supremacy in an age of strongly developing nationalism, they were potential keys to wealth and power.

During this great period of European exploration, therefore, rival kings, princes and merchant groups tried to keep secret many of their discoveries and at times expended both money and cunning to get hold of charts and navigators' journals. There was an active underground trade in maps, a kind of cartographic espionage, which could be very lucrative for spies or for mapmakers prepared to change their loyalties. When the son and assistant of a senior Portuguese cartographer fled the country after killing a man in a brawl, he prospered by selling his information to the Venetians and the English. Not even the promise of a royal pardon could bring him back to Lisbon.

The wharfside talk of sailors was another source for alert agents gathering information for their patrons. Dutch seamen working in Portugal passed on rumours and accounts of their own experiences to the representatives of merchant houses at home.

Some governments simply suppressed new geographic information. Charts and reports considered too valuable to fall into competitors' hands were sometimes filed in archives that would not be opened for years, even centuries.

In 1502 Portuguese cartographers produced an exceptionally fine map depicting the then known world in vivid colours and with surprising accuracy. The Duke of Ferrara, in Italy, an avid map collector who was fascinated by recent Spanish and Portuguese discoveries, secretly commissioned an agent named Alberto Cantino to secure a copy of this map from Lisbon. Cantino did this, paying the copier the substantial sum of twelve ducats. The map shows a portion of the coast of South America, including Brazil, claimed for Portugal by Pedro Alvarez Cabral in 1500. Farther north and well to the west of the Tordesillas demarcation line are the West Indies, a string of islands labelled 'The Antilles of the King of Spain', and to the northwest of these, the peninsula of Florida in the present United States, which was not discovered for Spain until 1513, eleven years after the appearance of the Cantino map, as it is called today. Imaginary coastlines were not unusual on sixteenth century charts, but this is a particularly accurate map, and Florida is quite correctly placed. Did Lisbon's cartographers know more about Spain's North American territory than did the Spanish? The Portuguese Corte-Real brothers reached

Labrador and Newfoundland in 1500–02, but the map seems to raise the possibility that even earlier Portuguese expeditions surveyed the American coast in violation of the Tordesillas Treaty. Or was the outline of Florida merely a stunningly well-placed bit of cartographic imagination? The Cantino map, which in the nineteenth century was found hanging in a butcher's shop in Modena, now resides in that city's Biblioteca Estense. So far it has kept its secret.

In 1592 the Dutch mapmaker Pieter Plancius published a large world map based on sea charts that had been obtained in some way from the Portuguese hydrographer Bartholemeu Lasso. In the same year, the Dutch merchant brothers Cornelis and Frederik de Houtman went to Lisbon as commercial representatives of Dutch trading houses and were caught trying to steal secret maps of Portuguese sailing routes to the East. They were imprisoned for three years, but nevertheless returned home with 25 of Lasso's nautical charts which undoubtedly they used on their subsequent voyages to the East.

Another example of the preoccupation with secrecy is the handling of a letter written in 1607 from Manila to Philip III of Spain by the navigator Luis Baéz de Torres. Torres had completed his voyage from Callao in Peru, across the Pacific and through the Torres Strait to Manila, where, as his orders specified, his ship was to be refitted and provisioned for his return to the Americas or to Spain. When this was not done, he wrote to his king, reporting on his voyage and sharply criticising the local Spanish administration. Importantly, he described his passage through the strait that now bears his name. The letter was apparently never answered. It was placed in state archives where neither the Portuguese nor Spain's English and Dutch enemies would ever find it. The price of such secrecy was that Spain never acted upon Torres's discoveries, which could have led to Spanish claims to Australia. Instead, the existence of the strait remained conjectural until James Cook went through it in 1770. Torres's letter was not seen again until the Spanish historian Juan Bautista Muñoz uncovered it in 1782. It remains in the royal archives at Simancas in Spain.

Several maps of the late sixteenth century, among them Ortelius's world map of 1570 and Rumold Mercator's of 1587, had, in fact, already depicted New Guinea as an island separate from Terra Australis. In each case, however, an almost round island is accompanied by a legend saying that it is not known whether this newly discovered territory is an island or part of the southern continent. Plancius showed New Guinea joined to the Great South Land on his map of 1594.

There are interesting details on a map entitled 'NOVA GVINEAE Forma & Situs', which appeared in an atlas, *Speculum Orbis Terrae*, published in 1593 by Cornelis de Jode. Here New Guinea is accompanied by an inscription in Latin saying that the country is so called by sailors because it resembles the Guinea coast of Africa, and that it is not known whether it is insular or joined to Terra Australis. Drawings of imaginary birds and fishes, a ship under sail, a crowned Neptune and, presumably, his wife Amphitrite adorn the ocean, while the South Land is located below the Tropic of Capricorn and decorated with mountains and valleys, an archer drawing his bow, a dragon, a lion and a serpent. The title page of this atlas is also interesting. Each corner is decorated with an animal—a horse, a camel, a lion and an odd, long-necked marsupial with two young in its pouch. Marsupials, of course, are found in the Americas and in New Guinea and its nearby islands, as well as in Australia. The variations and standard imaginary embellishments on all these maps indicate that their renditions of Nova Guinea and Terra Australis were mainly hypothetical and imaginative.

During this period of exploration and imperial expansion, improvements in mapmaking continued. Gerardus Mercator introduced his technique of projecting latitude and longitude onto a flat surface in a manner particularly useful for navigation. Some land shapes became more true and many coastlines more accurate. The imagined outline of the Great South Land continued to cap the southern hemisphere, with purely speculative variations and details. About the middle of the century, however, there appeared a series of maps which strangely seemed to be based on real information. Curiously, they came from France.

THE DIEPPE MAPS

France, during the sixteenth century, did not actively enter the race for the East and its trade. Initially excluded from exploration by the Papal Line of Demarcation and the Treaty of Tordesillas, and further deterred by continental wars and internal strife, the country moved into the wider world with restraint. Yet French cartographers now produced extraordinarily detailed representations of a southern land mass, where no known French or any other expedition had been.

Normandy, facing the Atlantic Ocean, had a long tradition of seafaring, with ship owners and builders, merchants and sailors crowding its ports. During this period the city of Dieppe became an especially important maritime centre, attracting a group of unusually gifted geographers. The outstanding Pierre Desceliers, a priest from the town of Arques, was Dieppe's leading cosmographer, as well as a teacher and examiner of pilots, and Jean Rotz, a hydrographer of Scottish background, made an exceptional contribution to mapping with his *Boke of Idrography*. Other highly skilled mapmakers followed, as well as many lesser talents who put out charts and portolans for the practical use of mariners. These common maps were in black ink on paper, received some necessarily rough handling, and rarely survived. Of the finer maps produced by such experts as Desceliers, only a few are extant. Executed on vellum, sometimes more than 2m long and perhaps 1m wide, they were works of art, with jewel colours, elegant script and finely drawn adornments—ships and sea monsters, mountains and exotic animals. Those that survive generally belonged to princes and aristocrats, and so were sheltered in great homes and perhaps later in museums. The splendid Dauphin or Harleian map, probably commissioned by the French king Francis I for his son, was later acquired by Edward Harley, Earl of Oxford. On Harley's death the map disappeared for a time, but eventually came into the possession of Sir Joseph Banks, the renowned eighteenth century naturalist, who presented it to the British Museum.

Whether beautiful creations or simple, practical charts, sixteenth century maps had many limitations. Their makers had to rely on a miscellany of maps drawn by other geographers or by mariners who might have sketched them at sea, their pens wavering as the ship pitched and rolled. There was no agreed system for recording place names or notations. North could be at the top of the chart or at the side or bottom. The scale on which a map was drawn was rarely indicated. If maps were subject to ignorance and error, so were the journals and sailing directions also given as aids to the mapmakers.

The mariner's equipment imposed its own limitations. Latitude was determined from observations of the sun or stars with the cross staff or astrolabe. The latter was nearly impossible to use on a moving deck, and both devices could produce errors of several degrees. There was no effective way of measuring longitude and usually navigators did not even try. Speed was gauged by the log, a line with a weighted piece of wood at the end, which unrolled as the vessel moved forward, and a sandglass used as timer. The amount of line that ran out in a given time, usually half a minute, was translated into nautical miles per hour, at best an approximate measurement. A variation of this was simply two marks on the side of the ship at a known distance apart; a chip of wood was thrown into the water and the time it took to pass between the two marks was measured by a minute glass, counting one's pulse or reciting a certain number of words. Some experienced mariners, especially among the Spanish, used only 'eye and judgment'. The compass, which at night was illumined by a candle in its box, was unreliable. A pilot estimated as best he could the effect of wind, current and tide; he had no means of measuring them. Watching a new coastline, the navigator had only his eyes. Galileo produced a telescope in 1609, and many experimental versions followed, but telescopes practicable for use on ships did not appear until the later 1700s. Thus a seaman might make out a promontory but miss low-lying areas entirely; he might mistake a headland for an island, or see a row of overlapping islands as a single land mass.

For the cartographer, then, drawing a world map or a large chart was something like assembling a jigsaw puzzle, for which the pieces were drawn by different people on different scales—and some pieces would be missing. Other variables came into play: personal judgment, mistakes in copying and perhaps faulty translation from another language. Despite all these limitations, the large maps produced during the mid-1500s in Dieppe are exceptionally good for the time. More than that, they seem to have a most interesting relevance to Australia.

These charts are *mappa mundi*, or world maps, and curiously, they all show a large land mass that could conceivably be Australia—a country whose discovery by Europeans would not be documented for another 60 or 70 years. Indonesia, known to Europeans by this time for more than half a century, appears in some detail, with Sumatra shown as a long island in approximately the right location, but Java, or 'Iave', as it is written, almost circular and separated by a narrow waterway called Rio Grande from a continental-sized land mass to the south, labelled Iave La Grande. Capes and bays are shown and named for some distance down the west coast of this land mass, after which the shoreline is a wavy stroke extending south. The east coast—which on these maps actually runs southeast and then turns southwest—extends about four times the distance of the detailed part of the west coast, but has fewer named geographical features. As the maps have neither specified scales nor any proper system of projection, distances can only be surmised. The continent's interior space is ornamented with trees, huts, animals and small human figures. Although on some of the maps the area seems to merge with a Great South Land to the south of it, it is not called Terra Australis or any variation of that term, but by a name apparently derived from Marco Polo, who wrote that sailors called Java 'the biggest island in the world'.[1] The question is whether this is a map of Australia produced half a century or more before the north coast was discovered by the Dutch and over 200 years before the east coast was seen by James Cook.

Scholars do not agree, and have developed a number of different theories on what Java La Grande represents. Some suggest that it is a kind of geographical hoax, others that it is a highly imaginative rendering of garbled Indonesian sailors' tales. Yet to dismiss a portion of the maps as deceit or fantasy runs counter to the fact that the Dieppe world maps are agreed to be as skilfully and knowledgeably done as the age permitted.

Another interpretation is that Java La Grande is really a combination of several Indonesian islands, put together from different sketches on different scales by mapmakers influenced by Marco Polo's notion of Java's size. An entirely different line of thinking uses the study of place names to identify Java La Grande as the coast of Vietnam. This scholar believes that navigators and mapmakers misunderstood native words and transcribed place names incorrectly, so their poor rendition of Vietnam is also mislabelled and has therefore been assumed to be something else.[2]

The scenes ornamenting Java La Grande on most Dieppe maps are certainly not Australian. They show mythical beasts, elephants, monkeys, camels, and Asian village life. More than anything else, they look Sumatran, some with added scenes of idol worship and cannibalism— again reflecting Marco Polo's tales. However, a large flightless bird decorates the 1555 map of Guillaume le Testu, and a Nicolas Vallard map, dated 1547, includes small, spear-carrying, scantily clothed men, together with a dog, crocodile, whale, iguana and turtle. All of these, however, could relate to a number of countries other than Australia. On the whole, then, the embellishments can be ignored as expected mapping conventions. It is more significant to examine the extent to which the details of the Java La Grande shorelines match those of Australia.

The north coast conforms only remotely. A number of details belonging to Indonesian islands appear to have been superimposed on the continent, so that Java, Sumbawa and Flores, for instance, appear where Arnhem Land and Cape York should be. Such transpositions may reflect efforts by cartographers, who knew little about the south coasts of Indonesian islands, to adapt the known north coasts to the shoreline of a rumoured southern continent. Then, because the mapmakers knew that Java itself was an island, since the ship *Victoria* from Magellan's fleet had sailed past its southern end, most of them added the Rio Grande seaway to separate Java from Java La Grande.

Less confusion attaches to Java La Grande's northwest coast. Here scholars have matched many features—

promontories, inlets, islands and estuaries—to those on modern maps of Australia's north. The long east coast of Java La Grande presents more difficulties. It projects sharply to the southeast for a considerable distance and then turns southwest. Some writers have assumed that Dieppe cartography can be adjusted mathematically for its sixteenth century distortions, and using this method they have managed to make Java La Grande, on the Dauphin and Desceliers maps in particular, better approximate the shape of Australia. Others have taken the Java La Grande coast section by section, matching the details with various parts of the present Australian coastline. There is, however, no consensus on how the results should be interpreted. Where the Java La Grande coast swings back to the southwest, the shoreline has been identified as that of Victoria from Cape Howe to Warrnambool,[3] but also as the east coast of Tasmania from Cape Portland south.[4] Two islands, Ye de Saill and Yslas de Magna on most of the Dieppe maps, have been variously identified—sometimes by turning the image upside down—as the Furneaux Group in Bass Strait, the main islands of New Zealand or New Caledonia, islands off the Mekong delta of Vietnam, or even possibly Sri Lanka and the Andaman Islands. It has also been suggested that the maps' distortions were deliberate, intended to place as much territory as possible within the geographic hemisphere of influence of the original mapmaker's country, Portugal, or to mislead the navigators of other nations. On the same theory, fictitious islands were added to indicate salient points of the real shoreline.

Whether or not Java La Grande represents Australia, the similarity of the Dieppe maps, drawn by several men over a period of about 30 years, and their difference from other contemporary work, suggest a common source for the information that went into them. Although the later maps undoubtedly derived from the earlier ones, and individual geographers clearly made adjustments of their own, sometimes updating certain details, the outlines of Java La Grande remain very similar. Where did they come from?

SOURCES

French sources have been propounded. In 1663 there was published in Paris a book describing the voyage of a long-deceased French mariner, Jean Binot Paulmier de Gonneville, in about 1503–05. Inspired by Da Gama's voyage of a few years earlier and financed by local shippers and merchants, Gonneville is known to have sailed for the East from Honfleur in Normandy. The rest of the story is based entirely on Gonneville's account given on his return. Driven for weeks by adverse winds, he arrived in a strange tropical land, where he and his men lived for six months. He described curious animals, friendly natives with bows and arrows who lived in cabins with doors locked with wooden keys, and great caves where the seamen sheltered. The local king was an elderly widower with six children, one of whom, a young man named Essomericq, joined the French on their departure.

Pursued by pirates on the way home, Gonneville's ship was wrecked and his charts and records lost. In the city of Rouen in 1505 he made a statement to the French Admiralty, the only official documentation of the journey. It contained no sailing directions for the route to or from an unidentified country. Thus the origins of Essomericq, who actually arrived in France and whom Gonneville adopted, were unrecorded.

Gonneville's tale was evidently laughed at by those who listened to him. During the next two centuries, however, many French came to believe that he had found Terra Australis. Modern historians generally dismiss the narrative as mainly a tall tale, although some suggest that the caves he mentioned may have been those seen by George Grey in Australia's northwest, while other theorists put him in New Zealand. More likely suggestions are that he reached either South America, perhaps Brazil, or Africa, possibly Madagascar, and told the story with many imaginative additions.

In 1529 a better-documented French voyage to the East took place when the brothers Jean and Raoul Parmentier sailed from Dieppe in the ships *Pensée* and *Sacré*. They reached Sumatra, where both men died of fever, and the ships, with the charts and journals of the voyage, were brought back to France by the pilot, Pierre Crignon. Later references to his now-vanished account suggest that Crignon heard some intriguing tales of Java La Grande but did not venture beyond Sumatra. His lost work, however, may have been the basis for a map, produced in about 1540 by Jean Mallard, which shows a large promontory of 'Terre Australlé' lying south of Malacca. Probably the maps and navigational guides produced by Crignon and the Parmentiers became available to Dieppe cartographers, but they would not have documented any land beyond Sumatra with any reliability. Another member of the Parmentier expedition may have been Jean Rotz, a mariner as well as hydrographer. In 1542 he published a world map on a hemispherical projection, on which Java La Grande's west coast terminates at approximately 35°S, close to Cape Leeuwin's 34°21'S, where the Australian southwest coast turns a corner, so to speak, to run eastward. The map's east coast, however, extends to about 60°S, much farther south than does the actual continent; Tasmania's southernmost point, the South East Cape, ends at 43°37' S. There is also the 1544 reference of Jean Fonteneau, a French sailor, who claimed to have seen 'la Grand Jave'— a continent, not an island—which, he had heard, extended south to near the antarctic pole. Married to a Portuguese woman and at times assuming Portuguese nationality and the name Jean Alfonse, Fonteneau spent many years at sea and later wrote of his adventures. The authenticity of his claims, however, was questioned at the time and remains suspect.

However limited their incursions may have been in the East, the French found the idea of an unknown world fascinating. The contemporary satirist François Rabelais is said to have used Fonteneau as the model for his character Xenomanes, 'the great traveler across perilous routes' who 'had mapped out . . . in his great universal hydrography, the route they would take'[5] as he travels with the giant Pantagruel on his mock-heroic sea-going adventures.

Jean Parmentier, a poet as well as a navigator, wrote,

> I often wonder why, for this odd fantasy,
> I Europe leave, and why it lies to me
> To circle Africa so near around,
> Nor can I yet contented be

Until the coasts of Asia shall be found,
To such an effort am I tied;
My head is fired, my spirit has not died.
So, making ready, I am filled with joy,
If questioning still the ends of my employ.[6]

A historian and cartographer, Lancelot du Voisin, Seigneur de La Popellinière, translated the text of Hondius's atlas into French, and referring to Terra Australis, argued in his treatise of 1582, *Les Tres Mondes*, that the greatest discoveries were yet to be made. France, he said, could still catch up with Spain and Portugal in securing colonies by settling the great southern continent. At the time France was split by civil war, and no one heeded his advice.

For the Dieppe maps Portuguese origins are better argued than French. Portugal was the principal European presence in the East Indies, and the maps and records of her mariners were assembled and held in Lisbon's Casa da India. The term Java La Grande may well be French, but Portuguese derivation is obvious in many of the place names on the Dieppe maps. 'Terre ennegade' comes from *tierra anegada*, meaning 'overflowed land', a term often used for shoals and reefs. 'Bahie bassa' is from *bahia bassa* or 'shallow bay', and *anda ne barcha*, 'no boats go here', is purely Portuguese. These, on the Dauphin map, show the failure of a French copyist to translate correctly from a Portuguese source. Some of the maps, notably those of Nicolas Desliens from 1561, 1566 and 1567, even display Portuguese flags on Java La Grande.

How Portuguese geographical information, preserved in Lisbon as a state secret, came into the hands of French hydrographers is an interesting question. Somehow, charts or parts of charts, or a prototype of some sort, reached Dieppe, possibly through the cartographical black market, but there is no sure answer. There is another question: if the material was originally Portuguese, what was their source of information? The voyages of Abreu, Sequeira and others and the work of such men as Rodrígues and Pires produced maps and considerable descriptive information on the Indonesian islands generally, but no surviving Portuguese map or document shows any trace of Java La Grande.

Here is a very large land area with an extensive coastline which somehow was charted. Was it pieced together from sundry Indonesian accounts, from chance sightings by Portuguese sailors blown off course over the years or simply from someone's imagination? Java La Grande, whatever it was, seems a very large country, with some parts almost excessively rich in coastal detail, to have been generated in this way. A number of scholars are convinced that such a mass of information must have come from a single definite and competent source, and they maintain that the mysterious 1521 voyage of Cristavão de Mendonça was that source. The journey antedates the first of the Dieppe maps by about 15 years, sufficient time for any information gathered to reach the hands of French mapmakers. According to this hypothesis, Mendonça and his three ships, coming from Malacca, might have stopped for water, firewood and provisions on the south coast of Java or in Timor, and from there caught the monsoonal winds to the south or southeast.

He would then have reached the Australian northwest coast, which he and his pilots would have charted as the ships steered north, and then east around Arnhem Land and across the mouth of the Gulf of Carpentaria. As none of the Dieppe charts show any detail to the south from what would have to be Australia's northwest corner, we could assume that the expedition did no exploration in that direction.

Could Mendonça then have made his way through Torres Strait 85 years before Torres and 249 years before Cook? Going from west to east, rather than east to west as they did, he would have encountered the same apparent barrier of reefs, shoals and islands as the Dutch explorer Willem Jansz did a few months before Torres found the passage. The problems of getting through the strait in little ships entirely dependent on wind and tide should not be underestimated.

The Mendonça hypothesis, however, maintains that he negotiated the strait and continued south along Australia's east coast. If the Dieppe charts show the results of his mapping, some labels may be significant. A portion of the northeast coast of Java La Grande is marked *Coste dangereuse* on the Dauphin map and *Coste perilleuse* on a Desceliers chart, suggesting the hazards of the Great Barrier Reef. On some of the maps rows of dots or small x's may show reefs or islets. Farther south, the label *Coste des Herbaiges*, or on another map *Cap des Herbaiges*—Coast or Cape of Vegetation—has stirred contention, some believing that *Herbaiges* suggested the name Botany Bay to Cook, who thus derived the name from his knowledge of the Dieppe maps. This, however, is unlikely, as Cook first named the bay for the stingrays his men were catching and chose the name Botany Bay only after he had seen the large botanical collections gathered from the area by Joseph Banks and his fellow naturalist Daniel Solander. Another interpretation is that the label belongs to today's Fraser Island, perhaps named for its wooded aspect. Farther south again, opinions on the Java La Grande coastline and thus a route for Mendonça vary. If the map's easternmost point corresponds to Tasmania, it might perhaps be argued that, if Mendonça came that far, he explored some of that shoreline. If, however, it represents Victoria's Cape Howe, then perhaps he followed Australia's southern coast westward and entered Bass Strait. Whatever the case, the coast of Java La Grande ends soon after.

Why Mendonça stopped at this point on his putative voyage is also much debated. Adverse weather, common in Bass Strait, or the long, strong rollers and prevailing westerlies that come in from the southern Indian Ocean might have been reasons. A serious accident has been considered. As to what he did next, most speculation centres on a return to Malacca by much the same route along which he had come, sometimes with a suggestion that he discovered Norfolk and Lord Howe Islands on the way. Whatever the case, a number of historians have maintained that Australia was discovered and some of its coasts were explored and charted by a Portuguese expedition in the early 1520s, all in utter secrecy from the rest of the world.

Were there other Portuguese voyagers on the Australian coast, so that the charting on which the Dieppe maps were based came from the logs, rutters and sketch maps of more than one navigator? One suggested candidate is Gómes de Sequeira, who was sent out from Ternate in the Moluccas in 1525 or 1526 and reached two islands that might have been off the Northern Territory or north Queensland coast. Were there others? To date there is no evidence of them.

The Java La Grande sections of the Dieppe world maps remain an enigma, and sources for its information seem not to exist. One reason for this may lie in the catastrophes that struck the town of Dieppe in the late seventeeth century. Almost 10 000 people died from plague in 1668, and in the following years the strongly Protestant seaport suffered severe religious persecution leading up to the revocation of the Edict of Nantes in 1685 and afterwards. Finally, in 1694 the city was almost completely destroyed in an attack by the Dutch and English navies. Maritime records, and perhaps the people who understood them, quite possibly perished in the devastation.

By then, however, the image of Java La Grande was already fading from European maps of the East, with only hints of it appearing in the legends and decorations of a few later charts. As Indonesia's islands became better known to Europeans, the form of its islands, particularly Java, became more realistic. Java La Grande shrank back into Terra Australis Incognita, and its name disappeared from the charts. The more powerful image of the Great South Land remained.

What became of Lisbon's great fund of primary cartographic material—the charts, portolans, rutters, reports and journals accumulated over so many years? Stubborn secrecy was maintained by the government through most of the sixteenth century. Despite persistent effort, the Italian scholar Giovanni Battista Ramusio was permitted in 1550 to print only parts of the works of the apothecary-geographer Tomé Pires and the Portuguese India official Duarte Barbosa—books, Ramusio said, which were 'concealed' for reasons he was not allowed to discuss.[7] Masses of material never came to light. As in Dieppe, a natural disaster may go some way to explaining this mysterious lacuna. On 1 November 1755 a massive earthquake rent Lisbon. The Tagus River poured into the city. Fires raged. An estimated 30 000 lives and 9000 buildings were lost. Probably some of the depositories of the Casa da India with their centuries' accumulation of maps and information were among them.

Some explanation may lie simply in Portugal's decline as a maritime power. The small Iberian nation fought to maintain its footholds on the shores of Asia into the twentieth century, but long before that, its limited resources were no match for those of stronger, richer nations. Documents that were no longer important may have been destroyed or simply allowed to deteriorate. Nevertheless, it is puzzling that no scrap of source material for the Dieppe maps and no information on Mendonça's 1521 journey have ever come to light.

There is so far no firm documentary or archaeological evidence of a Portuguese discovery of Australia. If there were landings they went unreported, except perhaps indirectly via the Dieppe maps, and had no effect on the affairs of the outside world. If indeed Mendonça's brief was to explore unknown lands for information that could be used in diplomatic negotiations, and if indeed he found Australia, that information was never put to use. Portugal did not pursue exploration or make any territorial claim to the south of Indonesia. The Portuguese crown may have found the spice trade lucrative enough, particularly as its grip on the Moluccas required constant attention and sometimes reinforcements of men and ships. Perhaps Portugal was neither interested nor prepared to look farther south until, paradoxically, her military and economic decline already precluded further voyages of discovery.

Still, there remain tantalising hints that some knowledge of southward exploration reached Europe. A curious comment accompanies Cornelis Wytfliet's world map, published in Flanders in 1597. Here New Guinea is an island narrowly separated from Terra Australis, which is described as 'but little known, since after one voyage and another, that route has been deserted, and seldom is the country visited unless when sailors are driven there by storms . . . [it] is maintained by some to be of so great an extent, that if it were thoroughly explored, it would be regarded as a fifth part of the world.'[8] Two other world maps also rather oddly suggest some knowledge of the Australian continent. One is a map of 1571 by the Spanish theologian and mapmaker Benedictus Arias Montanus on which a triangle of unidentified land rises out of the sea at the approximate location of northwestern Australia. The second is the English mathematician Edward Wright's 1600 world map, on which there is no Great South Land, but instead a short, curving, unnamed shoreline shown south of Java. Are these details based on fragmentary information about an otherwise unrecorded voyage? Or are they simply alternative, idiosyncratic representations of Terra Australis Incognita?

There may be a very tenuous link between Dieppe cartography and the later, well-recorded exploration of Australia's east coast. Joseph Banks, who accompanied

James Cook on his voyage of 1770, was an owner of the Dauphin map, which he apparently acquired from his fellow scientist Daniel Solander. In 1790 Banks presented the map to the British Museum. What is not known is how or when—or possibly even if—Solander obtained the map, or whether he gave it to Banks before or after the 1770 voyage.

To what extent, then, did Portugal contribute to the European discovery of Australia? Portugal pioneered the sea routes from Europe to Asia. Her kings were able to think in terms of the world beyond Europe, and her ships and men, often with great suffering and terrible loss, found and charted seaways halfway around the earth. Their contribution to geographical knowledge was immense. Their economic success aroused the interest and cupidity of other nations. These in turn pushed into the same region with conquerors and merchants but also geographers and men of science, who in the path of the Portuguese searched for the substance of an ancient tradition and discovered instead a strange and wonderful island continent.

7.

The Spanish Explorers

In the final years of the fifteenth century the fragmented land that was Spain came together as one country under the combined crowns of Queen Isabella of Castile and King Ferdinand of Aragón. The unification was complete on 2 January 1492 with the official surrender of Granada, the last of the Moorish kingdoms. The Spanish monarchs then turned briefly from the countless postwar domestic problems of their kingdom to the lure of overseas exploration. In April they signed documents extending their consent and support to the project of a Genoese mariner, now called Cristóbal de Colón, whose plan to reach Asia by sailing west had been approved by their advisers. Before the end of that year the foundation of a Spanish empire would be laid, leading to more than a century of epic exploration and conquest and, for a time, seemingly unbounded wealth. The men who built this empire came from a largely impoverished land that had spent eight centuries in recurrent wars against the Moors, a history which had bred into them intolerance and arrogance, superb courage and toughness, and a view of themselves as the defenders of Christendom. Through them, Spain would come to control the West Indies and Central America, the South American continent except for Brazil, and much of North America, giving her captains the ideal springboard for ventures across the Pacific.

THE PACIFIC OCEAN ROAD

Within 30 years of Columbus's first sighting of the Americas, Spain had consolidated her position in the Caribbean, claiming the entire arc of West Indian islands. In 1513 Vasco Nuñez de Balboa crossed the Panamanian isthmus to look down upon the Pacific Ocean, and a few days later, wading into its waters, took possession of the Mar del Sur or Southern Sea and its adjacent lands for the King of Spain. Six years later Hernando Cortés and some 600 soldiers and sailors invaded Mexico and established Spanish dominion from the Caribbean to the Pacific.

In 1519, as Cortés fought and parleyed in Mexico, an even more significant enterprise was launched from Spain. On 20 September Fernando de Magallanes—Magellan— sailed in command of five ships and approximately 270 men from Seville's port of Sanlúcar de Barrameda in a bid to circumnavigate the globe.

Magellan was a Portuguese of the minor nobility who had served his king in India, Malacca and North Africa, where he received a wound that left him with a permanent limp. Denied the token increase in his pension that would have signified promotion, he transferred his allegiance to Spain, offering King Ferdinand's successor, Charles V, a plan for finding a strait through South America to the Pacific and across to the Moluccas. Aside from discovering an important sea route from Atlantic to Pacific, he believed that he could provide practical proof that the Spice Islands were within the Spanish hemisphere.

Magellan was a complex man, sombre, remote and hard, given to fits of temper but possessed of enormous drive and an undeviating will. He had great physical stamina, and would stand for many hours on the open deck, eyes narrowed, great beard blowing in the wind. As a Portuguese in the service of Spain he encountered active resistance among the predominantly Spanish officers of his command. He handled this with no hesitation. When certain captains mutinied on the South American east coast, he had one killed at once, another executed and a third abandoned, together with a disaffected priest, on the desolate Patagonian shore.

Soon after that, one ship was wrecked, and as the fleet began probing westward through the rock-bound strait between the tip of South America and the island of Tierra del Fuego, another deserted. On 28 November 1520 the three remaining vessels emerged into Balboa's Southern Sea, which Magellan called the Pacific for its tranquillity. No one, however, understood its currents, which first drove them north, or its wind patterns. No one realised its immensity or the emptiness of an ocean where in three months and 20 days of sailing they found only two tiny, barren and uninhabited islands. Food and water ran out and men were dying. Antonio Pigafetta, whose journal records the agonies of the journey, believed 'that nevermore will any man undertake to make such a voyage'.[1] At the beginning of March 1521 the three ships made their first landfall across the great ocean, on the island of Guam.

Magellan's flagship, the Trinidad, *sailed from Spain in 1519. Two and a half years later in the Moluccas, with Magellan dead, its decimated crew surrendered the ship and themselves to the Portuguese. On their return to Spain, they were the first to circumnavigate the globe.*

A month later they reached and claimed for Spain the archipelago that would be called the Philippines. Here Magellan's own journey ended: before the end of April he was killed in a fight with the natives.

Without Magellan, the ships steered haphazardly for the Moluccas. Their combined officers and crews, about 260 men when they left South America, were now reduced to probably 115 and, unable to manage three vessels, they burned the worm-eaten *Concepción*. Finally reaching Tidore, they loaded spices, only to find that the *Trinidad* was leaking too heavily to go to sea. She was left behind for extensive repairs by her men. Attempting to recross the Pacific, she was forced back by gales, and the captain surrendered ship and crew to the Portuguese in Ternate. The few survivors reached Spain some six years later. The other ship, meanwhile, sailed alone on the second terrible half of the voyage, her crew ravaged by scurvy, starvation, storms and near mutiny. The three-year journey of circumnavigation was completed on 8 September 1522, when the single surviving ship, *Victoria*, and eighteen Spaniards reached Spain.

Magellan's magnificent venture brought the Pacific Ocean under Spain's dominion and claimed for the Spanish king a substantial territory in the Far East. However, the immediate interest of the king and his government remained focused on the valuable Spice Islands. The Moluccas did not, in fact, lie within the Spanish hemisphere of interest, but well within the Portuguese zone. Yet at the time the location of the Tordesillas line's counter-meridian was so uncertain that the issue raised ongoing debate. In 1559 an authoritative report assured the Spanish king that 'It is evident and clear that'[2] the Philippines lay within the Portuguese zone. Yet, a few years later, the respected Spanish cosmographer and mathematician Father Martín de Rada calculated degrees and distances at Cebu in the Philippines, and in a letter to Philip II declared:

> we find that not only the Philippines and the Moluccas, but also most of Borneo and part of Java, with the islands in between, fall within the jurisdiction of His Majesty [Philip II]. Needless to say, not only the entire

New Guinea, but also the best part of China and the
adjacent islands, with Loncor, Lequios and Japan, lie also
within His Majesty's jurisdiction.[3]

The claims and counter-claims would continue until the
mid-eighteenth century, when reliable chronometers
enabled navigators to see the time both at their location
and at their home port—or some other place of known longitude—at the same instant. From the difference in time
they could then calculate how many of the globe's 360
degrees of longitude they had covered. Until then, however, deciding where the counter-meridian fell depended
on flawed mathematical procedures. In 1524, the urgency
of resolving who owned the rich Moluccas led to a council in the Spanish and Portuguese border towns of Badajoz
and Elvas. Here theologians, cosmographers and navigators
mixed biblical quotations with the most advanced geographical information available, yet after seven weeks of
bitter argument could find no solution. Each monarch
thenceforth proceeded with his own plans.

The Spanish believed firmly in the Great South Land.
In 1546 Pedro Sancho de la Hoz, one of the conquistadors
of Chile, was appointed governor of a territory in a continent that was yet to be discovered. He was to administer
Beach, Ortelius's and Rumold Mercator's *'provincia
aurifera'*—'gold-producing land'—which the Spanish
believed lay on the Terra Australis coast southwest of the
Strait of Magellan. On a map, reaching Beach appeared to
be a fairly simple matter, but in reality there were great
navigational difficulties. A ship entering the Pacific from
the Strait of Magellan immediately encountered head-on

both storm winds from the west, the 'roaring forties', and the strong eastward-flowing Peru or Humboldt Current, which at this point swings north up the South American west coast. Modern engine-driven ships can overcome these forces. Clumsy little sailing vessels were almost invariably impelled northward, away from the imagined coast of the Great South Land. Expeditions were also expensive, and Spain had European wars to pay for and territories thousands of kilometres away to administer, sometimes at considerable cost. For some expeditions money had to be borrowed from the great German banking houses of Fugger and Welser.

Spain also assumed the responsibility of bringing Catholicism to these as yet undiscovered regions. In 1623 King Philip III's confessor, Juan de Silva, wrote to Pope Urban VIII,

> Requesting that the mission to the natives of the Austral Lands be confided to the spiritual care of the Franciscan friars, who would undertake their 'conquest' by spiritual and peaceful means.[4]

He added that 'understanding that the Crown of Castile is encharged with said propagation [of the faith]',[5] he had submitted detailed plans for the missionary program to the Spanish king and his councils. The distinguished Juan Luis Arias de Loyola urged Philip III to 'give no heed' to those who told him that for political reasons he was not in a position to undertake great, new and faraway conquests. Such advice, Arias wrote, should be condemned as 'mischievous to your greatness, your conscience, and to your crown'.[6]

The quest for this continent, encircling the lower reaches of the southern hemisphere, was to become a key motivator of Spain's Pacific exploration, but Spanish kings also had to heed economic considerations and were preoccupied with the immediately accessible riches of the Moluccas. In 1524 Charles V ordered a second expedition to make its way by Magellan's route to the Spice Islands.

Well equipped and provisioned, a fleet of seven ships under García Jofre de Loaisa sailed out of La Coruña in northern Spain early on an April morning in 1525. Aboard the flagship, *Santa Maria de la Victoria*, was a 28-year-old Basque soldier, Andrés de Urdaneta. As a youth he had prepared for a career in the Church, studying Latin and philosophy as his parents wished but after their deaths he followed his own preference, becoming a soldier in Charles V's wars in Italy and Germany. Urdaneta's bravery earned him the rank of captain, and during pauses in the turmoil of military life, he studied mathematics, cosmography and astronomy. Now, an alert and resilient young man, he had won a place in the expedition's military contingent.

Storms struck as the fleet made its way southward along South America's east coast. One ship was driven ashore and broke up, another disappeared, never to be seen again; a third turned and sailed back to Spain. The four remaining vessels made it through Magellan Strait and into the Pacific, but a few days later they were caught in a wildly storm-whipped sea. Urdaneta wrote in his journal: 'We were separated from one another, and we never saw each other again.'[7]

The smallest vessel dared not continue alone and headed for Mexico. Another ship, the *San Lesmes*, simply vanished. Loaisa died, but his flagship and one other vessel made it separately across the ocean. The second ship was wrecked in the Philippines, where most of the men were killed or enslaved, but the battered flagship reached Tidore where the survivors, including Urdaneta, spent the next eight years fighting off the Portuguese. Only seventeen men lived to be finally repatriated to Spain. Urdaneta gave his account to Charles V and travelled on to Mexico where he declined the command of a new expedition and in 1552, at the age of 54, joined the Augustinian Order of friars. In his portrait he stands in the voluminous black habit of the order, but his hawk-like nose and long, strong, pointed chin are those of an adventurer. Urdaneta was not to stay cloistered for long.

In 1527 Charles V directed Cortés, Governor of New Spain, or Mexico, to send out three ships to find Loaisa's fleet. Commanded by Alvaro Saavedra de Cerón, the ships went west on the northeast trade winds, but near the Marshall Islands they became separated, and two were never seen again. The commander and his flagship reached Tidore, and Saavedra attempted the return voyage to Mexico via the north coast of New Guinea. Driven back by adverse winds, he tried a more northerly route, but when he and his successor in command both died at sea, the remaining officers and crew returned to Tidore, where they joined the embattled survivors of Loaisa's fleet.

In 1529 Portuguese ownership of the Spice Islands was finally settled by a payment of 350 000 ducats from Portugal to Spain, and Spanish interest shifted to the

Philippines, an archipelago of 7000 little-known islands. Although the group was actually within Portuguese space, Spain had possession, and the islands were far enough from Portuguese bases to make policing them difficult, although the attempt was made from time to time.

The Spaniards' fervid passion for gold had been aroused once more as, in their conquest of Peru, they heard tales of islands westward across the Pacific that were rich in priceless metals. A Peruvian legend related how the Inca Tupac Yupanqui had once made a year's voyage across the sea, discovering two islands and returning with gold, silver, a copper throne, slaves and the hides of horse-like animals. This story had intriguing parallels with the European theory, supported by a noted astronomer, that Ophir, from whose mines King Solomon had obtained gold for the temple at Jerusalem, lay in the same direction, not in southern Arabia or India as had long been thought. Could these mysterious places lie in the undiscovered Great South Land? To find them would be one of the supreme achievements of discovery. And many Spaniards were convinced that this achievement belonged to Spain.

Against this background a somewhat obscure attempt to find new lands was made in 1536 by one Hernando de Grijalva, who, on a return journey to Mexico from an errand in Peru, turned his ship into the Pacific, possibly on orders from Cortés. As water and provisions grew short, Grijalva attempted to return, but was blocked by strong northeasterly winds. His crew mutinied, slew their commander and set a course for the Moluccas. Shipwrecked off New Guinea, they were either killed or enslaved by natives until a few survivors were ransomed two years later by the Portuguese.

In 1542 an expedition of six ships under Ruy López de Villalobos left the port of Navidad in Mexico under orders from the king to conquer and colonise the Islands of the West, as the Spaniards called the Philippines. Gold, spices and other products were to be sought, and peaceful relations and fair standards of trade established with the natives. The voyage across the Pacific took three months. Villalobos then spent more than a year in Philippine waters and on Mindanao and adjacent islands, trying to found a colony. Defeated by hunger, contrary winds and natives turned against him by the Portuguese, he finally took his survivors to the Moluccas, where he negotiated a treaty with its administrators and subsequently died of fever.

It was not until April 1565 that Spain founded a lasting colony in the Philippines. Sailing from Acapulco, Mexico, Miguel López de Legazpi crossed the Pacific and, after a three-month reconnaisance of the surrounding islands, landed at Cebu with three ships and some 300 men, exactly 44 years after Magellan's death. Legazpi established a settlement and six years later transferred Spain's administration to the port of Manila on Luzon island, where a Spanish city of straight stone-paved streets, balconied houses, churches and massive fortifications grew up. With Legazpi on the voyage had been Miguel de Urdaneta, summoned from his monastery to help to prepare and guide the expedition and to find a viable return route to the Americas. Urdaneta had asked that the expedition go first to New Guinea so as to discover whether it was part of the Great South Land that might extend into the

Antarctic or across the South Pacific to the Strait of Magellan. At the time, however, authorities in Mexico were interested in first securing the Philippines and then finding the winds and currents that would provide a Pacific return route.

Accordingly, on 1 June 1565 a ship navigated by the hardy 67-year-old friar sailed from Cebu and, steering north, found the prevailing currents and westerlies of the North Pacific, which over three months later brought the ship within sight of California and, on 1 October, to the Mexican port of Navidad. A breakaway ship of Legazpi's fleet, captained by one Alonso de Arellano, had raced on ahead and reached the Americas two months ahead of Urdaneta, but Arellano was considered a deserter and credit for establishing the route went to the Augustinian. Urdaneta reported to the governing board in Mexico City. Then, journeying to Spain, he reported to the king. On his return to Mexico he asked to be sent back to the Philippines for missionary work, but was deemed too old. He died in the Augustinian house in Mexico City in 1568.

Before 1565 several ships had crossed the Pacific from the Americas by riding the southeasterly trade winds but, faced with the same winds against them, they were unable to return the same way. Spain could not seriously consider either exploration or trade until a workable return route had been found. This Urdaneta accomplished. As yet no other European nation had trespassed upon the broad Pacific, and with her sea lanes established, Spain came to regard the ocean, and any lands that might be discovered there, as part of its widening imperial domain.

In 1563 the navigator Juan Fernández became famous

as a sailing *brujo*, or wizard, by completing the voyage from
Callao, Peru, to Valparaiso, Chile, in 30 days instead of the
usual 90. He then made several trips westward into the
Pacific and discovered a number of islands off the South
American coast, including the little group now named for
him. What Fernández was looking for is not clear, but his
fame as a navigator and accounts of his offshore adventur-
ings fuelled the belief that he had seen some part of Terra
Australis Incognita. In a petition to Philip III Arias de
Loyola described the 'very fertile and agreeable continent'[8]
and the gentle, well-clad people supposedly seen by
Fernández, and pressed for the colonisation and christian-
isation of 'that Austral Land'.[9] Later English writers
suggested that Fernández had reached New Zealand, but
that is problematic because Fernández reportedly made his
landfall after a month's sailing, too short a time for a sixteenth century Pacific crossing. The mystery of the
southern ocean remained.

In the late sixteenth and early seventeenth centuries
the dynamism that had carried the conquering Spanish
through the Americas seemed to shift to the Philippines. In
1606 a strong expeditionary force from Manila seized the
spice-bearing islands of Ternate and Tidore, which had
fallen to the Dutch. Another expedition restored to his
throne a deposed native ruler of Borneo and formally
claimed the country for Spain. The Caroline Islands were
explored and the Mariana Islands colonised, mainly on
Guam. There was a colony at Jilong in northern Taiwan,
and alternating invasions and peace treaties with Cambodia
and Siam, or Thailand. The dreams and schemes for
empire of governors and military men in Manila, as well as

the proselytising plans of the missionary orders, went further, even to projected invasions of Japan and China, but the immensely long supply lines from Spain, limited local resources and more prudent kings at home curbed their ambitions. Gradually the Spanish momentum faltered, to some extent giving way before the well-organised incursions of the Dutch. Before the end of the sixteenth century, however, a new cycle of discovery had revived the so far haphazard search for the Great South Land, taking at least one Spanish expedition almost to the shores of Australia.

WRECKS AND REMNANTS

Did the Spanish ever reach Australia or New Zealand?

Using the northeasterly trade winds north of the equator to carry their ships from the Americas to the East, and the North Pacific currents and westerlies for the return voyage, Spanish transpacific shipping fell into a circular pattern, staying largely within the northern hemisphere. At times over the years Spanish ships stopping at Pacific islands encountered castaways from earlier expeditions, but there is no record of any Spaniard's being picked up south of Indonesia. Nevertheless, countless ships were lost without trace, and some historians speculate that a few of these may have washed up on Australian or New Zealand beaches.

Of the seven ships of the tragic Loaisa expedition of 1525–26, all but one are accounted for. The *San Lesmes* simply vanished. In 1929 four small cannons were found embedded in coral in shallow water off Amanu Atoll east of Tahiti. Depending on just how they were manufactured, they could have been produced in Europe before 1550, during the following century or at a later date in China. This cannot be determined until the guns are scientifically analysed. Nevertheless, one writer[10] has argued that the cannons came from the *San Lesmes*, which he believes was wrecked on the atoll, 5000 to 6000km from where it was last seen. According to his theory, the survivors and their descendants gradually made their way through the Pacific Islands until they reached New Zealand.

Another researcher[11] conjectures that, attempting to return to Spain, the *San Lesmes* missed her reentry into the Strait of Magellan and was driven by powerful winds towards Antarctica, first to 62°S and then westward to New Zealand or the Australian east coast. If so, the *San Lesmes* would have had to battle her way through the wild westerlies between 40°S and 50°S, and then sail for months in subantarctic latitudes in the depths of the southern winter. On the other hand, the vessel might have made her way to New Zealand or Australia in more northerly latitudes. Two maps, one made by the Englishman John Speed in 1626—sixteen years before Abel Tasman's voyage—contain legends claiming Spanish or Portuguese knowledge of continental land in the area of New Zealand.

Around 1837 a missionary saw Maoris using the upper part of a bronze bell as a cooking pot. He was told that it had been in their possession for generations, and, indeed, the bell is today estimated to be 400 to 500 years old. Of a type used by the Tamils of southern India, it bears an inscription in archaic Tamil stating that it belonged to a member of the seafaring Marakkaiyar people of India and Java.

The bell has been speculatively linked to Cristavão de Mendonça, to descendants of *San Lesmes* survivors, and to a drifting derelict Indian vessel. More realistically, perhaps, an old bell picked up in the East might have come to New Zealand in the 1790s to 1830s, when sealing and whaling ships from all over the world were calling at New Zealand ports.[12]

Another source of speculation is the so-called Spanish helmet reportedly brought up from Wellington harbour some time before 1904 and currently dated by the National Museum of New Zealand to about 1580.[13] The helmet is of iron, a plain but crested example of the 'close helmet' popular throughout Europe in the sixteenth and seventeenth centuries. Rivets and rivet holes show that a visor, chinpiece and gorget were once attached.

How did it reach New Zealand? With one of Mendonça's men? With the *San Lesmes* or one of those other vanished vessels? Or at a much later date? We will probably never know. The long white beaches of Australia also invite imaginative theories, and rumours of the remains of Spanish ships among the sand dunes arise from time to time, but nothing identifiably Spanish—and usually nothing at all—has ever been found.

A NEW ROUND OF EXPLORATION

While Legazpi consolidated his settlements in the Philippines, a new round of exploration was beginning from Spain's ports on the South American west coast. Part of the motivation lay in the Inca tales of islands abounding in gold and silver and the theory that the mines of Ophir were somewhere in the Pacific. Of more immediate concern were the devastating raids on Spanish treasure ships by the English adventurers Francis Drake and Thomas Cavendish, and the inroads of the Dutch in the East, which had alerted Spain to the possibility that other nations might set up bases in its Pacific domain. A Spanish way station somewhere between Peru and the Philippines—conceivably on the coast of the Great South Land—would provide a strategic advantage. Glory, riches and the honour of spreading the Roman Catholic faith to new lands were seldom far from the minds of the Spanish kings, the high-ranking men who hoped to lead such expeditions, the missionary friars and the impoverished soldiers and seamen who would volunteer, whatever the risks. And the vision of a rich and welcoming southern continent, pictured for them on maps and by the acounts of previous adventurers, hovered luminously behind their aspirations.

Thus, between 1565 and 1605 three new expeditions were launched from Peru. Notably, their routes were to take them south of the equator.

The man behind the first of these expeditions was Pedro Sarmiento de Gamboa, a mathematician and scientist in whose adventurous life there are some blank spaces. For reasons unknown he fled suddenly from New Spain to Peru, where he became interested in the legends of the Incas, which he linked to the supposed lands of Lucach and Beach in Terra Australis. As a scientist and historian, he also supported the theory that King Solomon's mines were west of Peru. Possibly because of some scientific project, he found himself in 1564 facing the terrifying ordeal of arraignment for conjuration, or witchcraft, before the

Inquisition in Lima. Although he was exonerated and managed to retain his reputation as a historian and astronomer, he continued to be harassed by the Inquisitors as he stubbornly pursued his scientific interests. In 1567 Sarmiento's petitions to the viceroy of Peru resulted in the preparation of two ships, which sailed from Callao in November with instructions to find and settle the great southern continent. Sarmiento captained one of the ships, but to his angry disappointment command of the expedition went to Alvaro de Mendaña de Neira, the viceroy's young nephew. Mendaña was 26, and he believed as fervently as Sarmiento in lands of gold to the west. It was a dream that never left him.

In 80 days of sailing, the ships sighted only reefs and a small island, probably Nui in today's Tuvalu. In early February 1568 they made landfall on an island Mendaña named Santa Isabel, in the group that retains the name of the Solomon Islands. A settlement was established and a boat built to survey and chart the surrounding sea and islands. Very soon, however, the Spaniards roused the enmity of the islanders. Having found no gold and little food, and beset by attack and sickness, they shifted the colony to the site of today's Honiara on Guadalcanal. When this led only to further warfare with the natives, the community moved again, to San Cristóbal. Finally, in September, the Spaniards evacuated and returned in abysmal failure to Peru.

While Mendaña realised that he had not found the Great South Land, he was certain he had come upon its outlying islands, and he steadfastly refused to give up this conviction. For 27 years he pressed for another expedition, and finally, in 1595, then in his mid-50s, he sailed again for the Solomons, this time with four ships, from the Peruvian port of Paita. This was not merely a voyage of exploration. Its purpose was to begin the colonisation of Terra Australis, and in addition to 280 soldiers and sailors, the ships carried 378 men, women and children who expected to settle on the Islands of Solomon near the coast of the Great South Land. As his chief pilot and captain of the flagship, Mendaña had a man who would become even more zealously dedicated than he to the mirage of Terra Australis. This was Pedro Fernández de Quirós, a Portuguese navigator then about 30 years old.

Crossing the Pacific, the expedition discovered the Marquesas Islands, which Mendaña took to be the Solomons. Realising his mistake, he named the the little archipelago in honour of the Marqués de Cañete, Governor of Peru. After three more months at sea the Solomons had still not been sighted. Errors in observed latitude and failure to calculate longitude led the ships instead to Ndeni Island in the Santa Cruz group, today a part of the Solomons but several hundred kilometres southeast of Guadalcanal and the other islands of the first settlements. Mendaña now established his colony at Santa Cruz. The result was disastrous. The settlers fell victim to rampant disease and massacre by the natives. Ships were lost at sea and bitter dissension broke out. Mendaña was dead at the end of the first month, having named his wife, Isabel Barreto, as governor in his place. A month later the surviving colonists abandoned the settlement and embarked for the Philippines under Quirós. Six terrible weeks later one ship and about 100 people reached Manila.

The catastrophe of Santa Cruz in no way altered Quirós's dedication to finding Terra Australis. He firmly believed not only that the atolls and islands they had seen were on the fringe of the great continent, but that he was chosen by God, who would guide him to complete the discovery. He was particularly impressed by the people of the Marquesas, whom he found more civilised than other island people he had seen, and he developed a theory about their origins that Juan de Iturbe, who later sailed with him as comptroller and overseer, expressed:

> seeing that those islands lay in the middle of the ocean, they [Quirós] considered that they could not have been colonized from Peru nor from New Spain, which lay 600 leagues away, nor from the western part, in which direction they afterwards sailed for 1200 leagues. It seemed a very obvious fact and one which left no room for doubt that the mainland of the southern zone, whence these islands must have been colonized, was very near.[14]

The Spaniards did not realise that the early Polynesians had spread throughout the Pacific because they were able to navigate over vast stretches of ocean in open craft, without the instruments the Europeans possessed. Quirós concluded that the Marquesans' land of origin must be close, and that it had to be the Great South Land.

He spent nine years seeking the support of the Pope and the king of Spain for a new expedition. To the Pope he passionately urged the importance of taking the Catholic faith to Terra Australis and to the king he wrote repeatedly of a just and holy enterprise that could make

Philip III 'the lord, known, obeyed and served from one pole to another'.[15]

In 1605 he finally returned to Peru with the necessary documents to lay before the viceroy, who ordered two ships, the *San Pedro y San Pablo* and the *San Pedro*, and a smaller launch or tender to be thoroughly reconditioned and provisioned. Amid flying flags and banners and gun salutes, the little fleet left Callao on 21 December 1605.

Quarrels arose a fortnight out of port when in an otherwise clear sky low clouds—to many seamen an indication of land—were seen on the southwestern horizon. Quirós agreed to alter course in that direction, but during the night, he unaccountably turned west, and the other ships had to follow. Mutinous mutterings mounted as the fleet came to one barren, waterless islet after another. At the island of Taumako, in the Duff group of the Santa Cruz Islands, tempers flared again. The chief pilot, a surgeon and Diego de Prado y Tovar—one of several *entretenidos*, gentleman adventurers who joined expeditions at their own expense—transferred from the flagship, the *San Pedro y San Pablo*, to the *San Pedro*, commanded by Luis Baéz de Torres. Within a few days larger islands were seen, and on 1 May 1606 the three vessels entered an extensive bay on the coast of a land Quirós named Austrialia del Espíritu Santo, in acknowledgment of the Spanish king's descent from the royal House of Austria. It was, in fact, the largest island of present-day Vanuatu.

Quirós was certain that he had found the Great South Land. With the ardour of a visionary, he planned a marble city to be called New Jerusalem, created a knighthood with which he invested every member of the expedition and, according to the record of the *entretenido* Diego de Prado, announced that he would send for 3000 friars to convert the natives of the South Land to the Catholic faith. Dressed in the brown habit of a Franciscan friar, he spoke mystically of the glories of the land they had found. The realities were very different. The settlement was a cluster of makeshift huts and a chapel of green branches, and exploration outside the bay was frustrated by contrary winds and, on land, by mountainous, thickly wooded terrain and warlike islanders. Quirós's attitude towards the natives was both humane and conciliatory, in line with many Church and royal directives. In practice, these instructions often failed, here as elsewhere. The islanders simply did not want these strangers on their soil. There were misunderstandings, individual Europeans acted aggressively and, needing food but failing or not bothering to negotiate an acceptable exchange, the crews often seized whatever fruit, vegetables, or pigs they found, further incensing the inhabitants.

At the beginning of June the ships attempted to leave the bay to continue exploring. Violent winds drove them back, and on the night of 11 June 1606 the *San Pedro y San Pablo* became separated from the other two vessels and disappeared. Only months later did the men of the other ships learn that Quirós had recrossed the Pacific to New Spain.

Torres searched for the flagship for two weeks. On the fifteenth day, in the presence of all remaining officers, he opened sealed orders which made him commander of the expedition. The two ships then sailed far enough around Espíritu Santo to confirm that it was an island, not the Great South Land, and then bore southward to 21°S in the

Coral Sea, seeking the continent. There was only ocean.
Had Torres then sailed directly west he would eventually
have arrived on the Queensland coast close to where
Mackay is today. Instead he took the expedition north,
encountered the Louisade Archipelago at the eastern end
of New Guinea, and, unable to find a way through to the
north, headed west through the strait later named for him.
He then turned north again, stopped at the island of
Ternate, which had recently been taken from the Dutch by
the Spanish, and on 1 May 1607 dropped anchor in Manila
Bay.

Luis Baéz de Torres is one of the more attractive and
mysterious figures in the early history of Australia. Prado
called him a Breton, which suggests that he came from
Galicia, in Spain's northwest, long ago settled by Celts.
Other than that nothing is known of his origins. The earliest mention of him is Quirós's request that he be
appointed captain of the *San Pedro*, partly, it seems, because
prospective crewmen were asking for him. During the
transpacific voyage Torres had none of the shipboard
dissension that plagued the flagship, and in the seventeen-
month journey, brought his ship safely through the
difficult, uncharted waters between Papua New Guinea and
Australia and then north to finish the voyage with the loss
of only one man.

On arrival in Manila, Torres expected to have his ship
refitted for his return to either Spain or New Spain, where
he planned to report in person to the king or his representatives. He therefore wrote only a brief report to Philip
III, with which he enclosed five charts drawn by Prado. All
arrived in Spain, but only four survive. These show anchor-

ages where the ships spent ten days or more and are a combination of perspective and plan, with details of the coastal landscape meticulously drawn. Distances would have been largely estimated by sight and do not extend beyond perhaps 8 or 10km. All the locations are easily identified, including the present Big Bay at Espíritu Santo and places on the New Guinea coast. In addition to the missing fifth chart, some documents make fleeting references to others, all apparently lost. With Torres's letter and Prado's charts there were four watercolour sketches, allegedly of natives in each of the areas mapped. They are obviously not drawn from life, but were probably done in Manila from someone's general descriptions.

Torres wrote another letter, perhaps with more navigational detail, which he sent to Quirós. This letter has been lost, and only a rather confusing summary, written by Quirós, exists today.

Torres's letters, an account written by Prado, the maps and the drawings are the only evidence we have on whether Torres actually saw the continent of Australia and whether he believed he was at the edge of the Great South Land. He knew, of course, that the route he was following was new to Europeans. On the maps with which he was familiar he would have been sailing overland, as New Guinea was usually shown to be part of a larger South Land.

The surviving accounts, especially that of Prado, provide considerable detail on the islands, reefs and currents encountered by the Spaniards, but as the strait abounds in all of these, and one reef or islet looks much like another, identifying them is difficult. The latitudes given may not be accurate, and longitude is never mentioned. In one part of his narrative Prado simply wrote 'at the end of two days on the eve of S. Francis [1 October] we found other islands to the north and among them one bigger than the rest.'[16] With a little more precision Torres wrote, 'we had to go out turning south-west in the said depth, to eleven degrees, and the bank goes lower: there were very large islands and they seemed more on the southern part.'[17] Here the latitude, with allowance for a slight error, could put the *San Pedro* in the Endeavour Strait later traversed by Cook; if so, the 'large islands' sighted could include Prince of Wales Island or parts of the mainland of Australia. Torres and his ships were in this general area from 1 to 3 October, and if they were, in fact, passing the Australian coast, the Spaniards would have watched the scrub-grown bluffs and white beaches for at least two days.

However, scholars have not always agreed on the translation of the Spanish documents, nor on the interpretation of the remarks themselves. Some have set Torres's course close to New Guinea, while others have focused on passages just north of Endeavour Strait. In either case, Torres saw at close hand many of the Torres Strait Islands which are today part of Australian territory. Possibly he believed that he had left Terra Australis far behind in the South Pacific or somewhere beyond the range of his explorations in the Coral Sea, and that what he was seeing during those first days of October 1606 were no more than additional islands.

After June 1608, Torres, still in Manila, disappears from history. His account of his remarkable voyage was filed in Spanish archives, not to emerge for 175 years. Prado apparently showed his own *relación* of the voyage to the historian Hernando de los Ríos Coronel, who mentioned it in 1621. The paper then vanished from view until a copy was discovered among documents sold at a London auction in the 1920s.

Traces of information on the discovery of Torres Strait seem to have slipped through Spain's formidable curtain of secrecy, possibly by way of a now-lost chart. A map of the Pacific probably made in 1622 by the Dutch cartographer Hessel Gerritsz contains a note indicating that Spanish maps showed the passage of a small ship from Quirós's expedition south of the 'Coast of the Papuas' in 10°S. On a map the geographer Gilles Robert de Vaugondy published in France more than a century later, an obvious strait is shown between the Australian mainland, by then called Nouvelle Hollande, and the island of New Guinea. More significant is the juxtaposition of Dutch place names in New Holland with Spanish names along the southern coast of New Guinea. Some of these names and variations of them had already appeared on a French map of 1700. Here the New Guinea coast was shown between 9 and 10°S latitude. Since no other navigator traversed Torres Strait until Cook did so in 1770, it seems reasonable to suppose that the Spanish names and the idea of a seaway at approximately 10°S derived, directly or indirectly, from Torres, perhaps via charts brought secretly out of Spain or Portugal.

An interesting tie-in with Cook's first voyage seems also to exist. A brief but obvious reference to Torres's passage through the strait occurs in a memorial written by the Spanish scholar Juan Luis Arias de Loyola to King Philip IV in about 1630–33. A copy of this document came into the hands of the British geographer Alexander Dalrymple after the brief 1762 English occupation of Manila. Dalrymple included this information in his book *Discoveries Made in the South Pacifick Ocean, Previous to 1764*, printed and privately circulated in 1767, although not published until 1769.

Dalrymple gave a copy of the book to Joseph Banks before he sailed with Cook and the *Endeavour* in August 1768. Full recognition of Torres's achievement, however, had to wait for nearly 200 years after his unrecorded death.

The later story of Quirós, however, is well documented. He returned to Spain in 1607 to petition and negotiate for a new expedition, still unassailably wedded to his belief that he had come close to the Great South Land. Spanish authorities did not doubt the existence of Terra Australis, but they had serious reservations as to Quirós's ability to lead. Several of the officers who had served with him had harshly criticised his conduct as commander. For seven years his case was almost continuously before the king and his councillors, until in 1614 Quirós received authority for another voyage. He set out for Peru with a new viceroy in April 1615, but in Panama, on the threshold of his third expedition, Quirós died.

Quirós's vision of the Great South Land gave new substance to the speculations of Europeans, bolstering the concept of a marvellous new world in the south. Some 25 books on Quirós's voyages were published in Spanish, Latin, French, English, Dutch and German. When in 1615 the Dutch expedition of Willem Schouten and Jacob Lemaire set out in search of the Great South Land, Quirós's description of the magnificent southern continent was read to the officers. Some cartographers used Quirós's claims to substantiate their own belief in the South Land, and on certain later maps Vanuatu—that is, Espíritu Santo—appeared as the eastern edge of Terra Australis.

About this time an entirely different flight of imagination on the South Land took place in England. Joseph Hall, a bishop and moral philosopher, in 1605 published anonymously a satire of contemporary society, written in Latin and titled *Mundus Alter et Idem*, or 'The World Different and the Same', which was translated a few years later as *The Discovery of a New World*. Hall's protagonist is Marcus Britannicus, who spends 30 years in Terra Australis Incognita, a world consisting of four areas, one inhabited by gluttons, another by fools, a third by thieves and the fourth, Shee-landt, by women. A part of Shee-landt is Double-sex Ile, whose hermaphrodite inhabitants dress in a combination of men's and women's clothing and bear such names as Mary-philip or Peter-alice. Anyone of a single sex is publicly displayed as a freak and a monster. Few concepts of the Great South Land could have been more different from Quirós's notion of an innocent world awaiting Christianity.

Torres's voyage is the only documented approach to Australian shores by a Spanish explorer. Some lost or disoriented vessel could, of course, have reached the coast, and speculation on this possibility is revived from time to time with the finding of some fragment of an old ship or ship's gear. The expedition was also the last of the great Spanish sea voyages of exploration. Entangled in costly European wars, mired in outdated social and economic policies, wracked by plague, Spain abandoned any further dreams of new worlds.

The riddle of the elusive Great South Land would be confronted next by the men of another nation, rebels within Spain's European empire and a rapidly rising power on the oceans of the world. These were the Dutch, the merchant-mariners of a new nation, the United Provinces of the Netherlands.

8.

The Merchant Mariners

The northwestern corner of the European continent is a region of extraordinarily flat land, edged by the North Sea and gouged by the estuaries of the great rivers that flow through it—the Rhine, the Maas, the Scheldt. Over the centuries small principalities formed here—Flanders, Brabant, Liège, Hainault, Holland, Utrecht, Luxembourg and others. Populations grew, land was reclaimed from woods and bogs, and water boards organised the building of canals and dikes to battle the inroads of the sea, while the towns, many of them strategically placed for shipping on rivers as well as the sea, developed fishing, trade, banking and industries. Shipping became increasingly important, and the region's vessels plied the rivers and coastal waters of Europe.

In the fifteenth and sixteenth centuries the political strategies and dynastic marriages of Europe's greater nations brought these little states of the Low Countries into the sprawling Habsburg empire, to be dominated first by Austria and then by Spain with policies that steadily eroded the autonomy of the local princes and the states or assemblies of the provinces. Social and economic problems—wars with France, inflation, epidemics, floods and poor harvests—heightened the unrest. The issue of religion also came to the fore.

Religious debate and reform had long been part of the intellectual life of the Low Countries, and in the mid-1500s Calvinist Protestantism spread strongly. It was a stern, strict, highly disciplined faith whose adherents did not hold back from taking forcible action, freeing coreligionists from prison and on occasion attacking monasteries to remove their images and sometimes to close them. As Catholic Spain attempted to crush such disturbances with mounting brutality, rebellion spread, until in 1579 a number of the provinces and cities formed the Union of Utrecht and eventually embarked on a war of independence. From this alliance there emerged a new nation in the northern part of the Low Countries, seven of the little states becoming the United Provinces of the Netherlands or, more commonly, the Dutch Republic. Its central governing body was the States General, with members representing the assemblies of the provinces and headed by chief magistrates elected by the assemblies and later drawn from the princely House of Orange. The war finally ended in 1648 when Spain formally acknowledged the independence of the Netherlands. Flanders, Brabant and Luxembourg remained with Spain.

The VOC

Throughout the decades of war against Spain, Dutch commerce and economic growth had scarcely faltered. Excluded by the Portuguese and Spanish from lucrative trade with the East, Dutch ships had become important carriers of goods along the European coast, and Lisbon was among their principal ports of call. Here they obtained luxury merchandise from Asia for profitable resale elsewhere in Europe. In 1580, however, Philip II of Spain assumed the crown of Portugal, and four years later he closed the port of Lisbon to the Dutch. Dutch merchants now had to consider establishing a direct commercial link of their own to the faraway source of these important goods.

For many years Dutch navigators and geographers had been assembling what information they could about the East, mainly from sources in Portugal, guarded though they were. In 1595 the brothers Cornelis and Frederik de Houtman returned to Amsterdam from Portugal, where they had been imprisoned for espionage. In the same year Jan Huyghen van Linschoten, a traveller who had spent fourteen years in the Portuguese East, published a highly informative account of his adventures, accompanied by maps of the East Indies based on the work of Luis Teixeira, mathematician and cosmographer to the Spanish crown. Charts, sailing instructions and translations of imported navigational texts were circulated. As well, there were many Dutch mariners who had sailed on Portuguese ships and could describe the route from first-hand experience.

Of the Netherlands provinces Holland had emerged as the most prosperous, and its capital, Amsterdam, became the commercial centre of the republic and of much of Europe as well. A group of Amsterdam merchants now formed a syndicate to establish trade with the East Indies, and in the spring of 1595 sent out a squadron of four ships under the command of Cornelis de Houtman. They followed the Portuguese route around the Cape of Good Hope to Goa and the Indonesian islands and returned to the Netherlands in mid-1597. Despite serious losses and small profit, the voyage was an important breakthrough.

Other companies formed, and fleet followed fleet. In 1602 the companies amalgamated to create the United East India Company, the Vereenigde Oostindische Companie or VOC, which henceforth directed sea trade between the Netherlands and the Indies. The six principal Dutch seaports were represented by units called chambers, made up of directors, who held office for life and nominated their replacements as needed. The Company's executive was a seventeen-member council, often called The Seventeen, which determined Company policy, decided on the size and outfitting of the fleets, and allotted ships to the various chambers. The council had absolute power over the operations of the VOC and over the people it employed.

Having obtained from the States General a charter granting a monopoly on maritime trade between the Cape of Good Hope and the Strait of Magellan, the VOC set about extending the Netherlands' commercial domain with ruthless energy and astonishing speed. With authority to maintain armed forces, make treaties and declare war, ships and men of the VOC penetrated more and more deeply into Portugal's eastern territories, vigorously displacing the Portuguese and eventually other maritime powers from many of their trading centres. Forceful governors-general either fought or negotiated with native princes, battled English traders in Indonesian ports, raided Spanish ships and towns in the Philippines, and built a steadily growing chain of forts to guard their harbours and plantations. By 1599 Dutch captains had reached the Spice Islands. At settlements like Bantam, Jacatra and Gresik on the Java coast, Patani and Johore on the Malay peninsula, and Amboina, Banda and Ternate in the Moluccas, the Dutch obtained trade monopolies from local rulers. Their commercial centres, with garrisoned forts, port facilities and factories— trading posts with warehouses, offices and resident traders, or factors—studded the islands. In many places the ruins of the forts can still be seen, their thick stone walls now dark with mould and overgrown with vegetation.

At first the VOC had no permanent administrative centre in the East. Its admirals and their staffs travelled among the islands with their fleets, governing from their flagships and stopping from time to time at company trading stations, of which the one at Bantam, now Banten, at the northwestern tip of Java, was the most important. Among the rival trading groups in this part of the East, the VOC grew rapidly more formidable, with its competent organisation, reliable financing and well-armed ships. Indonesian ports, however, were generally open to other nationalities as well, and there were often street fights between sailors and exchanges of threats between ships' commanders. In 1618, after a months-long battle against the English and some Javanese, the VOC's governor-general in the Indies, Jan Pieterszoon Coen, captured the port of Jacatra on Java's north coast. Coen razed the settlement and built a new walled and moated town, which, as Batavia, became the centre of Dutch trade and administration in the Indies. Company ships, foreign vessels and local craft came to anchor in the bay before it. The entrance to the Jacatra

River, running through the town, was guarded by a moated citadel of coral rock. Wharves, warehouses and workshops lined the river, and along the neat, straight streets beyond stood churches, a town hall, and narrow-fronted Dutch-style residences of stucco-covered brick. Gates in a city wall and bridges over a broad, encircling moat led to suburbs occupied by Chinese, Indonesians, Dutch and other ethnic groups, and to the tropical countryside beyond.

Although in general much like other European vessels, Dutch ships were designed for the principal purpose of carrying freight. They varied in size from light, manoeuvrable little *jachts* and other small craft of up to 50 tonnes capacity to the medium-sized flute, or *fluyt*, to the larger East Indiaman or *retour* ship, built for the long return trip to and from the East and designed to carry about 600 tonnes, although many took on as much as 1000 tonnes. Most ships were three-masted, with the fore and main masts square-rigged and the mizzen lateen-rigged. Their relatively shallow draft enabled them to enter most harbours and even river mouths, and their greatly expanded hulls, tapering up to high, narrow superstructures, were built for maximum cargo space and, thus, profit. To deal with pirates, the Portuguese or local opposition, all ships were armed with swivel guns and cannons mounted a metre or more higher than in English vessels so that lower-deck gunports did not have to be closed. Their crews at this time were usually experienced Dutch seamen, and in addition they carried soldiers, who defended them from attack, accompanied shore parties and, once in the East, could be posted to centres in India or the Indies. Usually, with the intention of mutual support, the ships left Netherlands seaports in groups of three or more with a fleet commander, sometimes a ranking Company official on his way to a posting in the East. Once at sea, however, they were often separated by rough weather, the darkness of night, variations in speed, or accidents and other delays, arriving singly at the journey's ports of call and finally at Bantam or Batavia.

The VOC itself was an efficient and disciplined organisation, imposing strict regulations and extremely severe penalties on any of its own employees who erred, as well as on foreigners who violated its rules or failed to meet its demands. The Company's archives hold many mentions of heavy fines and other harsh financial penalties, the discharge of officers, permanent banishment from Company territory, lashings, torture and hanging. The long voyages in cramped conditions, together with hunger, thirst and exhaustion, bred violence, and with the shadow of mutiny often close to the surface, commanders responded ruthlessly to the slightest hint of insubordination. Negligence or failure in duty at sea, as on the part of a captain who lost his ship, or moral transgressions such as rape or homosexuality were punished with the same relentless justice.

Support from the Netherlands was strong and businesslike. Letters, reports and instructions travelled regularly between the governor-general and his council in Batavia and VOC headquarters in Amsterdam. New chartings by navigators went to Company cartographers, who updated the maps distributed to pilots and skippers. Embarking captains and commanders received explicit instructions, usually with alternatives in case the need arose. The principal aim of all VOC enterprise was trade, and this was clearly expressed in all directives. The Dutch were devout, and prepared at all times to attribute good fortune or bad to the gracious will of God, but their religion did not require the explorers to try to convert the heathen. Missions and churches might come later, at an established settlement. By contrast, the Portuguese, ineffectively supported from home and frequently lacking in money, manpower and other resources, were further burdened by the evangelical requirements of the Catholic Church.

THE FIRST ENCOUNTER WITH AUSTRALIA

The Dutch were never mesmerised by the elusive dream of a vast and extravagantly wealthy South Land. They did not send expeditions in pursuit of storied golden isles. It is clear from their maps that they accepted the existence of Terra Australis, and the discovery of 'south lands' was usually one of the aims of the Company's voyages of exploration. Yet their focus remained realistically commercial, and their voyaging in the East reflected this. Initially, they found it both easier and more profitable to seize existing trading posts from the Portuguese or to establish new ones through agreements with local rulers than to search for undiscovered territory.

Gold certainly held its fascination for the VOC's investors, but it was one of many commodities—including iron and lead, precious stones, pearls, rare woods, spices and other marketable products—that the Company's navigators were told to seek. VOC ships were invariably accompanied by a commercial agent, usually a higher-ranking upper merchant, who was responsible for the company's trade interests and carried considerable authority. Paradoxically, it would be the practical concerns of pragmatic merchants and officials, not golden fantasies, that would finally draw the veil from the Great South Land and uncover the reality of New Holland.

By 1605 the VOC was securely entrenched throughout the Indonesian island chain. Probably under orders from the Netherlands, Frederik de Houtman, governor of Amboina, today's Ambon, instructed Jan Willemsz Verschoor, director of the Bantam factory, to assist in refitting a vessel to explore seas and lands beyond the Company's current trading horizons, and specifically to discover 'the vast land of Nova Guinea and other east- and south-lands'.[1] The ship was a small three-master about nineteen metres long, smaller even than the average *jacht*. In 1595 she had, in fact, been the smallest vessel in the first Dutch fleet to reach the Indies, and after two long trips home and back, she had been used in exploration, benefiting from her small size, manoeuvrability and shallow draught. She was the Little Dove, or *Duyfken*.

Her captain was Willem Jansz. A career employee of the VOC, he too was a veteran of several trips to and from the Netherlands, and had been the *Duyfken*'s captain on her latest return to the Indies. Also on board was the company's commercial representative, upper merchant Jan Lodewijksz van Rosingeyn. The ship had carried a crew of twenty on her first voyage out from the Netherlands, and presumably a like number manned her now. Probably she was armed very much as on the first journey, with two bronze and six iron cannons together with two old-style stonepieces, so-called for their original stone cannonballs. These would have been small cannons, possibly arranged as swivel guns, set into stirrup mountings on the side rails of the ship, and able to be swung full circle, providing a wide field of fire and easy reloading.

In November 1605 the *Duyfken* sailed from Bantam. Lying in the Bantam roads at the time was an English ship, whose captain, John Saris, observed their departure. In his journal he wrote, '[On] the eighteenth heere departed a small Pinasse of the Flemmings, for the discovery of the Land called Nova Guinea which, as it is said, affordeth great store of Gold.'[2]

A few months later Saris noted that on 15 June an Indian captain 'in a Java Junke' from Banda had told him that 'the Flemmings Pinasse'

> which went upon discovery of Nova Ginny, was returned
> to Banda, having found the Iland: but in sending their
> men on shoare to intreate of Trade, there nine of them
> killed by the Heathens, which are man-eaters; So they
> were constrained to returne, finding no good to be done
> there.[3]

Thus, although no Dutch record of dates is preserved, the timing of the expedition is known through the observations of Captain John Saris. While he did not identify the *Duyfken* by name, the 'pinasse' he saw was most likely that diminutive ship. More, however, is known of the voyage, for a copy of Jansz's chart survives, and his discoveries were subsequently recorded on a map of the Pacific Ocean by the VOC's great cartographer, Hessel Gerritsz. These are probably the first maps that show an actual part of the Australian mainland.

Jansz sailed from Bantam to the Bandas, a cluster of nine little volcanic islands southeast of Ambon. Three of the islands are grouped to create a small, sheltered harbour, and on the largest of these a Dutch garrison guarded the nutmeg plantations.

From Banda Jansz sailed east southeast for the Kai and then the Aru Islands. He reached the coast of today's Irian Jaya in western New Guinea, in the region of today's Palau Yos Sudarso, formerly Frederik Hendrik Island—as it was later named by the Dutch—and coasted to the southeast, going ashore from time to time to seek information on the land, its people and possibilities for trade. The Dutch clashed with the natives, and eight of the Netherlanders were killed. At today's False Cape, or Tanjung Vals, Jansz set his course in the direction of Australia's Cape York. The emergence of a continent from millennia of isolation was about to begin.

Jansz soon encountered a barrier of reefs and islands running to the south, and, believing that he was following an extremely low coast, bore on southward, unaware that he was skirting the western opening to Torres Strait. In 1899 the Dutch historian Jan Ernst Heeres wrote:

> Did Willem Jansz look upon these narrows as an open strait or did he take them to be a bay only? My answer is, that most probably he was content to leave this point altogether undecided.[4]

Jansz did not alter course, and at some point came upon

Cape York Peninsula. He recorded his first landfall as 11°45'S at what is evidently the present Pennefeather River. It was the first documented discovery of Australia, the continent on which disparate visions would converge for almost two centuries to come.

Jansz continued south for almost 200km farther into the Gulf of Carpentaria, on his chart recording the low, flat coast he followed as an extension of New Guinea. He sent ashore landing parties, but they found little food or fresh water. Finally, near what he thought was an offshore island at about 13°51'S, Jansz turned his ship around. He named the island Keerweer, a nautical expression for 'turnagain', and Cape Keerweer—for a cape it is—it remains today.

On his return up the coast Jansz may have bypassed his first landfall at the Pennefeather River, but he set about exploring the mouth of the large Batavia River, now the Ducie River, which, although unnamed by Jansz, can be identified on his chart. The timing of the event is not clear, but here the Dutchmen had their first encounter with the Aborigines. A group investigating the land around the waterway was attacked and one man was speared to death. Now nine men had been killed, as John Saris was later to note. This would have almost halved the crew, and the country had offered nothing of value. Jansz returned to Banda. His journal of the voyage does not survive, nor does any record of his superiors' reaction to his report. In October of the same year, Luis Baéz de Torres took his two ships through the Strait.

While the voyage of the *Duyfken* had produced no commercial gains, Dutch authorities believed that the blank space beyond Keerweer on Jansz's chart should be

The little ship Duyfken, *barely nineteen metres long, brought the Dutch navigator Willem Jansz and his crew to the shores of the Gulf of Carpentaria. They became the first Europeans known to walk on Australian soil.*

investigated further. Letters between VOC directors in Amsterdam and Governor-General Laurens Reael in the Indies discussed plans that were set aside 'owing to other intervening business'—probably the continuing struggle with the Portuguese, the English and the Spanish—but in 1616 it was decided to take the project 'once more in hand'.[5] Reael's enthusiasm had been roused when in Ternate he spoke to Jacob Lemaire, whose expedition was searching for the Great South Land. On 8 October 1616 Reael issued orders for two ships to be prepared for a voyage of discovery, and two weeks later the important VOC official Cornelis Dedel was commissioned to lead them. By May 1617 the voyage for 'discovery of the Southern lands' had been ordered to proceed, but was suddenly halted. Two English ships had been sighted on their way to Banda for nutmegs. Dedel was given a squadron and sent to stop them. He died some seven months later, and the projected voyage was again postponed.

Jansz's map had another effect. When the journey was recorded on a chart by the cartographer Gerritsz, probably in 1622, Cape York Peninsula was drawn as an extension of Nova Guinea. For almost a century and a half to come, New Guinea and Australia would be assumed to be a single land mass.

An efficient and reliable man, Jansz continued to serve the VOC well, rising in rank and in the esteem of his employers. He sailed between Europe and the East, on one voyage encountering again the Australian coast, took part in engagements against the Spanish and the English, and served as commander of the island of Solor, a centre of the sandalwood trade. After being promoted to admiral he served for three and a half years as governor of Banda, where his administration was apparently peaceful and progressive. In 1628, aged 60, he returned to the Netherlands, after which there is no further mention of him in VOC or any other records.

Suddenly there arose a competitive threat to the VOC. In 1614 an Amsterdam merchant, Isaac Lemaire, founded a company appropriately named the Australian, that is, the Southern Company, in order 'to discover great and rich Countries, where they might lade their ships with rich wares and merchandise'.[6] Lemaire was certain that Quirós had found the great southern continent and was determined to reach it. Two ships, the *Hoorn* and the larger *Eendracht*, were equipped and, forbidden by the VOC monopoly from using normal Dutch ports, sailed on 14 June 1615 from the little offshore island of Texel. The expedition was led by Willem Cornelisz Schouten, an experienced mariner, and accompanied by Lemaire's son Jacob as merchant. The ships crossed the Atlantic and, denied access also to the Straits of Magellan by the VOC charter, went south and into the Le Maire Channel, between the island of Tierra del Fuego, at the southern end of South America, and the desolate peaks of Staten or Estados Island, which the Dutch named Staten Landt for the States General of the Netherlands. It would appear on some later maps as a promontory of the earth-encircling Great South Land. The *Hoorn* burned and, alone, the *Eendracht* rounded Cape Horn, which Schouten thought was the sharp, pointed end of a high, snow-covered mainland. In fact, it was one of the little islands that cluster to the south of Tierra del Fuego. In the fog Schouten could not see this, but he had found a new and safer route from the Atlantic to the Pacific. Three years later Tierra del Fuego was circumnavigated by two Spanish ships under the brothers Bartolomé and Gonzalo de Nodal.

The Great South Land eluded Schouten. He took the *Eendracht* too far north to sight any southern hemisphere land other than some islands in the Tongan and Samoan groups. Reaching Ternate, the ship loaded spices, but at Bantam, the governor-general, Coen, on orders from VOC headquarters, had ship and cargo seized, Lemaire having contravened the Company's monopoly. The crew either joined VOC ships or were sent back to Holland, the *Eendracht* sailed under the VOC pennant, and only after years of legal wrangling was Isaac Lemaire compensated for his vessel and cargo.

The earliest Dutch voyages to the Indies followed the Portuguese route around the Cape of Good Hope, up either coast of Madagascar and northeast across the Indian Ocean towards Goa. The African coast, however, was jealously guarded by a line of Portuguese forts, against which two Dutch attacks had failed. As well, Dutch captains were not usually headed for southern India but for the narrow Sunda Strait between Sumatra and Java. For them it was safer and more practicable to sail east of Madagascar and then almost directly across the Indian Ocean, although it was a sea lane of equatorial heat, frequent calms and treacherous shoals, reefs and islands.

In 1610 the VOC commander Hendrik Brouwer tested a new route that would dramatically affect the search for the Great South Land. With two ships Brouwer sailed south from the Cape of Good Hope to between 35°S and 40°S, where strong, prevalent westerlies swept him eastward. When he estimated his little squadron to be approximately south of Sunda Strait, he turned to the north. Brouwer reached Bantam in Java in five months and 24 days, compared with a year or more on the old route, and arrived with a healthier crew and provisions less rotted than usual. He reported the result to his superiors in

Amsterdam, and the new lane, after being trialled successfully by other ships, became in 1616 the mandatory route
for VOC shipping. The decision would be a key to unlock-
ing Australia's isolation, but at the time no one realised that
this route was a direct path across the ocean to an unknown
continent. Although world maps conventionally showed an
extension of the Great South Land in approximately the
location of Western Australia, on mariners' charts the
region was marked as open sea.

To speed the Indies voyage further, the Cape was made
the only permitted place for taking on water, firewood and
fresh food, and sizable bonuses in guilders were offered to
those who made the trip in nine months or less. In 1652
the Company sent Jan van Riebeeck to the Cape to establish a provisioning station for the ships on the Indies run,
a move that would play its part in the search for the Great
South Land. Set between Table Bay and the precipitous
walls of Table Mountain, the station consisted of a small
fort and hospital, warehouses and a shipyard, vegetable gardens and pens for cattle traded from local tribesmen. A
jetty and a few streets and houses appeared as Dutch settlers gradually arrived.

The new route presented one serious difficulty—determining exactly where in the Indian Ocean the vessels must
swing from an easterly heading to a northerly one to reach
Sunda Strait. Article 13 of the Sailing Instructions of 1617
stated that 'Having the Westerly winds, the ships will keep
in Easterly course for at least a thousand *mijlen*.'[7] No
instructions were given in terms of longitude, which could
not then be properly measured. Cartographers did estimate
the length of a degree of longitude, but these calculations

varied considerably, some with built-in errors that could mean miscalculations of hundreds of kilometres over long distances. Yet another source of difficulty lay in charts on which the meridians were drawn the same distance apart from the equator to the poles. This made the breadth of the southern Indian Ocean, for instance, much greater than it really was. Some navigators recognised the problem, but generally it was overlooked, and even when improved map projections were devised, they were adopted only very gradually. In practice, therefore, gauging the passage of 1000 Dutch miles, well over 7000km, from the deck of a ship in an empty ocean depended on dead reckoning alone, subject to the varying skills of the pilots and all possible conditions of weather. The ships of the VOC usually found Sunda Strait, but those that overshot the 1000-*mijlen* point could find themselves driven by the westerlies onto the empty, alien shores of Western Australia.

On 25 October 1616 the VOC ship *Eendracht*, sailing east under the command of Dirck Hartogs, came upon the startling sight of several unknown islands, apparently uninhabited. The ship dropped anchor at one of the islands, a narrow strip with high overhanging limestone cliffs on the ocean side and sloping sand dunes on the side facing a long, low coastline hazily visible across the water. Intrigued, Hartogs and his men explored the island for two days. At its northern end the captain had a flattened pewter plate affixed to a pole. The plate carried the inscription:

1616, the 26th of October has arrived here the ship Deendracht of Amsterdam; the upper merchant Gillis Mibais of Luick; skipper Dirck Hatichs [Hartogs] of

> Amsterdam; the 27th ditto having set sail for Bantam;
> the under-merchant Jan Stins; the upper steersman
> Pieter Doekes van Bil; anno 1616.[8]

Eighty-one years later the inscribed plate was found still in place by another Dutch explorer.

Dirk Hartog Island, as it is called today, lies southwest of Carnarvon and on the seaward side of Western Australia's large, shallow Shark Bay. The northern tip, where the pewter plate was nailed to its pole, is now Inscription Point. A small monument marks the spot where Australia's first known piece of writing was left.

With the inscribed plate, the Dutchmen had unequivocally marked their presence on this lonely shore, but to the question of what shore this was and of where they were, Hartogs and his men had no answers. Contemporary world maps showed that at approximately this location a peninsula of the Great South Land projected towards Java. Did they conclude that they had arrived at the edge of the legendary continent? Hartogs took his ship north, up the western Australian coast to 22°S latitude, near North West Cape, carefully observing and charting what he saw of an unknown shoreline. His discovery was reported in official letters to VOC headquarters, and his journal and charts, now lost, would have reached Amsterdam, but no account survives that reflects the impressions and speculations of Hartogs and his men. Only the pewter plate is first hand evidence of their landing.

A year and a half later, another Dutch ship sailed too far east before turning north on the new East Indies route. The *Zeewolf* had steered eastward from the Cape of Good

Hope until 29 April 1618, when the captain, Haevick Claeszoon van Hillegom, calculated that he had covered the necessary 1000 *mijlen*. He changed his heading to the north and twelve days later, at approximately 21°S latitude, the topmast lookout unexpectedly sighted land, 'a level, low-lying shore of great length'.[9] The landfall was again in the vicinity of North West Cape, but the report of the accompanying upper merchant shows that the astonished men on the *Zeewolf* knew nothing of Hartogs's earlier discovery. He wrote,

> it might well be a mainland coast, for it extended to a very great length. But only the Lord knows the real state of affairs. At all events it would seem never to have been . . . discovered by any one of us, as we have never heard of such discovery, and the chart shows nothing but open ocean as this place.[10]

Two and a half months later, at the end of July, Willem Jansz on the ship *Mauritius* saw Australia for the second time, but without realising that it was the same continent on which he had trod when in 1606 he had landed on the beaches of Cape York Peninsula. The *Mauritius* encountered the west coast at about 22°S, and its men went ashore on what they described as an island, where, with mixed excitement and fear, they saw human footprints. It is likely that their landing was on the peninsula which forms one side of Exmouth Gulf and terminates in North West Cape.

The ship then continued for a considerable distance up the coast. By one account, the captain called it Landt van d'Eendracht when he later learned that Hartogs on the

Eendracht had seen the new land before he did. Another record ascribes the name to a VOC official. In any case, the region appeared under the name Eendrachtsland on Hessel Gerritsz's 1622 manuscript map of the Indian Ocean. Small and detached as was this scrap of shoreline, it was the first geographically authentic map representation of the Australian continent, Willem Jansz's earlier chart having shown Australia as a continuation of New Guinea.

Yet no one knew what the meticulously drawn, isolated little line represented. What lay beyond the sandy flats and the bluffs dropping down to the sea and the intimidating line of restless surf that Dutch navigators would mention again and again? Was this some desolate stretch of the Great South Land? Or some other unknown place? A few years later, additions to a 1599–1600 map by Hendrik van Langeren showed 'Terra Australis—Magallanica' with a large north-projecting peninsula labelled traditionally with the names Beach, Maletur and Lucach, and in a different script with the name 't'Landt van Eendracht'.[11] Whoever reworked the Van Langeren map evidently believed that the continent had been found.

Like the Spanish and the Portuguese before them, the Dutch tried to keep their routes and discoveries secret. Written reports were filed in VOC archives and officers' notes and journals were retained by the company. Charts, too, were guarded, but somehow details found their way into commercially produced maps. Other seafaring nations copied Dutch information when they could. In the mid-1600s the Portuguese Albernas João Teixeira produced a map with coastlines identical to those on a map by Gerritsz that showed the *Duyfken* discoveries.

*Detail from a surviving fragment of a map originally published circa 1599
and reworked after 1623 to show new Dutch discoveries. It shows the
legendary names of Beach, Lucach and Maletur as well as the recently
discovered and newly named Landt van Eendracht. (Gowrie Galleries, Sydney)*

Around 1625 Jodocus Hondius produced an engraved
chart on which the recent Dutch discoveries appeared and
in 1633 his son Henricus published a similar one. On these
maps Terra dos Papous and Nova Guinea—Land of the
Papuans and New Guinea—is a long, narrow peninsula, separated from Cape York Peninsula by a small, uncharted gap,
while 't'landt van Eendracht' appears across open sea far to
the west as three small, separate and unattached bits of
coast.[12] On a 1635 map by the VOC cartographer Willem
Jansz Blaeu these are replaced by two slightly longer little
stretches of shoreline. The first known globe on which the
Dutch discoveries appear was produced in about 1625 by

Arnold Florent van Langeren, whose information must have come from some private VOC connection.

Other charts continued to show the Great South Land in the traditional way. Maps published in 1630 by Hondius's partner Jan Jansz and by Blaeu's firm omitted the recent discoveries, and depicted Terra Australis as a vast, sprawling land labelled with mythical place names and with New Guinea firmly attached. While the careful observations of practical mariners were steadily adding to geographical reality, the dream persisted.

In December 1618 a fleet of eleven ships left Texel, in the Netherlands, under the command of Frederik de Houtman. Houtman was now in his late 40s and a senior officer of the VOC. His portrait shows a stout, heavily bearded, richly dressed gentleman standing with absolute self-assurance beside a world globe. Also with the expedition was an important official, Jacob Dedel. In the course of the journey the ships became separated, and in mid-July two vessels, one with Houtman and Dedel on board, had crossed the Indian Ocean when, as Houtman later wrote to Prince Maurits of the Netherlands,

> we suddenly came upon the Southland of Beach in 32 degrees 20 minutes. We spent a few days there in order to get some knowledge of the same, but the inconvenience of being unable to make a landing together with the heavy gales, prevented us from effecting our purpose.[13]

Faced with an unknown land in the south, Houtman evidently believed that he was seeing some part of the Great South Land, and called it by a name common on maps of

Terra Australis. Actually, he and Dedel had found the Australian coast in the vicinity of modern Perth, apparently a little south of the Swan River. An island that appeared later at the mouth of a river on a VOC map was probably Rottnest Island.

The strong winds continuing, the ships steered north until the shoreline disappeared into the distance. In the early hours of the 30th, however, land was suddenly sighted again. Here it was 'a low-lying coast, a level, broken country with reefs all around it. We saw no high land or mainland.'[14]

On his chart Houtman wrote the commonly used Portuguese expression for caution, *abrolhos*, and on modern maps these reefs and islets appear as the Houtman Abrolhos or Houtman Rocks, lying in three loosely connected groups about 60km west of Geraldton. Dedel, who, as a ranking VOC official, knew of Hartogs's voyage, also wrote to the managers of the VOC. The ships, he said, had come

> upon the south-lands situated behind Java . . . We have
> seen no signs of inhabitants . . . in 27 degrees we came
> upon the land discovered by the ship Eendracht, which
> in the same latitude showed as a red, muddy coast, which
> according to the surmises of some of us might not
> unlikely prove to be gold-bearing, a point which may be
> cleared up in time.[15]

On the whole, Houtman and Dedel wrote favourably of the land they had seen, but their views were necessarily limited to what could be observed from the deck of a ship. Now shaping their course for Java, the two vessels arrived in Batavia at the beginning of September.

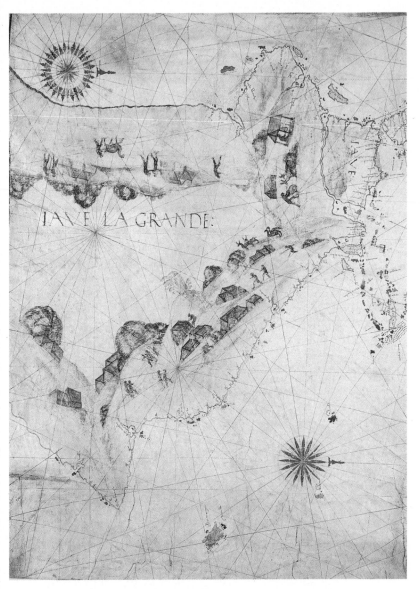

A section of the Dauphin Map, a world map of 1536 showing a large, mysterious area called Iave or Java La Grande which was thought to represent Australia. A narrow waterway separates Iave from Java itself. This map was later owned by Joseph Banks. (The British Library, London)

Fray Andrés de Urdaneta, the Spanish friar and navigator whose discovery of a favourable west-to-east sea route across the Pacific made possible Spain's colonisation of the Philippines and other activities in the Far East. (Museo Orientral, Colegio PP. Augustinos Filipinos, Valladolid, Spain)

Jan Pieterszoon Coen, governor-general of the Dutch East India Company who founded Batavia in Java, and aggressively expanded the Dutch commercial empire in the Indies. Following his instructions, his successor sent the Pera *and* Arnhem *to explore the mysterious South Land. (Westfries Museum, Hoorn, Netherlands)*

Willem Jansz Blaeu's 1635 map, India quae Orientalis dicitur et Insulae Adjacento, shows New Guinea separated by an unexplored break from the west coast of Cape York Peninsula. Far to the southwest, disconnected bits of shoreline indicate early Dutch discoveries on Australia's west coast. (Mitchell Library, State Library of New South Wales, Sydney)

Curious bits of evidence suggest that two more ships may have touched on the Australian mainland within three years or so of Houtman's explorations. A damaged letter found in VOC archives made a tantalisingly brief mention of discoveries by a ship called the *'t Wapen van Amsterdam*, that is, the *Arms of Amsterdam*, between May 1618 and September 1620.[16] Sailing instructions issued in 1644 to the navigator Abel Tasman also referred to a ship of that name:

> in the year 1619 the ship *'t Wapen van Amsterdam*, passing Banda on her way thither, was cast on the south-coast of Nova Guinea where also some of her crew were slain by the barbarian inhabitants so that no certain information respecting the situation of the country was obtained.[17]

What coast was this? We do not know whether it was in Papua New Guinea as we know it today or in Australia, perhaps on Cape York Peninsula.

Another ship of which little is known has left its name on Australian maps down to the present. In April 1621 fourteen ships left Texel for Batavia, and although one of the vessels reached its destination in the remarkable time of four months, the straggler, the *Leeuwin* or *Lioness*, took thirteen months, undoubtedly earning the stern displeasure of company representatives. The *Leeuwin*'s journey is known only from Hessel Gerritsz's map of 1627 and from instructions given to Tasman in 1644, both of which indicate discoveries on the Australian coast at about 35°S, placing them on the south coast of Western Australia. The point at the far southwestern corner of the Australian continent is clearly drawn on Gerritsz's chart, where it is marked Landt van de Leeuwin, today's windy Cape Leeuwin, where a spur of rocks and a few wave-washed boulders extend into the southern Indian Ocean. The nearest land from here is Antarctica.

What did Europeans, or more precisely, the Dutch, now know of Australia? They still believed that New Guinea was joined to Cape York Peninsula. VOC mapmakers were aware of some Spanish map or account of Torres's journey through the strait between the two but, evidently not trusting its accuracy, ignored the information. The peninsula's west coast, however, was charted from Willem Jansz's landfall at the Pennefeather River to a point some 200km farther to the south. Thousands of kilometres to the southwest, drawn with a wide, blank space separating them from Cape York Peninsula, disconnected segments of the coast of Western Australia had been seen and charted. In the south the Dutch were aware of the shoreline from west of Albany, on the underside of the continent, to Cape Hamelin, a few kilometres north of Cape Leeuwin. The next known section began roughly 200km farther north, possibly at Mandurah, and extended to present-day Perth, the Swan River and Rottnest Island. There had been sightings of several parts of the shoreline as far north as the Houtman Abrolhos outside Geraldton, but what parts these were is uncertain. Although Houtman noted the dangerous rocks, he did not see the mainland to the east. Farther north, Dirk Hartog Island southwest of Carnarvon was mapped and, beyond it, North West Cape and what may be the Ashburton River. Other sections of the coast in this area came into the view of later ships, but it is not possible to determine whether they were new sightings or places previously seen by Houtman or Hartogs. There is some evidence that there had been sightings even farther north, but again, this is not certain.

Between these various recorded points there were numerous gaps—bays and inlets that were not probed, stretches of coastline that had not been spotted by the ships' lookouts owing to bad weather, nightfall, the decision to put farther out to sea or to quit the coast altogether. Individual captains may have known more than VOC charts and reports suggest. Certainly on meeting they would have discussed their headings, observations and the navigational hazards they had encountered.

From the deck of their ship, from a ship's boat or in the course of a beach landing, the officers made rough plots of the shoreline which they later refined in scale and detail. At the end of the voyage the captain submitted to the local Dutch governor his journals together with the hand-drawn maps, the reports of the merchant who had accompanied the expedition, and sometimes drawings or a few unusual objects—fruit, sea shells, native weapons, oil pressed from a scented wood. These were dispatched to Batavia, and from there went with the governor-general's letters and reports to VOC headquarters in Amsterdam.

When a ship arrived in the Netherlands, its officers handed over the charts, journals and notes on the journey home from the Indies. Company directors reviewed the material, written reports were filed and new cartographic details were passed on to the hydrographic office in Amsterdam, where mapmakers amended their charts accordingly. Even charts for journeys among Asian ports were handled in this way until the 1680s, when the production of local maps was assigned to an office in Batavia. As ships prepared to sail from the Netherlands, updated charts were handed to the principal officers, who signed for them. After 1655 lists were kept of the charts and navigational instruments issued, and officers were fined for any not returned in Batavia.

Inevitably, the dispersal of new information was slow, at least by modern standards. The journey from Batavia to Amsterdam took months and in the VOC workrooms the copying of manuscripts and maps was slow and meticulous. A ship's captain could be unaware of the discoveries of a previous explorer, as was the case when the *Zeewolf* came upon the coast recorded by Hartogs eighteen months earlier.

No map of this inscrutable continent as yet recorded anything beyond the shoreline. Behind the neatly drawn beaches, headlands and estuaries, there was only empty space. For seamen, unknown coasts usually meant danger and delay, and their concern was only with whatever affected the ship—the wind, the tide, a light or heavy surf, the depth of the water. Overall, their principal interest was to get as quickly as possible onto the heading that would take them toward their intended destinations. Yet curiosity and sometimes necessity drove some to investigate the barren shore more closely. Despite gaps and omissions, the outline of a mysterious continent was growing.

THE FIRST OF THE ENGLISH

In the course of three days in July 1622, two ship's boats arrived in Batavia carrying the survivors of an English vessel wrecked off Australia's west coast. A shocked governor-general and Council reported to VOC authorities in the Netherlands:

> They state that they have lost and abandoned their ship with 97 men and the cargo she had taken, on certain rocks situated in Latitude 20 degrees 10 minutes South, in the longitude of the western extremity of Java.

Two years earlier several ships of both the VOC and the English East India Company had arrived to take on water and other supplies in Saldahna Bay on southwest Africa's Atlantic coast some 130km north of the Cape of Good Hope. The bay was deep and virtually landlocked, with abundant fish and seals, an exceptionally safe anchorage, good opportunities for provisioning, and level areas ashore where mariners could pitch tents and prepare food for the rest of the journey.

Towards the end of June, when the Dutch fleet sailed, only the English vessels, bound for Bantam, remained. Shortly afterward, the Dutch ship *Schiedam*, also bound for Bantam, entered the bay. At first the English suspected that the newcomer was a pirate, but when this proved not to be the case, their officers and the Dutch captain, John Cornelius Kunst, became very friendly. Kunst suggested the Brouwer route across the Indian Ocean to the English commander, Humfry Fitzherbert, and on 26 July the English fleet departed from Saldanha Bay in company with the *Schiedam*. The trip was successful, and the Brouwer sea road was adopted for subsequent English crossings, the

English East India Company ordering that the directions of Fitzherbert's Journal were to be carefully followed.

In early September 1622 the EEIC ship *Trial*, under the command of John Brookes, left Plymouth and at the beginning of May made an unexpected landfall at Australia's North West Cape, the first known sighting of the continent by Englishmen. In difficult winds they continued north, seeing a 'great Iland with his 3 small Ilands' on the 24th. Almost certainly the 'great Iland' was the Australian mainland between Point Cloates and North West Cape. At about 11 o'clock the next night, in fair weather and on a quiet sea, the *Trial* rammed onto rocks and rapidly began filling with water. Two boats were launched—the skiff with ten men in it, including Brookes, and the longboat, with 36 men led by the factor Thomas Bright. The rest, close to 100, were abandoned. The men in the boats sheltered for several days on islands, and then, in a journey of almost two months, made their way to Batavia.

This was Australia's first authenticated shipwreck. Where did it take place? The officers, Brookes and Bright, described seeing islands that have been identified as the Monte Bellos, low, sandy, mangrove-grown coral islets about 100km west of the modern city of Dampier—and used in 1952 and 1956 for British atomic tests—and the larger Barrow Island, 16km to the southwest, with its grassed-over sand hills. They lie several hundred kilometres east of the course prescribed by Fitzherbert's Journal, the course the English East India Company required for its ships.

At the subsequent inquiry Brookes falsified his evidence to show that he had been on the mandatory route.

A dangerous reef in an accepted sea lane concerned both the English company and the VOC, so the ships of both nations were instructed to look for it. The Trial Rocks were not found, and became a deepening mystery, although tentative sightings were occasionally reported and the rocks sometimes appeared in different locations on charts. Modern surveys finally found them about 16.5km northwest of the Monte Bello Islands.

Between 1969 and 1971 several expeditions located, examined and recorded wreckage at the Trial Rocks, but puzzles remain. While documents point to the foundering of the *Trial* at this site, no evidence has been found that conclusively identifies the wreckage as belonging to that particular ship, and there are seeming inconsistencies in some of the surviving equipment. Whether some unrecorded shipwreck took place here remains an open question.

No report from an English ship on the Australian coast is preserved from the next 60 years or so, until a Captain Daniel on the ship *London* wrote a description of what was apparently the Wallabi or northernmost group of islands and shoals in the Houtman Abrolhos. The date is given variously as 1681 and 1687, and his map of the Abrolhos, although far from accurate, is the first known English charting of the continent.

To explore the Great South Land

In his fortress at Batavia the VOC governor-general, Jan Pieterszoon Coen, studied the charts on which Company ships' officers had recorded the coasts to the south that they had passed. There, well beyond the arena of ordinary Dutch commerce lay short, disconnected, worm-like markings which might, if joined, trace the shoreline of a southern continent—possibly the Great South Land itself. It was time, Coen decided, to investigate this region more thoroughly.

Coen was a man of great energy, ability and ambition. Raised in a modest and strict Calvinist home in Hoorn, Holland, he was sent as a youth to be trained as a merchant in Rome. Clever and strong-willed, he learned Latin, French, English, Italian, Spanish and Portuguese as well as becoming well grounded in commerce, and in 1607, aged 20, made his first voyage to the East as an under merchant with a VOC squadron led by Pieter Verhoeff. Verhoeff and 50 of his men were later murdered while negotiating with the chiefs of the Banda Islands. Coen was not there, but it was an event he never forgot.

Coen returned home in 1610 and submitted a discerning report on trade possibilities in Southeast Asia. Impressed, his superiors sent him back to the Indies as an upper merchant, and a year later he was at Bantam, head of the VOC's most important trading post. By late 1617 he had been appointed VOC governor-general in the East Indies.

In 1619 Coen seized the settlement of Jacatra from an occupying sultan, destroyed the town and founded Batavia on the burnt-out ruins, creating a permanent seat for VOC government and a central base for its shipping. Here Coen wanted to build a true Dutch community. The Netherlands, however, lacked the people and other resources necessary to carry through so ambitious a project.

The Dutch expatriate population remained small, and both daily life and the basic economy of the colony rested on the skills and labour of the vastly larger numbers of Indonesians and Chinese. Nevertheless, Coen was considering a plan that he believed would draw more of his countrymen to the Indies and which he would later present to the Company.

Coen was also ambitious to develop a VOC network powerful enough to control the huge volume of intra-East Asian trade, as yet hardly tapped by other European nations. Here again the results would fall short of his hopes. Coen never succeeded in creating the mercantile empire that he envisaged, but he set a pattern of expelling rival Western powers from the Indies, securing and ruthlessly enforcing monopolies, reinforcing trade with Japan and China through a base in Taiwan and building a chain of fortified trading posts that by the end of the seventeenth century had established Dutch domination in the Indonesian archipelago for over two and a half centuries to come.

Coen's actions were guided by a potent combination of commercial ambition, ruthlessness and a severe Calvinistic outlook. To the company directors he wrote, 'Do not despair, do not spare your enemies, as there is nothing in all the world that can hinder or hurt you, for God is with us.'[18]

When the Banda islanders broke their trade agreement with the Dutch by selling nutmeg to others, he seized the islands, killing or enslaving virtually the entire population of several thousand. His contemporaries were shocked and the Company, although gratified by his acquisition of the islands, condemned the barbarity of his methods. In his personal relationships Coen was mercilessly puritanical. When he discovered that his foster-daughter had been intimate with her fiancé, he had the girl lashed and the young man executed. Coen's portrait forcefully projects the flint-like severity of the man. He stands, hand on his sword, humourless and utterly confident, his long, lean face deeply lined and implacably stern.

Coen's ambitions for the VOC lifted his interest in exploration. New resources and new markets were important in expanding the Company's trading sphere, and its own maps showed there was land to the south with unprobed possibilities. Yet no deliberate exploration had been done since the voyage of Jansz and the little *Duyfken* a decade and a half before. It was clearly time to investigate further.

Thus, at Batavia in 1622 two ships, the *Haringh* and the *Hazewint*, were prepared and Jan Vos appointed commander of the expedition 'for the purpose of making discovery of the South-land'.[19] Vos and his officers were to take formal possession of the territory, marking their claims with inscribed stone pillars, which suggests that Dutch authorities had in mind future colonies. The instructions went on to emphasise the tremendous risk run by Company vessels on an uncharted coast, pointed up by the recent wrecking of the *Trial*. Thus the expedition was to discover and survey the coast of the Great South Land from its northernmost extremity to between 45°S and 50°S, carefully mapping 'all capes, forelands, bights, lands, islands, rocks, sandbanks, depths, shallows, roads, winds, currents and all that appertains to the same'. Expeditions ashore were to be made

> to ascertain whether or not [the land] is inhabited, the nature of the land and the people, their towns and inhabited villages, the divisions of their kingdoms, their religion and polity, their wars, their rivers, the shape of their vessels, their fisheries, commodities and manufactures, but especially to inform yourselves what minerals, such as gold, silver, tin, iron, lead, and copper, what precious stones, pearls, vegetables, animals and fruits, these lands yield and produce.[20]

The instructions added that according to the writings of Jan Huyghen van Linschoten and 'the opinion of sundry other persons, certain parts of this South-land are likely to yield gold'.[21] The explorers should also secure some adult natives, preferably young, to be trained in Batavia as interpreters and go-betweens for future expeditions. The commercial thrust and purpose of Dutch exploration are clear from these instructions and, with variations, they remained basic to the orders given to later commanders.

Vos's vessels sailed in September. In the strait between Java and Sumatra they found a Dutch ship at anchor and, a little farther down the Java coast, another adrift. Here, almost at the end of their long journey from the Netherlands, what remained of their sick and starving crews were too weak to set the sails. Vos brought the ships to Batavia, other delays occurred and, as the monsoon season arrived, the voyage was postponed. Coen, who was leaving Java, left instructions for his successor, Pieter de

Carpentier, to dispatch two ships later in the year. The project was organised by Herman van Speult, governor of the clove-growing island of Amboina in the Moluccas, which the VOC had seized from the Portuguese. He was allotted two small ships, the *Pera* and the *Arnhem*. On 21 January 1623 he sent these from the harbour in Amboina's near-circular bay with orders to visit and establish friendly relations with the people of the islands of Kai, Aru and Tanimbar, to map more of Nova Guinea and, as in the case of Vos's ships, to explore 'the South-land'. Samples of pearls and gold, silver, copper and other metals were provided to use in questioning local people as to possible sources, and as in Vos's orders, a few natives were to be brought back to Amboina. Dirck Melisz captained the *Arnhem*. Jan Carstensz, aboard the *Pera*, commanded the expedition.

Carstensz had arrived in the Indies at the age of about 20 to serve as an under merchant at Bantam. He rose to upper merchant, commanded a troop of soldiers in Governor-General Coen's invasion of the Banda Islands in 1620 and briefly left the Company to become a free citizen in Banda. Work opportunities in a Company-dominated economy were very limited, and at the end of 1622 Carstensz returned to VOC service and accepted command of Van Speult's expedition.

The two ships concluded trade treaties with the Tanimbar, Kai and Aru islanders and sailed on to the southwest coast of New Guinea, today's Irian Jaya. Here the natives were fiercely hostile, and when a party of Dutchmen went ashore to fish, nine were killed and the remaining seven wounded, including Melisz, who died agonisingly of his wounds the next day. He was replaced as captain of the *Arnhem* by the *Pera*'s second mate, Willem Joosten van Colster, and the expedition resumed its eastward course. Repeated clashes with natives ended in casualties on both sides.

In late March the ships reached seemingly impassable shallows. Their boats sounded for deeper water without success, and Carstensz, seeing only shoals and mud flats, concluded that he had found a large, shallow bight lying between the coast they had followed and the rest of Nova Guinea, which Jansz had shown extending to the south. In his journal Carstensz wrote:

> the space between us and Nova Guinea seems to be a bight to which on account of its shallows we have given the name *drooge bocht* [shallow bight] in the new chart; to the land which we had run along up to now, we have by resolution given the name of 't Westeinde van Nova Guinea (Western Extremity of N. G.), seeing that we have in reality found the land to be an unbroken coast.[22]

Of their efforts to examine the entrance to what was, of course, Torres Strait, Carstensz wrote, 'Here we managed with extreme difficulty and great peril to get again out of the shallows aforesaid, ... for which happy deliverance God be praised.'[23]

On a new chart Cartensz labelled the presumed bight and indicated its reefs. Unable to see where the supposed Nova Guinea coast curved to the south, he left an empty space beyond the reefs, writing '*drooge*' at its western end. As the VOC cartographer Hessel Gerritsz had some knowledge of the 1606 transit of the strait by Torres, Carstensz may have had with him a chart indicating the possibility of such a passage. Nevertheless, he seems to have concluded that what he saw was a bight and, like Jansz, turned south. In his notes he commented that the land they were nearing could be a land of gold, perhaps referring to fabled Beach.[24]

Early on 12 April 1623 the ships came upon the western side of Cape York Peninsula and, thinking that they had again sighted the New Guinea coast, they continued confidently southward.

A dry southeasterly wind blew over the land, and under a cloudless sky the swamps and lagoons had begun to contract and the grass to turn yellow. The Dutchmen saw long, white beaches and grey mud flats. 'Great volumes of smoke becoming visible on the land,' it seemed likely that there were people here. Two boats with armed men were launched to make contact with the natives, who could now be seen watching from among the trees, but deep mud 'into which the men sunk to their waists'[25] prevented the landing. By 14 April the ships were close to Cape Keerweer.

Carstensz went ashore many times, walking through dry grass and the scattered forest of unfamiliar trees and shrubs and then conscientiously recording what he saw. On the seventeenth, he noted:

> we went a considerable distance into the interior, which we found to be a flat fine country with few trees, and good soil for planting and sowing, but so far as we could observe utterly destitute of fresh water. Nor did we see

any human beings or even signs of them; near the strand the coast was sandy, with a fine beach and plenty of excellent fish.[26]

The following day a landing party was met on the shore by a large group of natives, unafraid enough to try to grab the sailors' muskets and other gear. When the Dutch seized one man and took him back to the ship, a great clamour went up on the beach, and the next day a shore party chopping down trees for firewood was attacked by over 200 men. The Dutch fired two shots. One Aborigine fell; the others fled. The Dutch explored a little farther inland, coming upon 'great quantities of divers human bones',[27] which they took as evidence of cannibalism, and picking up some native weapons as souvenirs.

The ships continued south along a partially submerged coastal landscape. A salt river which they named the Staaten is probably either today's Staaten or Gilbert River. On 23 April a noonday sighting of the sun gave them a latitude of 17°8'S. They had coasted some 600 to 700km along Cape York Peninsula and were possibly within 125km of the bottom of the Gulf of Carpentaria.

Carstensz was increasingly disenchanted with the land before him. In his journal he wrote:

> the land between 13 degrees and 17 degrees 8 minutes is a barren and arid tract, without any fruit trees, and producing nothing fit for the use of man; it is low-lying and flat without hills or mountains; in many places overgrown with brushwood and stunted wild trees; it has not much fresh water.[28]

Carstensz now called a council of his officers and it was decided to end the southward journey and head back along the coast to examine points of special interest, before returning to the Indies. To fulfill the company's instructions on the capture of natives, the sailors were to be given ten pieces of eight, probably close to two months' pay, for each captive brought on board.

Before the expedition headed north, well-armed parties were sent ashore to look for fresh water, which was running low. Without result, they dug holes for water and followed the salt river in boats for about a kilometre and 'then marched a considerable distance into the interior',[29] which they found flooded in many places, reminding them of inundated areas of Holland. They saw huts made from what appeared to be dry hay, footprints and dog tracks, and a few inhabitants who would not approach them. To mark the southernmost limit of their exploration, they nailed to a tree a wooden tablet carved with a brief statement: 'A. D. 1623, on the 24th of April there arrived here two yachts dispatched by their High Mightinesses the States-General.'[30] Carstensz and his men had probably explored farther inland on the Australian continent than any Europeans before them.

Two days later the ships set sail on a northerly course. By the late afternoon of the next day the *Arnhem* had fallen a cannon 'shot astern',[31] as Carstensz wrote in his journal. In the evening the *Pera* anchored, and he had a lantern set out to guide the other ship. Instead, the *Arnhem* 'cut away from us against her instructions'.[32] Seeking a more direct course for Batavia, the ship struck northwest across the Gulf of Carpentaria, passing the northeastern extremity of Arnhem

Land—which Van Colster and his men mistook for a series of islands—and the Wessel Islands. Upbraided by company officials on his return, Van Colster insisted that his much-worn ship was in no condition for the longer route. Carstensz was furious at the desertion. In his journal he made special note of the poor seamanship and uncooperativeness of Van Colster and his mate, who had many times delayed the voyage by straying off course, forcing the *Pera*, which itself was leaking and kept afloat only with strenuous pumping, to go out of its way to find its companion ship.

Alone, the *Pera* continued northward up Cape York Peninsula's west coast. Fresh water was found, and in further confrontations with the Aborigines another man was kidnapped. Off an undetermined point on the peninsula the *Pera* left the coast of Australia and steered for Amboina. Carstensz had by now formed a very negative view of the country, which he described as monotonous and unproductive, inhabited by extremely primitive people who went naked and had no knowledge of metals or spices.

On 8 June the *Pera* dropped anchor in the safety of Amboina's fort-guarded harbour, and Carstensz completed his charts and his record of the voyage, a journal which is the earliest extended description of an Australian scene. Two years later in Amsterdam a short notice of the journey appeared in a historical publication, *Historisch Verhael aller gedenkwaardighe geschiedenissen*, by Nicolaas van Wassenaer. It was the first printed account of any part of Australia. No further public mention survives. However, the considerable geographical impact of Carstensz's discoveries can be seen on the world and East Indies maps that appeared over the next several years.

SIGHTINGS AND A SOUTHERN COAST

The long sea road from the Netherlands to the Indies continued to carry ships across the South Indian Ocean in the path of the swift-moving westerlies, and sightings and disasters continued along Australia's west coast.

In 1624 an English ship came upon the *jacht Tortelduyf* drifting in Sunda Strait and, finding her crew dead or too ill to handle the sails, brought the little vessel into Batavia. On a VOC chart published four years later a small island named Tortelduyf appeared in the southernmost part of the Houtman Abrolhos. No record explains the naming of the island, but quite likely it was discovered by the stricken men of the *Tortelduyf*. In 1623 and again in 1626, the ship *Leijden* sighted the coast somewhere south of Dirk Hartog Island. In late July 1623 the *Leijden*'s trip became notable in that a baby boy was born to a young emigrating couple, Willem and Willemijntje Jansz. Seebaer van Nieuwellandt, or literally, Seabirth of Newland, as they named him, was the first European child to be born in the vicinity of Australia, but nothing is known of his later life.

Scant comments in official correspondence, on charts and in later instructions to an explorer provide other glimpses. The *Wapen van Hoorn* came frighteningly close to Eendracht's Land, 'which lay quite differently from what the chart would have us believe', and one evening some days later, 'when it had got dark, the water suddenly turned as white as buttermilk, a thing that none of those on board of us had ever seen in their lives'. This unsettling phenomenon, the men finally decided, was due to a pale sky, although the cause was more likely limestone-rich calcareous mud from coral reefs, stirred up from the seabed. A letter adds, 'we made all sail and ran on full speed'.[33]

On certain maps the names Iacob Remens and Jacop Remmessen appear in connection with a river on the Australian west coast, and a Jacob Remmissen is mentioned as a mate aboard a ship that rode at anchor there, but whether he discovered the river, and if so, under what circumstances and when, are not known.

Governor-General Coen was aboard the ship *Galias*, returning to Batavia from the Netherlands, when in 1627 it encountered the Australian coast. In Coen's long-planned scheme for Dutch commercial hegemony in the East, the time had come for the introduction of private enterprise to be conducted within Asia by independent Dutch colonists. This, he believed, would attract more Dutch settlers and investments. In 1623 Coen had presented his plan to the VOC directors, who at first approved, then abruptly rejected it. Dutch authorities on Amboina had seized, tortured into confession and executed several Englishmen accused of plotting to seize the island's VOC fort. The English government was outraged and, although he was in Europe at the time, held Coen, long their most implacable enemy in the East, morally responsible. To preserve a very tentative peace with England, the Dutch government dropped Coen's plan and detained him in the Netherlands. In 1627, however, with the knowledge of only a few Company directors, the determined Coen took an assumed name, slipped aboard the ship *Galias* and secretly sailed for the East.

Almost at his journey's end he stood on the deck of the ship, watching with alarm as breakers came suddenly and

unexpectedly into sight no more than two or three kilometres away, when by the pilot's reckonings using the
charts on board, the ship was hundreds of kilometres from
land. 'If we had come upon this place in the night-time, we
should have been in a thousand perils with our ship and
crew,'[34] Coen wrote indignantly to the directors, sharply
requesting corrections on the charts. The ship had almost
collided with the Abrolhos reefs. Coen's encounter with the
edge of the shore seen by Hartogs and Houtman may have
rekindled his determination to probe the South Land, but
although he soon regained power in Batavia, a local war
absorbed his time and resources until his death two years
later.

One of the most significant of Dutch discoveries along
the Australian coast is known only from a passing mention
in the instructions given in 1644 to Abel Tasman: 'the
south coast of the great south-land had accidentally been
discovered in the year 1627 by the ship 't Gulden Zeepaert
(which came from home) for an extension of 250 miles.'[35]

The Gulden Zeepaert, or Golden Seahorse, had sailed
from the Netherlands on 22 May 1626 and arrived in
Batavia almost a year later on 10 April 1627. Thirty men
were dead and many others desperately ill. Later Dutch
maps suggest that the Gulden Zeepaert came upon
Australia's long southern coast somewhere near Cliffy Head
and Point Nuyts, southeast of Cape Leeuwin. Her captain,
François Thijssen, then took her some 1600km to the east,
past the broad, deep sound that leads to modern Albany
and the bay along which Esperance now rises, into the
Great Australian Bight. Passengers and crew watched the
high, deeply eroded cliffs as Thijssen brought the ship

close enough to map the shoreline. After several days they came upon a little island group, today's Nuyts Archipelago, off Ceduna and Denial Bay in South Australia. Thijssen named the two largest islands St. François and St. Pieter, apparently after himself and Pieter Nuyts, a member of the Council of the Indies who was on board. An updated version of a 1618 VOC map is marked along the coast with tiny anchors to show where the *Gulden Zeepaert* paused in its journey.

What caused Thijssen to take his ship on this long detour from the accepted route, undoubtedly with Pieter Nuyts's consent? What wondering thoughts filled the minds of the *Zeepaert*'s people as they viewed what was quite possibily the fabled Great South Land? No letter or journal survives to answer either question. At the Nuyts Archipelago the *Zeepaert* turned back to sail west round Cape Leeuwin and then north for Batavia. Nothing more is known of the voyage, but on Dutch charts there soon appeared a long extension to the southern shoreline of the unexplored continent, a coast labelled 'Landt van P. Nuyts'.

Hessel Gerritsz's map, official letters and some later instructions to Tasman also contain all we know of the ship *Vianen*, which, as a letter of 3 November 1628 remarks, had 'come upon the Southland beyond Java'.[36] Under Gerrit Fredriksz de Witt, the ship left Batavia late in the sailing season and, unusually, headed for home on the route normally taken only by outbound ships. Buffeted by headwinds, she was driven onto a sandbar on the Australian coast and only refloated by jettisoning quantities of valuable pepper and copper. De Witt then followed the coast south for some 370km to about the latitude of modern

Onslow, before heading west. On Gerritsz's map 'G. F. de Wits Landt' appears on the northwestern Australian coast in the general vicinity of today's Port Hedland. Probably this was the first European sighting of that part of the continent.

Gradually short stretches of coast on maps of the South Land lengthened and merged. The known regions were growing, but so was the mystery. Was this the outline of the legendary Great South Land? Or was it something else?

THE *BATAVIA*

At the end of October 1628 the ship *Batavia*, sailing in a convoy of eight vessels, left Texel on her first trip to the Indies. The ship was new, one of the larger VOC vessels, high-pooped and square-rigged. She probably held about 600 tonnes of cargo, including twelve chests of silver coins, the equivalent of about half a million Australian dollars.[37] Crowded on board were more than 300 officers, crew, soldiers and passengers, among them families with children, a young woman on her way to join her husband in Batavia, several wives of the soldiers, and two maids. The captain was Adriaan Jacobsz, who had sailed to the Indies before. Also on board was the upper merchant François or Francisco Pelsaert, who was returning to the East to assume the senior VOC position of Councillor Extraordinary of India, in which he would serve as a member of Governor-General Coen's council.

Pelsaert's career in the East with the VOC had been exceptionally successful. He had earned a reputation for his administrative work and commercial success, and for a lengthy, discerning report on affairs in the Mughal court of the Indian state of Agra. All this won the approbation of the Company, although some further influence may have been exerted by the respected Hendrik Brouwer, now a VOC director, to whose sister Pelsaert was married. As well as being the *Batavia*'s upper merchant, he was commander, or fleet president, of the eight ships.

Pelsaert's passage on the *Batavia* was, however, unfortunate. There was serious enmity between him and the captain, Jacobsz, going back to a quarrel in India. Throughout much of the journey Pelsaert was ill, and, although he was the senior official on board, he found himself almost powerless in a welter of violent arguments, an attack on a young female passenger and mutterings of mutiny, which worsened as the ship made its way across the Indian Ocean. The eight vessels had become separated early in the voyage, and the *Batavia* was sailing eastward alone.

In the pre-dawn darkness of 4 June 1629 the lookout saw what he thought was the sheen of moonlight on the water. It was, in fact, the pale glimmer of surf breaking on the curving outline of Morning Reef, in the northern Wallabi group of the Houtman Abrolhos. The *Batavia* struck violently. Pelsaert described in his journal, 'a rough terrible movement, the bumping of the ship's rudder, and immediately after I felt the ship held up in her course against the rocks, so that I fell out of my bunk'.[38]

As daylight came, strenuous efforts were made to free and refloat the ship, without success. Groups of people were taken in the ship's boats to two of the nearby islands.

Others remained on the wrecked ship. When it eventually broke up, some made it to the island by swimming or clinging to wreckage, while others drowned. The islands offered little shelter. They were small, reef-encircled platforms of broken white coral, only metres above the surface of the sea, patched here and there with the green and brown of succulents and low shrubs. They were home to vast numbers of birds, lizards, geckoes, a species of python and the small tammar wallaby, unique to a few Australian islands—but little else.

Drinking water was the immediate concern, and Pelsaert and Jacobsz set off in the larger of the boats to search the neighbouring islands. They were followed by some of the men in the smaller boat, which left the others stranded.

Finding no water, the searchers steered for the mainland, some 60km away, which they sighted at noon. The next day they neared a shoreline of broken-edged cliffs,

> a bad Rocky land, without trees, about as high as Dover in England. Here we saw a small Inlet, as well as low dune land, where we intended to land, but approaching, noticed that there was a big surf and many breakers near the shore.[39]

They could not land. A storm struck and the smaller boat was lost. High winds continued, the sea flinging itself in a churning white band against the precipitous red edge of the continent, which 'seemed to be a dry cursed earth without foliage or grass'.[40] At the sight of smoke rising inland, their hopes rose. Six sailors swam through heavy surf to seek help in finding water. Four naked black men fled at the sight of them. There was no water, and at nightfall the crewmen swam back to the boat. Eventually Pelsaert made a landing on 'a dune foreland of about one mile width before one comes to the High Land'.[41] Finding a little rain-water in holes in the rock, the Dutchmen camped for the night, perhaps the first Europeans to do so on Australian soil, and in the morning pushed inland to find more water. Pelsaert wrote:

> beyond the heights the country was flat again, without trees, foliage or grass, except for high anthills thrown up of earth, which in the distance were not unlike the huts of people. Was also such a host of flies, which came to sit in the mouth and the eyes, that they could not be beaten off. We next saw eight black men, each carrying a stick in his hand . . . but when we went towards them, they ran away.[42]

Still finding no water, the men decided to head for Batavia in the open boat. Quitting the coast, they steered seaward northwest by north. Eleven days later they were following the south coast of Java into Sunda Strait, and on 3 July Palsaert reported to Governor-General Coen in his fortress at Batavia. Coen was outraged at the sequence of events. He threw Jacobsz into prison for negligent navigation and gross misbehaviour on board, hanged the chief boatswain—who had been involved in the attack on the woman and in the planned mutiny—and dispatched Pelsaert in the small ship *Sardam* to rescue the survivors. The *Sardam* had been hurriedly prepared for the mission with water and provisions, two good Dutch swimmers and four Gujarati divers to salvage the silver coins, and a minimal crew to provide room for the castaways. Bad weather slowed the trip, and it was 49 days—three months since the wreck— before the *Sardam* reached the Abrolhos on 13 September.

In those three months the survivors had been plunged into an unbelievable vortex of violence, torture, rape and murder. The senior official left on Pelsaert's departure was the upper merchant Hieronymus Cornelisz, who had been one of the last to leave the wrecked *Batavia* as it broke apart. Unable to swim, he had floated ashore on a spar. With the departure of Pelsaert and Jacobsz, he took charge, and with a group of followers began killing the other survivors. Apparently, they planned to seize any rescue ship that arrived and use it for piracy. In the meantime, they would eliminate as many others as possible, partly to make their task easier when the time came, and partly to preserve food supplies until then. Bizarrely dressed in pieces of rich clothing that had drifted onto the beach from the wreck, they established a rule of terror, sparing no one. When Pelsaert returned he found that of the 250 people he had left behind half had been brutally slain—men, women and children shot, axed, beaten, and cut down with swords. According to a contemporary record, 60 of the *Batavia*'s original complement had died on the islands of illness or drowning, and 125 had been murdered. On one small island a group of about 50 men, mainly soldiers, had built themselves an enclosure of flat coral rocks and held off the attack of the mutineers. When Cornelisz himself approached them to negotiate, the soldiers had captured him and his group, and held Cornelisz prisoner while they executed the others.

Pelsaert disarmed the remaining mutineers. Eight men, including Cornelisz, were immediately condemned to be hanged after having their hands cut off. One was spared because he was only 18 years old. Others were flogged, dropped from the yardarm or keel-hauled. The salvage operation, meanwhile, was reasonably successful. Ten of the twelve chests of coins were retrieved, together with other monies, jewellery, two cannons and additional goods. On 15 November the *Sardam* left for Batavia. On the way two of the mutineers, one of them the youth who had been condemned to death, were marooned on the Australian mainland. Later captains were instructed to look for them, but they were never seen again.

Pelsaert arrived in Batavia on 5 December with 74 survivors. Governor-General Coen had died in the interval, but the Council of Justice imposed ruthless sentences, including torture and hanging, on the remaining mutineers. Jacobsz was left in the fortress dungeons. Pelsaert was reprimanded and disgraced. His departure from the scene of the shipwreck was questioned, as was the justice he had meted out on returning to the island, and rumours later circulated that he had engaged in private trade, forbidden to VOC officers. He did not receive the promised position as councillor. A broken man, he died the following year in Sumatra.

The *Batavia* disaster was to capture the imagination of generations, but at first news of it was only rumour. Pelsaert's journal of the wreck and its aftermath vanished into the obscurity of VOC files, and for the next twenty years the strange, sensational story of a sea catastrophe at the absolute edge of the known world circulated only in tantalising fragments. A brief mention of Pelsaert's account appeared in a journal in 1635. Twelve years later an Amsterdam editor, Jan Jansz, secured the principal facts as written by Pelsaert and published as *The Unlucky Voyage for the East Indies under the Command of Françoys Pelsaert, shipwrecked on Frederik Houtman's Abrolhos, 28 1/3 south of the equinoctial line*. It was a small vellum-bound book lavishly illustrated with copperplate engravings depicting the horrors of the tale. The barbarities were recounted—how Cornelisz had sent his men to cut the throats of the sick and to throw others into the sea; how, calling the cabin boy out of his tent, he had given him a beaker of wine and a dagger and told him he must stab the carpenter 'to the heart'. One night he entertained the minister and his eldest daughter at a meal while his men beat in the skulls of the man's wife and two other daughters with an adze and stabbed their maid. Another man cut off a boy's head with a single blow of a sword, while Cornelisz 'stood laughing'. The book was immensely popular. European readers were both shocked and fascinated by the idea of savagery erupting among civilised people on the desolate coast of a remote, isolated, almost legendary land.

Competing booksellers rushed to put out their own editions of the story. Joost Hartgers's version in 1648 included similar pictures and, more sensationally, a letter-account by Gijsbert Bastiensz, the minister who had been travelling on the *Batavia*. His wife and younger children slain, he and his eldest daughter had survived, he wrote, but 'Every night I told my daughter: "Come in the morning to see whether I have been murdered!" [43] Jansz immediately republished, prefacing his book with an indignant open letter to Hartgers accusing him of piracy. The following year a third rival, Lucas de Vries of Utrecht, entered the race with another illustrated edition that included a list of the rewards granted to the loyal members of the *Batavia*'s company. Hartgers and de Vries then published again, joined by yet another competitor, Gilles Saeghman. In 1663 and 1664 Pelsaert's story was translated into French and published in *Relations de divers voyages curieux* by the French historian and cartographer Melchisédec Thévenot.

In practical geographical terms, Pelsaert's account provided evidence of European sightings along an extended strip of Australia's west coast, which filled in sections not previously seen by the Dutch. On leaving the Abrolhos, Pelsaert had found the mainland to the northeast, and followed it probably to just north of Point Cloates. On the return trip in the *Sardam* he first met the coast to the south of the Abrolhos, and then tacked back and forth along a portion of the mainland probably not seen by previous mariners, until he reached the islets. Again he saw little more than sand dunes and a long, level, bare-looking profile of land against the sky.

In Europe rumour and fragments of fact about the southern continent began to catch the popular imagination and led to lively speculations that in 1676 took a literary form. Gabriel de Foigny, a reform-minded French priest living in Geneva, published the fantastical adventures of an imaginary French sailor named Jacques Sadeur, shipwrecked in Terre Australe. At first suppressed for indecency, the book was eventually translated into other languages, appearing in England in 1693 as *A New Discovery of Terra Incognita Australis; or the Southern World*, and promoted as a tale which had long been kept 'secret in the closet of a Great Minister of State'.[44] Sadeur, the tale's narrator, describes his 35 years in Australia, as the English translator called the continent more than a century before Matthew Flinders championed the name. Much of the land supposedly stretches southward from the latitudes 40°S and 50°S, with massive mountains towards the South Pole. Skies are forever cloudless and insects, spiders, serpents or venomous beasts are unknown. The people are hermaphrodites with red skin, almost two and a half metres tall, naked, athletic and war-like, living under a utopian communistic system. Sadeur eventually escapes on the back of a large bird. De Foigny's conceit is that his hero perishes on the way home but his manuscript is saved. With its almost heretical views, the book attained only modest popularity.

THE *BATAVIA* FOUND

The sensational story of the *Batavia*, however, remained alive for the next three centuries, together with the knowledge that the ship had been destroyed in the Houtman Abrolhos. The exact location, however, was forgotten.

In 1840 the British naval survey ship HMS *Beagle* found the Abrolhos to consist of three groups of small islands and coral reefs, for which the commander, John Lort Stokes, recorded names: the northern cluster as the Wallabi Group and the middle one as the Easter Group.

When the survey party came upon the wreckage of a very old ship and a VOC coin on an island in the southernmost group, they concluded that this was where the *Batavia* had struck. Accordingly, Stokes named these islets the Pelsart Group. His thinking was reinforced by the fact that survivors of the Dutch ship *Zeewijk*, wrecked in the southern Abrolhos in 1727, had reported seeing the remains of a previous shipwreck in the same area.

Half a century later, F. C. Broadhurst, a Geraldton businessman with a lease on guano deposits in the Wallabis, became interested in old items turned up by his labourers. His curiosity led him to a first edition copy of Jan Jansz's 1647 book on the *Batavia* disaster, which seemed to put the site of the wreck in the Wallabi Group, not farther south.

In 1955 a more extensive documentary search was done by Henrietta Drake-Brockman. Talks with local fishermen and Pelsaert's description of two large islands and of the tammar wallaby, both found only in the northern group, convinced her that the wreck had taken place there. In 1963 the wreck site was identified on Morning Reef, just south of the Wallabis, and diving expeditions brought up cannons, navigational instruments, pewter tableware, coins, parts of the ship itself, and even enormous sandstone blocks, cut into various shapes, that the *Batavia* had carried as ballast.

Displays at Western Australian museums bring vividly to life the men and women who voyaged along the lonely and dangerous coast of a continent they had never before seen and did not understand. There are a ship's bell that sounded the changing of the watch, anchors that promised safety, cannons that speak of the human hostility that could threaten a ship. Pewter dishes, glazed pottery cups, bottles and buckles bear witness to a daily life that was in many ways crude and difficult. Deeply moving is the reconstructed stern and hull section where Pelsaert, Bastiensz and his family, Jacobsz and so many others lived, now a sweep of bare and broken oak timbers rising above a model of a ship like the *Batavia* as it was, richly decorated, sails set, the pride of its builders. The huge, oddly cut sandstone blocks have been assembled into the towering arched gateway intended for the Waterport, which linked the moat of Batavia's citadel to the harbour.

BACK TO THE NORTH

Coen was succeeded by two short-term governors-general who seem to have had neither the wish or nor perhaps the opportunity to initiate further discovery. The VOC itself was not encouraging, for not a single product of value had been seen by any voyager.

In 1636 a new governor-general, Anthony van Diemen, took office in Batavia, and, disregarding past disappointments, roused a vigorous new spirit of investigation and adventure. Interest in the Great South Land was suddenly revived.

Van Diemen, son of a noble family, had already put behind him a varied career of business failure, bankruptcy and soldiering when at 25 he entered the service of the VOC as a clerk under an assumed name. His identity, however, was eventually discovered, for the Company directors warned the Indies government against this seemingly unreliable young man.

Van Diemen sailed from the Netherlands on 4 January 1618 in the East Indiaman *Mauritius*. On board as upper merchant was Willem Jansz, who twelve years earlier had taken the *Duyfken* into the Gulf of Carpentaria. The *Mauritius* rounded the Cape of Good Hope, ran its 1000 *mijlen* across the Indian Ocean in 38°S latitude, then headed north. On 31 July, Anthony van Diemen saw Australia from the deck of the ship.

'We discovered an island,' Jansz wrote to the Amsterdam Chamber of the VOC, 'its northern extremity is in 22 deg. S. lat.'[45] In fact, the *Mauritius* had come upon the Western Australian peninsula that terminates in North West Cape. Men from the *Mauritius* landed, and Van Diemen may have walked on Australian soil with Jansz when the group found 'marks of human footsteps'.[46] One can wonder what comments the young Van Diemen might have heard from the veteran Jansz, who unknowingly had seen more of the continent than all but a very few other Europeans.

Eighteen years after his journey on the *Mauritius*, Van Diemen was appointed to one of the most powerful positions in the East, governor-general of the Dutch Republic's great trading empire in the Indies. He was then in his early 40s, and a portrait shows him soberly dressed in dark material, with modest versions of the then-fashionable white lace-edged collar and cuffs, a brimmed hat, a sword, and a small, neat beard and moustache. It is the expression on his face that catches one's attention. Van Diemen looks out at the world with an oddly sceptical, yet faintly humorous, quizzical expression, one eyebrow expressively lifted and the suggestion of a smile on his lips. In office Van Diemen was very much a man in Coen's mould, forceful, able, energetic, with great ambition for the commercial expansion of the company and keen curiosity as to the real extent and possibilities of the Great South Land.

Despite the lengthening charted coastlines on Dutch maps at the time, the identity of the continent—if, in fact, it was a continent—was still unresolved. Was this part of Terra Australis Incognita, and thus somehow joined to the vast southern continent of earlier European maps? Or was it a different, hitherto unknown land mass, which left the actual Terra Australis yet to be discovered? What were its resources, its possibilities for trade, its potential for commercial bases and investment? Were there kings and princes with whom trade treaties could be made—or were there only the primitive peoples so far encountered by navigators? These were the questions in Van Diemen's mind, reflected in the instructions he gave his explorers.

There was another practical question. Was there a sea passage through or around the charted coastline that would carry ships from the East Indies to the Pacific? Spain, the Netherlands' longtime foe, held the Pacific littoral of both American continents. Van Diemen entertained two possibilities—trade with the Spanish colonies if they were prepared to break the monopolies of the Spanish crown, as was rumoured, or harassment of richly laden Spanish ships and wealthy seaside settlements if they were not. These goals required an uncontested route from the Dutch-held Indonesian ports to South America that ran well away from the Spanish-dominated North Pacific sea lanes, which were securely anchored in Spain's hold on the Philippines. The Dutch had attempted several times to shake that hold, but despite occasionally successful raids—even a sea victory—the effort had failed. Perhaps the means of gaining their objectives lay in finding a new route through or around that great, cryptic land mass to the south. Thus a new phase in exploration began.

In April 1636, three months after Anthony van Diemen became governor-general, two small ships, the *Klein Amsterdam* and the *Wesel*, under Gerrit Thomasz Pool and the upper merchant Pieter Pieterszoon, were dispatched from Banda to sail to the eastern extremity of today's Arnhem Land—believed to be islands—and from there to cross the upper Gulf of Carpentaria and follow Jan Carstensz's route down the west coast of Cape York Peninsula. Where Carstensz had turned back, however, they were to continue along the coast of the continent to the Houtman Abrolhos and beyond. Clearly, the Dutch did not know that the expanse of Arnhem Land and the entire northwestern corner of Western Australia existed. They believed that the coast of the South Land ran continuously from New Guinea to Cape York Peninsula and south, then slanted roughly southwest to the middle of the Australian west coast, where Pool was instructed to look for the two men Pelsaert had marooned there seven years before. It was thought, however, that at some point a sea channel might divide the South Land in two, and instructions were provided for exploring such regions. Charting and close investigation of new territories were part of Pool's task, but no native person was to be taken against his will from any of the lands.

At a landing in New Guinea, at very much the same place where Dirck Melisz of the *Arnhem* had died with his men thirteen years before, Pool and three others were killed by natives. Pieterszoon took command, but he did not pursue the more ambitious aspects of the expedition. Faced with opposing winds, the ships ran west instead of east, skirting the northern coasts of the present Coburg Peninsula and Melville Island. These were new lands for the Dutch, and they could only guess at what lay behind the white beaches and mangrove-laced shores, whether islands or a mainland. At Melville Island's northwestern tip, they swung north, surveyed Timor and some smaller islands, and continued to Batavia.

The expedition had failed badly to meet the objectives set for it. Nevertheless, Dutch officials in Batavia were able to report to VOC headquarters that great lands had been found in 11°S latitude.

9.

Discovery Widens

At the beginning of 1642 there were in the fortress-guarded port of Batavia three men whose energy and capabilities would add a dramatic new chapter to the European discovery of Australia, New Zealand and the Pacific Islands—and to the unveiling of the Great South Land.

The first of these men was Governor-General Van Diemen, who, undiscouraged by the relative failure of his first expedition, was by mid-year putting into motion a much more ambitious plan.

Central to this plan was the second man, Abel Janszoon Tasman, an experienced navigator and captain who was then 39. He was born probably in the small village of Lutjegast, to parents who were able to give their son enough schooling so he could read and write. In 1632 an Amsterdam church register recorded that Abel Tasman, widower and ordinary seaman, had married Jannetie Tjaerss or Tjaerts. Jannetie could not write, and their home was in Teerketelsteeg, a narrow street in a poor neighbourhood. A few months later, having joined the VOC, Tasman sailed for the East.

Rising in position, Tasman went on several voyages, including one sent to find two islands northeast of Japan that were said by Spanish sources to be fabulously rich in gold and silver. The islands did not exist, and Tasman's subsequent sailing involved carrying supplies and messages, watching for clove smugglers, occasional military operations and trade journeys to Sumatra, Cambodia, Taiwan and Japan. Once, at least, he was reprimanded for lacking the self-confidence necessary to have carried out properly the company's 'far-reaching' commands. In later years, though, his superiors had enough faith in his skill and experience to give him verbal rather than written instructions and considerable leeway in making decisions at sea. He returned once, briefly, to the Netherlands, to bring his wife, and evidently a little daughter from his first marriage, with him to the Indies, where he would spend the rest of his life.

A later portrait of Tasman portrays him as the solid citizen, successful navigator, landowner and businessman he became in Batavia. He is standing with his wife and daughter, all three dressed in fine, dark clothing. Tasman, alert and confident, extends a hand holding a pair of dividers towards a world globe, to which he points with the other hand. It was in 1642, however, several years before he had attained such prosperity, that he was chosen by Governor-General Van Diemen to command a squadron of two ships, the *Heemskerck* and the *Zeehan*, in the VOC's most ambitious voyage of discovery—and what would also be the most important and revealing voyage of discovery to Australia until that of James Cook 128 years later.

The third man was Frans or François Jacobszoon Visscher, chief pilot of the expedition. In 1623 Visscher had come to the Indies as steersman or mate with a fleet of Dutch ships that, unusually, had sailed the Cape Horn route to the East. In subsequent years he had gained wide experience in North Pacific and Southeast Asian waters, as is shown by the surveys and charts he produced of islands and coastal areas in both regions. He also wrote navigational tracts, advice on discovery in northern Japanese waters and a dissertation on compasses which earned the special commendation of his superiors. His knowledge and experience of the sea and of navigation and cartography were considered exceptional. In January 1642 he had prepared a 'Memoir concerning the discovery of the South-land', a memorandum that possibly encouraged Van Diemen in his schemes for exploration. When the expedition was organised later that year, Van Diemen charged Visscher with writing the record of its discoveries.

The flagship of the expedition was the *Heemskerck*, a 'small war-yacht' of about 120 tonnes, with 60 officers and crew and Ide Tjerkszoon Holleman or Holman as captain. Tasman and Visscher would be on board as well as an under merchant, Abraham Coomans. The second ship, the *Zeehan*, was a flute of about 200 tonnes with a characteristically Dutch rounded hull tapering up to a narrow top. She carried 50 men under Gerrit Jansz, and on board as well was the merchant Isaack Gilsemans, whose duty was to assess and develop mercantile opportunities for the Company. During the voyage Gilsemans also produced maps. The best seamen available in Batavia were assigned to the ships.

Instructions for the voyage were addressed to Tasman as skipper-commander, Visscher as pilot-major, and the

Council of the Ships, as the officers of the two vessels were officially called. The expedition was to explore further the known South Land, discover and explore the unknown South Land, and find a new Pacific route to South America. It was a project of enormous scope. Long stretches of the Australian coast were known to the Dutch, but the extent of the unseen shoreline could only be imagined, while detailed information on the country itself would require extensive penetrations inland. The finding of a new transpacific route was in itself a major enterprise. As well, there were particular problems to be solved, such as whether this South Land was part of an even larger continent, where and how New Guinea was joined to it, and if a seaway ran through the continent from the final point reached by Carstensz in the Gulf of Carpentaria to Pieter Nuyts Landt on the south coast (in a modern approximation from near Burketown in nothern Queensland to Adelaide in South Australia, a distance of roughly 2000km). The expectations of Van Diemen and the Company were considerable.

Procedures and requirements were set out in detail:

All the lands, islands, points, turnings, inlets, bays, rivers, shoals, banks, sands, cliffs, rocks, etc., which you may meet with and pass, you will duly map out and describe, and also have proper drawings made of their appearance and shape, for which purpose we order a draughtsman to join your expedition.[1]

On reaching land, they were

to gather information concerning the situation of the country, the fruits and cattle it produces, their method of building houses, appearance and shape of the inhabitants, their dress, arms, manners, diet, means of livelihood, religion, mode of government, wars and the like notable things, especially whether they are kindly or cruelly disposed.[2]

Van Diemen's instructions were tempered by the experiences of past expeditions and shaped as well by shrewd business sense. Officers and crew were to exercise caution at all times in landing, as they could encounter extremely dangerous savages, but they were to make every effort to show kindness, and no unwilling natives were to be taken. Essentially, the Dutch were to win the good will of the people they met so that peaceful and profitable trading relationships could be established. At the same time, they were not to betray too much interest in the desirable commodities they might find. If local populations did not understand their worth, a more advantageous deal might be struck.

Besides provisions for a twelve- to eighteen-month voyage, the ships carried small quantities of 'commodities and minerals',[3] including spices and metals, and perhaps sandalwood and other luxury goods, to be shown to local people as samples of the sorts of goods the Dutch were interested in. Cloth, metal tools and trinkets would almost certainly have been included as items for barter.

THE FAR VENTURE

The squadron sailed from Batavia on 14 August 1642 for the island of Mauritius, almost 6000km away in the Indian Ocean. This small, oyster-shaped, volcanic island had been known to Arab sailors since at least the tenth century and to the Portuguese possibly from 1500, but was still uninhabited when in 1598 the Dutch occupied it as a convenient stopping place for ships on their way to and from the Indies. Numerous streams provided abundant water, and although the island was rocky, fertile patches made possible gardens yielding fresh fruits and vegetables for the ships. The island's fauna included the flightless dodo.

When they reached Mauritius on 5 September, the ships were found to be in surprisingly poor condition. Repairs were made and some essentials, including firewood, canvas and cordage, taken on. The vessels put to sea on 8 October, steering south into the belt of strong westerlies between 40°S and 50°S, that would carry them eastward. At 49°S the weather was tempestuous and the seas huge. On Visscher's advice, Tasman turned north. The heavy seas rolling in from the south led him to believe there could be no large land mass in that direction.

The weather swung from mist and drizzle to storm with hail, snow and bitter cold. They saw whales and drifting seaweed, and their compasses became alarmingly unsteady. At about four o'clock on the afternoon of 24 November they saw under a clear sky high land rising east by north at a distance of perhaps 65km. Mesmerised, the men watched as two and then three mountain peaks emerged against the pale sky of early evening. Here was a new land, solitary, nameless, thousands of *mijlen* across an empty ocean from the world they knew. Was it the Great South Land? As darkness drew on the mystery and the loneliness must have been frightening. For the night, the ships stood off from the land.

The explorers had reached the west coast of what would much later be called Tasmania, probably in the vicinity of Cape Sorrell and Macquarie Sound. A hundred and fifty-six years later two of the mountains they had seen were named after their ships.

In the bright calm of the following morning, signal flags summoned the senior officers and steersmen of the *Zeehan* to a council on board the *Heemskerck*. Among the decisions made was a name for the new land. Tasman's journal notes:

> This land being the first land we have met with in the South Sea, and not known to any European nation, we have conferred on it the name Anthoony van Diemenslandt in honour of the Hon. Governor-General, our illustrious master, who sent us to make this discovery.[4]

Nearby islands were named for the Councillors of the Indies, and a chart and profile sketches of the coast were completed.

For several days the ships followed the green, craggy and often rainswept coast to the south and then east. They rounded the Tasman Peninsula in the island's southeast, and on 1 December the joint ships' council resolved on a landing to find water, wood and fresh food, as well as to assess the land. An hour after sunset they found a good anchorage with a bottom of fine grey and white sand.

The next morning Visscher went ashore with the two ships' boats, ten musketeers and six rowers armed with pikes and sidearms. The country was high, level and thickly grown with trees and undergrowth that showed no sign of cultivation. A running stream cut across the forest floor, and they saw animal tracks startlingly like those of a tiger. Through the dark green shadows came the sound of some kind of horn or drum, and they had the eerie feeling of being watched. No one appeared, but they found other signs of a human presence—trees deeply burnt into and two especially tall ones with the bark peeled and the trunks bearing step-like gashes cut a metre and a half apart. The inhabitants had to be either very tall or especially adept at climbing. To men accustomed to the flat, open spaces of the Netherlands and of the sea, the forest was gloomy and intimidating.

In the later afternoon, the men returned to the ships with edible greens, some animal droppings and a strongly scented tree gum, presumably eucalyptus. From the ships they saw smoke rising inland.

The next day crewmen prepared to make another landing, this time taking with them a stake carved with the Company's mark and the Prince flag, the flag of the Dutch Republic's princely magistrates, to be set up, so that, as Tasman wrote, 'those who shall come after us may become aware that we have been here, and have taken possession of the said land as our lawful property'.[5] The tumbling surf, however, was so rough that the *Zeehan*'s small boat had to turn back, and when even the larger ship's boat was unable to land, the carpenter swam ashore with the stake and the flag, which he erected near a semicircle of four tall trees. The boat then came as close to the beach as possible and the carpenter swam through the breakers to reach it. There is general agreement that the marker was set up on the shore of the present Prince of Wales Bay.

The ships continued along the coast for two more days, turning north with the shoreline. On 5 December the coast trended to the northwest, which brought the wind against them. The ships' council decided to quit the coast and set a course due east. Tasman's ships left Australia in the vicinity of St Patrick Head and sailed into the Tasman Sea.

Eight days later the lookouts sighted the high mountains of the west coast of New Zealand's South Island, the first recorded sighting of that country by Europeans. A gun was fired and a white flag raised. There was no sign of human life. What land was this?

Proceeding up the coast, on 18 December the ships anchored in Golden Bay at the north end of South Island. Here men appeared in several large canoes, but remained at some distance despite efforts by the Dutch to entice them closer. Probably with the intention of meeting the natives, the *Zeehan* sent out its small boat with several crewmen. In a sudden, flashing burst of speed the canoes paddled forward, rammed the little boat and furiously attacked the sailors. Four Dutchmen died and the quartermaster and two others swam for their lives, to be picked up by the pinnace of the *Heemskerck*. Tasman named the inlet Moordenaersbay, or Murderers' Bay, and ordered his ships out.

The coast now turned eastward, and the mariners found themselves in what they took for a deep bay. It was, in fact, the entrance to Cook Strait, between New Zealand's South and North Islands. Bad weather and contrary winds discouraged them from venturing farther east, so Tasman resumed his generally northward course, now along the west coast of North Island. There seems to have been some question, in Visscher's mind, at least, as to whether the broad inlet they had seen was really a bay. Tasman's chart indicates the shore as a continuous line, but on his map Visscher drew a dotted line. At New Zealand's northernmost point the ships rounded the cape to which Tasman gave the name Maria van Diemen. To the northwest they saw a little group of small islands, which they called the Drei Coningen or Three Kings. Tasman's ships were now in the Pacific Ocean.

Behind them lay a new land, forest-rimmed shores and snow-topped mountains, which they had failed to realise consisted of two islands separated by a strait that was, in fact, a shortcut to the Pacific. Their rounding of Van Diemen's Land had indicated that Australia was not part of the Great South Land girdling the bottom of the earth, but New Zealand seemed to Tasman to be different. Studying his charts, he concluded that this new territory could be a large promontory of the true Terra Australis Incognita, perhaps a continuation of the mountains in the sea that Willem Schouten had seen on the other side of the world before doubling Cape Horn in 1615. Tasman clearly thought this was likely, for he gave his discovery the same name—Staten Landt—as Schouten had given his. It is not known when or how the name New Zealand was later attached to Tasman's discovery.

Tasman and Visscher sailed northeastward into the Pacific. They encountered the Tonga islands, visited 27 years before by Schouten and Lemaire, and some of the Fiji islands. Here they met with enthusiastically friendly receptions and obtained abundant fresh food in exchange for trade goods. But of spices or precious metals there were none.

Tasman's ships then steered for the northwest and sailed along the north coast of New Guinea. From New Guinea's westernmost point they should have turned southeast, in effect doubling back to explore the Gulf of Carpentaria beyond the point reached by Carstensz, but prevailing winds were against them, and the ships' council decided to probe no further. They followed the familiar Indonesian island chain and reached Batavia on 14 June 1643, ten months after they had left.

What had Tasman accomplished? He had circumnavigated the Australian continent, albeit in a great, sweeping arc that at times put him thousands of kilometres from its shores. He had shown that it was not part of South Pole–encircling Terra Australis, a name that, in the region of Australia, would soon be supplanted by the VOC's Hollandia Nova. He had seen Tasmania and discovered the existence of New Zealand and its Maori people. He and his pilot Visscher had made extensive and detailed charts which, despite errors in longitude that put the Australian coast farther east than it is, contributed enormously to a more complete knowledge of the geography of the world in this far region. And he had put on the map a possible part of the Great South Land.

Nevertheless, Van Diemen and the Council in Batavia were neither pleased nor satisfied with the results of the voyage. Tasman had not established the connection or lack of it between Australia and New Guinea, nor investigated what lay at the extreme south end of the Gulf of Carpentaria. He had made no contact with the forest dwellers in the new Van Diemen's Land and had had only a brief and violent meeting with the men of Staten Landt. He had obviously made little effort to establish good relations with native people, to explore on land, or to seek out commercial commodities and opportunities. In a letter to the directors in the Netherlands, Van Diemen wrote with clear annoyance, 'Tasman has not made many investigations regarding the situations nor form and nature of the discovered lands and peoples, but has in principle left everything to a more inquisitive successor.'[6]

From a modern standpoint too, Tasman had failed to exploit fully the possibilities of his expedition. He had circumnavigated Australia without seeing any of it except a part of Tasmania. He was fully aware of the existence of the south coasts of Western and South Australia, yet, after finding Tasmania, he made no attempt to discover whether the two areas were connected. Similarly, on the east coast of Tasmania he turned his ships away from land, instead of exploring farther to the north, in which case he would probably have learned that Tasmania is an island and, had he continued, might have hit upon the east coast of the Australian mainland. Tasman also showed insufficient curiosity as he coasted New Zealand to discover that it was two islands and not part of an antarctic land mass that he thought might extend beyond Cape Horn. Nor did he later investigate the north coast of Australia. The landings he made were relatively few; he showed little desire to venture inland and on meeting resistance was quickly discouraged, unlike Torres, Jansz and Carstensz, who had pushed on despite native attacks and serious loss of men.

Some explanation for Tasman's actions may be found in the manner in which authority was shared in the fleet. On the choice of routes to be taken, Tasman was subject to the advice of Visscher, the respected and influential pilot-major. More important, the decisions made by the ships' council of officers carried considerable weight. Tasman's journal records frequent meetings, at which individual opinions were sometimes requested in writing. After the stops in Tonga and Fiji, for instance, a consensus had to be reached on whether to turn west towards New Guinea and, if so, the course to be taken and the latitude at which the coast should be met. Visscher and the *Heemskerck*'s officers provided written and signed statements of their opinions. Then the pilot-major and his secretary rowed across to the *Zeehan* for the written recommendations of its officers. All these statements were made part of the overall record of the voyage.

Such councils of ships' officers were common in European fleets at the time. A lack of agreement among his officers could be very frustrating for a commander who lacked the leadership qualities to bring them around to his own decision. Sir Francis Drake is said to have called his councils often and enjoyed hearing their views, but afterwards to have issued his own orders. At the other extreme the bitter and destructive quarrel between Quirós and his officers cut short the commander's participation in the voyage with something apparently akin to mutiny. If, as has sometimes been suggested, Tasman lacked initiative and imagination, the general sharing of responsibility may have led him at times to opt for the easier and perhaps safer course. However, the problems of navigation at the time should not be forgotten—the very real difficulties of not being certain of one's location at sea, of fighting contrary winds and handling clumsy, sea-worn little ships, of dealing with exhausted and sometimes very frightened crews. In these areas Tasman apparently conducted the voyage capably, and the way in which such adversities could shape a commander's decisions is not always appreciated by detached onlookers, whether they be VOC dignitaries in Batavia or modern historians.

Inveitably, Tasman's findings changed Europeans' view of the southern hemisphere. The land they had been calling the South Land, together with Van Diemen's Land and possibly New Guinea, was now seen as a vast island or islands quite separate from the reputed Great South Land, which mapmakers now moved farther to the south and endowed with the promontory of Staten Landt. Most Europeans still had little doubt of its existence, and its elusive, provoking image would continue to draw explorers for another century and more, until Terra Australia Incognita vanished before their wider charting, to reveal in its stead the two continents of Australia and Antarctica.

THE SECOND VENTURE

Whatever his reservations about Tasman's drive and initiative, Van Diemen decided to send him out again with another fleet. Although the results of the first voyage had been disappointing and impressions of the newly discovered lands inconclusive, the energetic governor-general was certain that so large a territory must hold worthwhile commercial opportunities.

Plans for the new expedition were set in motion shortly after Tasman's return to Batavia. Three ships were prepared: the *jachts Limmen* and *Zeemeeuw*, both small ships, and the still smaller *Bracq*.

The *Limmen* was assigned 45 officers and crew and eleven soldiers, the *Zeemeeuw* received 35 seamen and six soldiers, and the *Bracq* was manned by just fourteen sailors. Tasman was captain and commander, Visscher pilot-major, and Isaac Gilsemans merchant. In January 1644 they received their instructions.

Exploration was to begin to the north of Australia. The ships were to proceed eastward along the south coast of New Guinea and at 9°S latitude, to approach the shoaly areas with caution. The bigger ships were to anchor while shore parties explored the islands, and the *Bracq*, with its slight draught, was to enter the 'shallow bight' which was, of course, the western entrance to Torres Strait, and search for signs of a seaway to the Pacific Ocean. If it succeeded, the other ships were to follow, making every effort to settle once and for all whether New Guinea was separate from the continent to the south. If at all feasible, Tasman was to sail through to the Pacific and then down the South Land's east coast to Van Diemen's Land, and to ascertain whether there was any passage between the two that might afford the Dutch a shorter far-southern route to South America than Tasman had found so far. From here he was to circle the continent counter-clockwise, that is, along the coasts of today's South Australia and Western Australia, before returning to Batavia. On the way he was to retrieve a chest of silver coins not salvaged in the Abrolhos after the wreck of the *Batavia* and to look for the two men Pelsaert had left on the mainland in 1629. Once again, he had been charged with a very ambitious mission.

Tasman's instructions on exploring the shoals at 9°S show that the Dutch still did not know whether or not Torres Strait existed. Van Diemen and his advisers were evidently unaware of the account of Prado, who in 1606 had traversed the strait with Torres. Yet Hessel Gerritsz in Amsterdam apparently published one of Quirós's many memorials[7] and produced a map, dated 1634 but probably from 1622, on which an inscription refers to 'the yacht of Pedro Fernando de Quiros', which sailed

> about New Guinea on 10 degrees westwards through many islands and dry banks and 2, 3, and 4 fathoms for full 40 days. Presuming New Guinea not to stretch over the 10 degrees to the south—if this were the case—then the land from 9 to 14 degrees must be separate and different from the other New Guinea.[8]

The yacht Gerritsz referred to was, of course, a ship taken through the strait by Torres, not Quirós, who had already left the expedition. This confusion suggests that Gerritsz was drawing conclusions from Spanish charts or other records that had reached him, but to judge by further remarks in his inscription, he questioned their accuracy. The documents were 'very different from one another, and not fitting well with these parts'.[9] Most likely Dutch geo-graphers had some information on the Spanish captain's transit of Torres Strait, but did not put much faith in it.

In fact, it was not generally thought likely that New Guinea and the South Land were separated by water; more probably they were one great land. If Tasman's probe of the shoals at 9°S confirmed this view, he was to follow the north coast of Australia around to the west and then sail south to the Abrolhos. Failing this, he was to carefully investigate the Gulf of Carpentaria, Arnhem Land and Melville Island, and outlying islands, areas seen in 1623 by Joosten Van Colster on the ship *Arnhem* and by Pieter Pieterszoon in 1636 on the first expedition Van Diemen had sent out.

The ships sailed in February. Little of the intended dis-covery took place. The *Bracq* found no channel south of New Guinea, and the entrance to Torres Strait remained a shallow bight as far as the Dutch were concerned. Failing to find a way through, they never reached the coasts of Queensland or New South Wales. Tasman did examine the Gulf of Carpentaria, and then, sailing north, evidently rounded Arnhem Land and continued down the continent's west coast to 23°5'S, roughly off Point Maud and Ningaloo Reef, before heading back to Batavia, where the ships arrived on 4 August. Van Diemen and his council were keenly disappointed. In a letter to VOC headquarters in the Netherlands, dated 23 December 1644, they reported that the expedition had found nothing of value, 'only poor, naked people walking along the beaches; without rice or many fruits, very poor and bad-tempered people in many places'.[10] But, they conceded, Tasman and his men had only seen the coasts; the interior remained to be explored—and would have to be done on foot. Given the immense size and the range of climates covered by this land, it seemed inconceivable that it should contain nothing of profit.

Tasman's second voyage is sparsely documented. Neither his journals nor his charts are known to survive, although his discoveries were soon appearing on Dutch maps. Only a year or two after his second voyage, in 1645 or 1646, the copperplates of a map by Willem Janszoon Blaeu were reworked by his son Joan, a cartographer to the Company's Amsterdam chamber, to show the new outlines of the southern continent, called not Terra Australis, the South Land, but Hollandia Nova, New Holland, apparently the first use of the name.

Van Diemen died in 1645. Tasman's subsequent career with the VOC included high position, dismissal and reinstatement, trading voyages and command of a war fleet sent unsuccessfully against the Spanish in the Philippines. He left the Company's service in 1653 and lived in Batavia, a wealthy and prominent citizen, until his death in 1659.

Despite the VOC's efforts at secrecy, word of Tasman's voyages filtered through to the rest of Europe. Just months after the return of the second expedition to Batavia, an English resident in Bantam had picked up news of the journey. In January 1644 he sent to the English East India Company in London a rough sketch map of Van Diemen's Land, titled 'A Draught of the South Land lately discovered in 1643'. His letter added that 'The Dutch have lately made a new discovery of the South Land,' which they were going to 'fortifie, having mett with something worth looking after'.[11] England at that time was in the grip of civil

war, and the report stirred little interest. A somewhat confused version of the voyage by the surgeon Henrik Haelbos
was published in Amsterdam in 1671. The narrative contained little geographical information and was more
concerned with the attack on the explorers by the
'Southlanders' of New Zealand, but an English translation
appeared in London the same year. Here the editor stated
that while no Spaniard had set foot on the unknown South
Land since Quirós's time, the VOC had 'with great eager-
ness sent thither two ships'.[12] Two years later a German
edition came out. A better account of the journey, based in
part on Tasman's journal, was published in the Netherlands
in 1674 and, appearing several years later in the journal of
the Royal Society, England's prestigious scientific academy,
apparently formed some of the background information
that later encouraged the British government to support
William Dampier's expedition to New Holland. In France
Melchisédec Thévenot incorporated Tasman's and other
Dutch discoveries into his map of 1663, which showed
Hollandia Nova attached to a great blank space labelled
Terre Australe.

THE DUTCH ON AUSTRALIAN SOIL

In the darkness of the first part of the morning watch on
28 April 1656, the VOC ship *Vergulde Draek*, on its way
from the Netherlands to Batavia, drove onto a reef off
Western Australia's Ledge Point, just over 100km north of
Perth. The ship broke up, its cargo—including silver
coins—spilled into the surf, and of the 193 crew and passengers on board only 75 managed to swim or float on

wreckage to shore. Seven men were chosen to make the 2500km voyage to Batavia in the remaining ship's boat to fetch help. The captain, Pieter Albertsz, stayed on the steep, rocky shore with the others.

The boat arrived in Batavia two months later, and the governor-general and his council immediately dispatched two ships to locate the rest of the survivors. The effort failed, as did renewed attempts in 1657 and 1658. Some scattered wreckage from the *Vergulde Draek* was eventually found, but none of its people. During these searches, however, some interesting and largely unexplained events took place.

Although ordered to stay together, the two ships sent out in 1656 became separated. When the smaller vessel, the *Goede Hoop*, made a landing, three men vanished in the bush. Eight others sent in a small boat to look for them also disappeared, and when their shattered craft was found on the shore, they were assumed to have drowned. There was no sign of the three who disappeared on land. By the end of the year, 78 Dutch people had been left on the beaches of Australia's west coast, in addition to the two men marooned by Francisco Pelsaert. And there were those, like the eight in the *Goede Hoop*'s boat, who could only be presumed dead. None of them was ever seen or heard from again.

During his stopover at the Cape of Good Hope in 1657, the captain of the ship *Vink* was asked to look out for wreckage of the *Vergulde Draek* as, on his way to Batavia, he ran along the Australian coast about where the disaster had occurred. Rough weather prevented the *Vink* from approaching closely, and the captain reported low-

ANTONIO VAN DIEMEN
Gouverneur Generaal Van Nederlands Indiën

M. Balen Delineavit ad Offig. I. Anginoo fecu

Anthony van Diemen, governor-general of the Dutch East
India Company, dispatched two ships to explore the northern
coast of Australia, and, in 1642 and again in 1644, sent
expeditions under Abel Tasman to explore, chart and thoroughly
investigate the unknown coasts of the Great South Land.
(Australian National Maritime Museum collection)

The Dutch explorer Abel Tasman with his wife and daughter. In 1642–43 Tasman,
commanding two ships, reached Tasmania and the west coast of New Zealand, his
journey showing that Australia was not part of a great continent to the south.
(Rex Nan Kivell Collection, National Library of Australia, Canberra)

William Dampier, the English buccaneer and writer who explored parts of the coasts of Australia's northwest, New Guinea and New Britain. In England, the published accounts of his adventures in strange lands were immensely popular and aroused England's interest in the southern continent. (Rex Nan Kivell Collection, National Library of Australia, Canberra)

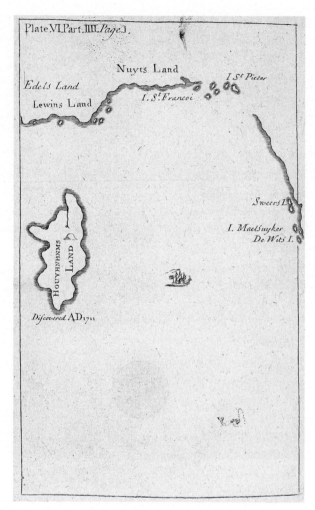

The 'map of the Houyhnhnms' Land' which appeared in
Jonathan Swift's best-selling novel Gulliver's Travels,
London, 1726. Swift placed this imagined island off
today's South Australia. (The British Library, London)

lying dune country but no sign of the lost ship or its people. On 1 January 1658 two more ships, the *Emeloord* and the *De Wakende Boei*, were sent out on the search, and they too parted. Reaching the Australian mainland separately and at a considerable distance from each other, the men on both ships saw fires on shore at night and discharged gun shots as signals, but although additional fires sometimes flared as if in response, when the seamen came ashore the next day they found only cold ashes. A landing party from the *Emeloord* briefly encountered five natives described as tall, almost naked and very black. The Aborigines and the Europeans regarded each other warily and kept their distance. Meanwhile, the *De Wakende Boei* had made a landing on Rottnest Island, which the captain, Samuel Volkerts, drew on his chart. In his journal, he noted that it was

> a big island . . . which has high hills, with much bush and thorns, so that it is difficult to traverse, where were seen some animals, and much excrement, with two seals and a wild cat.[13]

Volkerts and his men also made several landings on the mainland, and on 26 February, almost two years after the *Vergulde Draek*'s disappearance, they discovered some of that ship's wreckage. There was no sign of its passengers, officers, or crew. They continued searching and turned up other remains from the ship—planks, bits of timber chests, buckets, a small barrel. Heavy weather then carried the *De Wakende Boei* south, and worsened as the ship's boat and fourteen men were on their way to a beach. To avoid being driven onto the shore by the wind, Volkerts headed his ship for open sea. When he returned five days later, there was no one on the beach. That night a fire came to life in the darkness. A cannon was discharged from on board and a second fire appeared on the shore, but without the ship's boat, the men on the *De Wakende Boei* could not land. By morning the wind had pushed the ship some distance to the north. Volkerts then left the area, and just over three weeks later, the two search vessels met off Java and arrived together in Batavia. An inquiry later found Volkerts guilty of gross negligence for abandoning the men in the boat.

The story of men in the ship's boat was not over. High wind and surf had driven them northward until they finally succeeded in landing on an island. From here they had seen their returning ship, lit a fire and, hearing the cannon shot, lit a second one. They then waited for daylight and a chance to sail out to the *De Wakende Boei*. When morning came, the vessel was gone. The men waited for rescue for eleven days before provisioning themselves with seal meat and building up the sides of their boat with seal skins to make it more seaworthy. Thus prepared for a long, rough voyage, they set out for Batavia. Three men died on the journey and seven were lost ashore in Java, but the remaining four, after walking for two months along the coast, were helped by Javanese tribesmen and finally reached Batavia. There were no further efforts to locate the survivors of the *Vergulde Draek*. Later in 1658, however, another unexpected bit of the Australian coast came to be charted.

About the middle of 1658 the flute *Elburgh*, on its way to Batavia, came upon the Western Australian coast and, beset by strong winds and a dangerously heavy sea, found a sheltered anchorage, probably in today's Geographe Bay, north of Cape Leeuwin. The captain, a mate, the sergeant and six soldiers went ashore, where they saw three black men dressed in skins. The natives moved away, but their campfire was left burning, and the Dutch saw spears and small hammers made from wood and stone fastened together with a pleasant-smelling gum—'the whole strong and heavy enough to knock out a man's brains'.[14] A little farther inland the Dutch saw some empty huts and fresh-water springs. Some days later the *Elburgh* was able to put to sea, and arrived safely in Batavia in mid-July. In 1678 a more northerly sighting of New Holland was made by the ship *De Vliegende Swann*. Sailing from Ternate to Batavia, she was driven into the Indian Ocean, evidently by storms, and saw land probably between Exmouth Gulf and Carnarvon. Aside from a brief mention of her arrival in Batavia in a letter of the governor-general, a chart marked with little anchors is the only evidence of the journey.

Remains of the *Vergulde Draek* did, however, reappear nearly three centuries later. In 1931 a young boy walking among the sand dunes near Cape Leschenault found 40 coins of several types used in seventeenth century trade. Although the nearby town of Moore River changed its name to Guilderton as a result, the interest aroused by the find soon dimmed, and it was 1963 before scuba divers, coming upon an elephant tusk on the sea bottom off Ledge Point, rekindled the excitement of discovering a lost wreck. Cannon, anchors, yellow ballast bricks and more elephant tusks were found on the seaward side of a reef some 6km out to sea and 12km south of Ledge Point. The immediate result was an undisciplined rush of looters and souvenir hunters, some of whom used explosives to get at the objects they wanted. The following year, historic wrecks came under the protection of Western Australia's Museum Act, and after 1972 organised and scientific diving and retrieval began. All that was left of the ship itself was unrecognisable bits of timber smashed by three centuries of waves as well as by the looters. Little can be learned now of just how the ship was damaged when it struck, but the wreckage tells something about the material comforts enjoyed by the Dutch community in Batavia. The cargo included a shipment of leather shoes, hundreds of clay pipes, and 40 German bellarmine jugs with their moulded faces. Animal bones, copper kettles and pewter spoons were recovered, but of the passengers and crew who used these things no trace has ever been found.

By now Dutch navigators had virtually filled in the western outline of the continent. Thus, on the 1680 sea chart of the Indian Ocean and the East Indies by the cartographers Pieter Goos and Johannes van Keulen, the mighty curve of New Holland extended from the shores of the Great Australian Bight around Cape Leeuwin, up to the Kimberleys, across the top of Arnhem Land and into and around the Gulf of Carpentaria. Much remained uncertain. At the top of Cape York Peninsula the line stopped, leaving a blank space between the peninsula and the coastline of New Guinea. In the south, there was a long emptiness between the Nuyts Archipelago islands in the Bight and the V-shaped coast of what was known of Van Diemen's Land. The vast interior remained a featureless void that extended eastward. There was no attempt to show where it ended and consequently no east coast.

In July 1693 the VOC ship *Ridderschap van Hollandt* sailed from the Netherlands for the East Indies with 325 people on board. Having stopped at the Cape of Good Hope in January 1694, she set out across the Indian Ocean. She was never heard from again.

Nicolaas Cornelisz Witsen, a director of the VOC who had previously urged an extensive survey of the New Holland west coast, seized on the disappearance of the *Ridderschap*—and the implied dangers of incomplete charts—to organise an expedition aimed more specifically than any before at scientifically observing and surveying not only the coast but the interior, both on foot and by sailing up rivers as far as possible. Witsen had a genuine interest in natural history and looked forward to receiving both specimens and information.

Three ships were put under the command of Willem Hesselsz de Vlamingh. Born on Vlieland, an island of sand dunes and small farmsteads on the edge of the North Sea, De Vlamingh, now in his 50s, was an experienced sailor, a veteran of whaling trips to Greenland and years of Company service. The new *Geelvinck* was his flagship, and with it would sail the smaller *Nijptangh* and *Weseltje*. Also assigned to the fleet was Victor Victorsz, described as a lay priest, whose responsibility was to chart precisely every coast sighted between the Netherlands and Batavia. The three ships' combined complement was about 194 men.

The squadron set sail from Texel at daybreak on 3 May 1696. By the middle of September it had anchored in Table Bay at the Cape of Good Hope. There the captain of the *Weseltje* died and was replaced by De Vlamingh's son Cornelisz. Catching the westerlies into the Indian Ocean, the ships steered first for the tiny mid-ocean islands of St Paul and Amsterdam. On St Paul, the remnant of a volcano that exploded millennia ago, the Dutch trod an eerie, steep-sided ring of blackened, tortured rock around a sea-filled caldera. Quarrelling Antarctic fur seals were so thick on the ground that the men had to kill some so they could move about in their search for wreckage or signs of cast-aways. There was no trace of either. De Vlamingh had an engraved plate set up to commemorate their visit, and the ships moved on to the greener island of Amsterdam. Again, De Vlamingh had a plate set up. Again, there was no sign of the *Ridderschap van Hollandt*.

At dusk nineteen days later the coast of New Holland was sighted. A few days later an island emerged from the mist. The ships anchored and the men spent the last days of 1696 exploring the curious island with its sharply scented trees. De Vlamingh called it Mist Island, but Gerrit Collaert, captain of the *Nijptangh*, dubbed it Rotteneilandt for the many nesting quokkas, which to him looked like rats. The name Rottnest stuck. They found a piece of timber with nails in it and a length of wainscot, possibly some of the widely scattered wreckage of the *Vergulde Draek*, lost up the coast 50 years before. No human beings were seen, and no identifiable remains of the *Ridderschap van Hollandt* were found.

To the east stretched the mainland, seemingly without

The three ships of Willem de Vlamingh's fleet reached Australia
in 1696, anchoring in the vicinity of Perth after an eight-month voyage.
Following the coast northwards, De Vlamingh and his captains chartered the
Western Australian shoreline to North West Cape, more than a century
before Cook chartered the island continent's eastern shores.

end. The first reconnaissance there was brief, in a single boat that landed probably near today's Coogee Beach. A few days later 86 men under Collaert set off at sunrise on a four-day excursion with the ships' boats and the small *Weseltje*. They landed on a beach probably in the vicinity of modern Cottesloe, north of the Swan River. Making their way into a wooded area to some small salt lakes, they found the footprints of children and adults and the remains of a hut. They then split into separate groups and for the next two days pushed on through seemingly deserted bushland. The men following the shore found a piece of ship's timber sheathing and presently discovered the mouth of a large river and extraordinary black swans, some of which they caught and brought to the flagship the next morning to show an astonished De Vlamingh.

De Vlamingh himself now took three boats up the river, which widened impressively as they travelled upstream for perhaps 70km until shallows blocked their way. The Dutchmen saw no natives nor anything else of interest beyond the sloping, wooded river banks, and after three days they returned to the anchorage. De Vlamingh named the broad river Zwaanerivier or Swan River. Above the beach at Cottesloe today a modern monument commemorates the explorers' landing.

The little fleet resumed its journey northward along the coast, keeping as close inshore as possible, mapping the visible shoreline and making several landings, while Victor Victorsz painted a number of fine watercolour profiles of the coast. It was high, waterless duneland, which reminded De Vlamingh of his home island. Occasionally the mariners saw people, but they remained at a distance and all attempts at contact failed.

On 30 January the fleet reached a long, narrow island, which, studying his charts, De Vlamingh decided was the one discovered 81 years before by Dirck Hartogs. The ships' boats were dispatched to sail around the island to scout and seek a good anchorage, and De Vlamingh himself took a landing party ashore. On 3 February the excited boat crews returned with a thrilling find from a hill at the north end of the island. The upper steersman had discovered a flattened pewter plate still hanging on a 'pole, which though half rotted stood still erect'.[15] Its inscription announced the arrival of Dirck Hartogs on the island in 1616, and it was with something like awe that the seamen stared at this remnant of their countrymen's presence three generations earlier in this empty, desolate land.

The fleet now sailed confidently into the shelter of Dirck Hartogs's Roads in the lee of the island and spent nine days exploring and charting the farther reaches of Shark Bay, which divides into two long, shallow inlets. One man was drowned when one of the boats capsized in a sudden, violent gust of wind. Despite the enthusiasm stirred by the discovery of Hartogs's plate, the men found little of interest. Hartogs's island was rich in bird and marine life, particularly turtles, but was uninhabited and without any products of value. Nor did the surrounding territory, dry and uninviting, yield anything more. De Vlamingh decided to sail on, but first had a replacement made for Hartogs's plate. Again a pewter dish was flattened and engraved, first with a copy of Hartogs's announcement of his and his ship's arrival and departure on 25 and 26 October 1616, and then with a few lines commemorating the arrival of the ships *Geelvinck*, *Nijptangh* and *Weseltje*, their commander and captain and his principal officers, and their departure from the island to continue exploring New Holland on the way to Batavia. The symbol of the Amsterdam chamber of the VOC was added. A new pole bearing the new plate was erected at the same spot where Hartogs had raised his almost a century before.

The next day the ships hauled up their anchors, set

their sails and steered north. They made only one more landing, although they kept as close to land as was safe. At Australia's North West Cape De Vlamingh quitted the continent and headed for Batavia, seeing and charting what was possibly Christmas Island on the way. The Dutch called it Mony Island, and Victorsz sketched its profile. The little fleet arrived in Batavia on 20 March 1697, eleven months after leaving Texel.

Once again Company authorities in Batavia and subsequently in Amsterdam were disappointed in their navigator's achievements, particularly Nicolaas Witsen, who had instigated the expedition and who now accused De Vlamingh of drunkenness. The meagre evidence of almost a year's voyaging included eleven fine watercolours by Victorsz, seven of them profiles of New Holland against the sky—the first set of pictorial views of Australia—the journals of the voyage, Dirck Hartogs's pewter plate, a bottle of oil pressed from the fragrant wood of Rottnest Island, and a box of fruits, plants and shells collected from the beaches of the continent. Three black swans were to have been sent as well. A letter from Batavia to the Amsterdam chamber of the VOC reports that the ship's company

> have seen a species of black swan, three of which they
> have brought to Batavia alive, which we should have
> been glad to send over to Your Worships, but that
> shortly after their arrival here all of them died one after
> another.[16]

De Vlamingh's mapping was accurate, but he named few

places. A skilful, honest but unimaginative seaman, he simply reported what he saw. The following year he returned to the Netherlands in command of a fleet of three ships, after which there is no further word of him. The Dutch public learned of the voyage through a brief report by Mandrop Torst, surgeon of the *Nijptangh*, published in 1701. There was still no news of the lost ship *Ridderschap*. Later rumours maintained that the vessel had been seized by pirates off Madagascar, although two ships from the VOC base at the Cape of Good Hope had searched that area without result.

In terms of geographical knowledge, De Vlamingh's journey had provided some gains. His charting had been thorough, and the Australian west coast was soon a more detailed reality on European maps. As its contours grew more definite, however, its potential seemed to grow less exciting. This part of the continent evidently held nothing of commercial value, nor people even remotely interested in trade. Settlements might have been a possibility if the coast had appeared more hospitable, but without strong incentives and at such a great distance from the homeland, and even from Batavia, it was not seen as worth serious consideration. Jan Pieterszoon Coen had had such a vision for the East Indies—and perhaps tentatively for the South Land—but even at the hands of that ruthlessly forceful governor-general, the scheme had been beyond the capabilities of the VOC and the Netherlands.

Victor Victorsz's watercolour paintings disappeared not long after the voyage, but in 1970 they were found in the Prins Hendrik Maritime Museum. Dirck Hartogs's pewter plate is in the Rijksmuseum in Amsterdam. The plate De

Vlamingh set in its place was found in 1801 by Louis de Freycinet, serving under the French explorer Emmanuel Hamelin. It had fallen from its disintegrating pole, and Hamelin had it nailed to a new stake. In 1818 De Freycinet revisited the island, found the second pole decayed and took the plate to Paris, where it was given to the Academie des Inscriptions et des Belles Lettres. The plate was misplaced, found again and in 1947 presented to the Australian government. It can now be seen at the Western Australian Maritime Museum in Fremantle.

Again the north

Dutch interest in New Holland flagged after the disappointments of De Vlamingh's journey. Then in 1687, 1703 and 1709 an English adventurer, William Dampier, published accounts of his visits to the northwestern coast of the continent, a region the VOC saw more or less as its own. The Company was not particularly perturbed by an intrusion into an area where it saw no opportunity for profit for anyone, but a possible threat to the north of New Holland, whose commercial potential was still uncertain, was another matter. This area had not been investigated since Tasman's voyage 60 years before, and the Dutch still did not even know whether New Guinea was joined to New Holland or not. The Company's interest revived and two expeditions were organised. One was to sail along the north coast of New Guinea; the other was to explore the north coast of New Holland.

Three vessels, including an Indonesian-rigged boat with a very shallow draught, were prepared for the

Australian journey, and in 1705 sailed from Batavia under the command of Maarten van Delft. For over three months they coasted Arnhem Land and the shores of the Gulf of Carpentaria. Spear-throwing Aborigines opposed a landing on Melville Island, but amicable relations were later established and maintained for some weeks. As the ships prepared to depart, however, two sailors were attacked and wounded for their clothing. Van Delft wrote at some length, describing the people and what he saw as their extreme poverty.

Sickness then struck all three ships, killing more than half of the flagship's company of 62, including Van Delft, and leaving only four men strong enough to handle the sails. The little fleet staggered back to Batavia.

The Dutch now concluded that the reports of earlier navigators had been right: the region was worthless to them and to anyone else. It had no minerals, metals, spices, valuable timbers or even fertile areas, and although its people were not unremittingly hostile, there were clearly no commercial opportunities to be gained from relations with them.

CASTAWAYS

The well-armed VOC ship *Zuytdorp* left the Netherlands on 1 August 1711 in convoy with four other vessels headed for Batavia. Aside from other cargoes she carried large sums of money for VOC expenditures in the East— guilders, gold and silver bullion, reals and other coinage.

The voyage southward through the Atlantic was disastrous. Caught in calms and countercurrents, the *Zuytdorp* drifted off Africa for weeks in terrible heat, its people ravaged by sickness. One hundred and twelve of the 286 on board died before reaching the Cape of Good Hope and 22 had to be left in hospital there. During July 1712 the other ships reached Batavia one by one. The *Zuytdorp* did not appear. The authorities waited, hoping for the arrival of survivors who could direct them to where the ship had undoubtedly been wrecked. None appeared, and after a time the *Zuytdorp* was virtually forgotten.

In 1927 an Australian stockman, Tom Pepper, climbed over the tumbled rocks that spill down the face of the high cliffs on the Western Australian coast north of the Murchison River. On a rocky platform at the water's edge he was surprised to find pieces of timber wreckage, curious metal discs and several bronze objects he could not identify. Cleaning revealed the discs to be Dutch coins of 1711. In the years that followed Pepper and others from neighbouring stations visited the place, carrying away a carved wooden figure of a woman, lead, more coins and other objects. In 1939 an expedition from Perth examined the site, but little was done to explore the surrounding area or the sea bed. The nearly inaccessible location of the wreck discouraged investigation. The sea crashes heavily onto the rocky shelf at the base of the cliff, and the cliff face itself is a jumble of broken boulders. The clifftop and the region around it are seamed with gullies and densely covered with scrub.

In 1954 Tom Pepper described his find to Phillip Playford, a young oil geologist working in the area. Playford inspected the location and realised that it was worthy of serious investigation. Researching ships lost in the period indicated by dates on the coins, he determined that this was the wreck of the *Zuytdorp*.

Since then numerous expeditions to the wreck site have been made despite the difficulties. Divers have brought up bronze cannons and thousands of silver coins from the sea floor, while breech blocks, musket fragments, buckles, coins, keys and many other items have been found at the bottom of the cliff. Examining the sand, investigators turned up ashes, a sign that there had been survivors.

Even more vivid evidence of survivors—and of a desperate struggle to live—was uncovered on the clifftop. Here again there had been a fire, larger than the one at the base of the cliff, and numerous objects from the ship were found—brass dividers, barrel hoops, nails, fragments of green glass bottles, long-stemmed stone pipes, pieces of slate and lead—all painfully carried up from below. Drenched, terrified, some of them no doubt injured, the *Zuytdorp*'s castaways must have struggled up the tumbled rocks to the top, frantically gathered a pathetic miscellany of belongings, hunted for water, and lit fires against the chill and the fear-filled darkness of night. What became of them? How long, with meagre supplies and no knowledge of the land, did they manage to survive in that harsh, alien environment? No solid answer has ever been found. Like the lost people of the *Vergulde Draek*, some of the men who searched for them, and the two young mutineers marooned by Pelsaert, the survivors of the *Zuytdorp* simply vanished.

In 1834, settlers in Perth heard through local Aborigines the story of a wreck up the coast and in one version a description of survivors. Assuming that the wreck was recent, they sent out search parties, but without result.

Evidently the tale had been handed down among the Aborigines for more than a century.

The Great South Land may have claimed many more victims than anyone knows. The general area in which a ship perished was often known—for instance, six vessels were lost in 1722 in a cyclone off Mauritius—but in 1724 and in 1726 the ships *Fortuyn* and *Aagtekerke* just disappeared. Did the South Land's breakers carry more shattered timbers or a few survivors onto its unforgiving shore? It is a secret the continent has kept to itself.

Fourteen years after the disappearance of the *Zuytdorp*, in November 1726, the ships *Zeewijk* and *Barbesteyn* sailed from Flushing, bound for Batavia. The *Zeewijk* was new and one of the VOC's larger ships, armed with 36 cannons and six swivel guns, and carrying ten chests of Company money—guilders, schellings and stuivers. She was skippered by Jan Steyns, an experienced seaman, and had at least 212 men on board. The voyage south through the Atlantic was uneventful apart from the usual deaths and illness and the separation of the two ships. At the Cape of Good Hope the *Zeewijk* took on fresh water and provisions and sailed on alone, heading east-northeast according to Company directions. This route would bring the ship to Eendrachtsland at 17°S latitude—a point on the coast which by now had become something of a marker on the ocean road to Batavia. When land came into view, the ship was to steer the northerly course that would bring it to Sunda Strait. Ships' captains were routinely cautioned that, since winds and currents would normally be with them and nautical charts did not show long distances accurately, New Holland could appear sooner than expected. Moreover, the

Eendrachtsland coast was dangerous, with shoals and a rocky sea bottom. Captains were advised to have lookouts posted, to frequently sound for depth and to be generally very cautious, especially at night or in heavy weather.

The *Zeewijk* was sailing east-northeast early on the clear night of 9 June 1727. A lookout had been sent aloft and the sails shortened for the night. The captain, Jan Steyns, was standing on deck when he saw a ghostly line of surf directly ahead. He shouted orders, but the heavy ship could not be stopped. She plunged forward, crashed and swung around, her starboard side wedged on the reef.

In the light of morning, refloating the ship was seen to be impossible. There were several small islands a few kilometres away, and although rough surf frustrated several attempts to get off the wreck, drowning a number of men, most of the people were eventually brought to the largest of the islands. Here they set up tents, gathered their salvaged provisions and found fresh water, left by rains.

The *Zeewijk*, like the *Batavia*, had crashed onto one of the reefs of the Houtman Abrolhos, but well south of the *Batavia*'s position. The ship's company knew that no search would be made for them unless the officials in Batavia had some idea of where to look, so eleven men were selected to sail to Java in a small boat to raise the alarm.

The rest of the castaways set up their camp on a flat rock of an island just a few metres above sea level and rimmed with mangrove thickets. Smaller islets protruded from among the reefs around them. Work parties were organised to salvage the ten chests of Company money and other goods and materials and finally to dismantle the wreck. Other groups dug wells, fished and hunted seals and muttonbirds. Discipline wavered at times, but for the most part order was maintained, to the extent that two men accused of homosexuality were marooned separately to die on tiny islands to the north.

After six months with no sign of rescue, it was decided to build a new ship from the timbers of the *Zeewijk* and wood from the islands' mangroves. The building of the ship was pivotal to maintaining both the spirits and the discipline of the group. Through months of planning and hard work the *Zeewijk*'s carpenter and his assistants put together the *Sloepie*, 12 to 16m long, with one mast, two square sails, a bowsprit and a jib, a kind of cabin under the after deck, and two swivel guns mounted near the stern. The scene is depicted on a chart drawn by the captain, Jan Steyns, the *Zeewijk* high on the the reef, the sea dotted with small islands and a flag flying from a mound on the largest. At the bottom of the picture appears the *Sloepie*, flags fluttering cheerily from bow, masthead and stern.

On the morning of 26 March 1728 the men of the *Sloepie* triumphantly made sail. Eighty-eight survivors watched the island dissolve into the distance. On 30 April the little craft entered the Batavia's harbour with 82 men. Six had died on the way, but the Company's ten chests of money were on board, untouched.

Months of judicial investigation followed. Jan Steyns was condemned for carelessness and failure to follow Company instructions in his approach to New Holland and for an attempt to falsify the ship's journals to protect himself. The prosecution demanded a heavy lashing, chains and hard labour, financial penalties and eternal exile, but Steyns got off with confiscation of his money and belongings, discharge from his post and banishment for life from all Company territories. He probably had no choice but to return home.

The eleven men who had left the island to seek help were never heard from again.

The *Zeewijk* wrecksite was not discovered until 1968. During the 1970s diving teams found planking and other remains, and investigators tentatively identified the place where the *Sloepie* had been built. The silent, secretive continent had not claimed everything flung upon its shores.

THE LAST SEARCH OF THE NORTH

By the early 1700s the VOC's interest in New Holland had almost evaporated. No prospects for profit had eventuated, and a passage between New Guinea and New Holland, which might have opened new market opportunities, had not been found. In 1718 one Jean Pierre Purrij made a proposal for the exploration of Pieter Nuytsland with a view to settlement. The only known suggestion for a Dutch colony in New Holland was rejected.

Yet some curiosity persisted. In 1751 the commander of the Dutch fort on Timor, Daniël van den Burgh, reported to the governor-general and Council that one of his Chinese traders, on his way to hunt turtles at nearby Roti Island, had been driven south by strong winds. He had reached a low shore and had friendly encounters with some of the local people before returning home.

This report fanned the embers of interest in the potential of New Holland's north coast, and in 1756 two ships, the *Rijder* and the *Buis*, were sent from Batavia to explore the Gulf of Carpentaria. Separated in a storm at Banda, each continued alone. On 17 April some of the *Rijder*'s company, under Captain Jean Etienne Gonzal, landed on the Gulf shore. They found several bark huts, a small bark canoe, bone-tipped spears and fishing gear of twisted fibre and animal claws. An Aboriginal man fled on their approach. Gonzal described the land itself as attractive, with high grass, little valleys, tall trees, good soil and small streams of fresh water. At what is probably the site of today's Weipa, the *Rijder* was approached by two canoes, each holding two men who called and made signs for the Dutch to come ashore. When on the following day the Europeans did so, the Aborigines fled, but then returned armed and accompanied by several women, and sat down on the sand. When the Dutch indicated that they were seeking fresh water, the people got up and led them along the beach and into a little green valley where there were women and children and bark shelters under the tall trees. Water welled up in hand-scooped pits in the ground.

Returning to the beach, the Netherlanders were joined by nineteen Aborigines daubed in red, to whom they offered spirits sweetened with sugar. The result was a highly amicable interchange, the two groups sitting on the sand while the natives 'struck up a kind of chant, at the conclusion of which they retired to the wood again'.[17] When the Dutchmen returned to the beach two days later, 'the natives came up to them dancing and singing, sat down close to them, laid aside their ... weapons, and again enjoyed the liquor'.[18] Good will, however, ended with that bout of socialising, for Gonzal tried to seize some Aborigines to be trained as interpreters and informants. In the fighting that ensued, muskets were fired and spears thrown. One captive escaped by biting the sailors who held him, but in the end Gonzal had one man securely on board.

Continuing southward, the Dutch found a stream gushing down over rocks and a lake where they saw numerous birds and the footprints of large animals. They learned something about the diet of the Aborigines—wild fruits, roots, tubers and fish—and thought that the people recognised gold as such when shown some lumps of it. Gonzal's impression of the Gulf region remained generally favourable, but when he had lost all but two of his anchors and the season began to turn, he decided to head for Timor.

Meanwhile, the second ship, the *Buis*, under Lavienne Lodewijk van Asschens, had sailed down the eastern side of the Gulf. Off Cape Keerweer eight men were lost in the ship's boat when it drifted away in the late afternoon and the ship was unable to follow it into the shallows. Guns were fired and a light kept burning at the topmast at night to guide the men back. They did not return, but joined the toll of almost 90 Dutch men and women lost on Australian shores. After twelve days, running low on water and firewood, Van Asschens ordered the sails unfurled and the anchor raised, and steered for Batavia.

Gonzal's favourable observations were exceptional. They hinted at the possibility of farming in northern New Holland and achieving amicable relations with the Aborigines, although the good will he saw was encouraged by spirits and destroyed by his decision to capture some of the native men.

Gonzal's optimism did not prevent the Company's

heavy-handed criticism of his expedition. Gerrit de Haan, master cartographer in Batavia, carefully studied the two captains' maps and journals and found only fault. In his report to the governor-general he excoriated both men for lack of initiative, Gonzal for failing to press farther into the interior, and Van Asschens, in particular, for scarcely approaching the shore. The expedition was never followed up. The Dutch no longer had the interest nor, perhaps, the resources for further exploration.

By 1756 the Netherlands, through its United East India Company, the VOC, had been visiting and surveying the coasts of New Holland off and on for one and a half centuries. Some of its probes had been deliberate. Others were accidental—unintended sightings, tragic catastrophes, searches for lost ships that happened upon something new. For the Netherlands' seafarers, merchants, investors and ordinary citizens, the rewards of all this effort had been scant. A strip of the western coast had come to serve as a useful marker on the ocean voyage from the Cape of Good Hope to Batavia, yet its perilous surrounds had led to the loss of ships, lives and cargoes. No landing had ever found anything of economic value. The native population existed at a subsistence level, and had no interest in nor understanding of trade as the Dutch practised it. For the Dutch, New Holland had meant cost without return. By unfortunate chance, most Dutch investigations had been confined to some of the most inhospitable regions of the country. Place names and the wreckage of a few ships were thus the principal legacies of the Netherlands—and of Europeans—in Australia for another half century.

Dutch voyages of exploration were now at an end.

During the second half of the eighteenth century the financial might of the VOC had been eroded by smugglers' violations of the Company's monopolies, internal corruption, mounting administrative costs and growing competition from the English. In 1794 the French Revolutionary Wars swept over the Netherlands, bringing political upheaval. Five years later the charter of the VOC was revoked, and the government took over the Company's possessions and obligations.

Dutch discoveries had brought the Australian continent into the realm of known geography, giving a vast region shape and reality. In the process they had shifted the imagined South Land south. Now it would fall to other nations to complete the charting of Australia and to finally remove the ancient vision of the Great South Land from the maps.

10.

A Changing Image

The sober charts of realistic Dutch mariners, meticulously processed by VOC geographers, had filled in bit by bit the outlines of New Holland—the southern coast along the Great Australian Bight, the huge bulge of the western seaboard, and the indented and island-strewn northern littoral. There remained gaps and inaccuracies. An incomplete Van Diemen's Land still floated alone in the south. An elongated New Guinea, considered probably connected to New Holland, extended fingerlike into the Arafura Sea to the northwest with a small, hesitant break in the coastline at its base, where it almost joined Cape York Peninsula. Unlike many of their predecessors, the Dutch cartographers of this period preferred to make omissions than to indulge in fictionalised details. Their charts, despite the handsomely lettered legends in scrolled frames and little ships under sail on the oceans, were carefully assembled from the direct evidence supplied by seafarers who had seen and recorded each island or portion of coast. There remained, however, the enormous blank space of the continent's interior, that stretched towards an unknown east coast that must somehow extend from south of New Guinea to, perhaps, Van Diemen's Land.

Many Europeans now linked this region to the idea of the Great South Land. On Melchisédec Thévenot's map of 1663 there spread almost explosively to the east of New Holland a vast, empty, undefined space labelled Terre Australe, and maps published in Amsterdam and London during the next century depicted Terra Australis in much the same way. Thus, for many, New Holland was merely the western part of a greater continent. The question was, where exactly did this continent end?

A number of European discoveries had, of course, been made in the Pacific. Tasman had found New Zealand, a promontory, as he thought, with a west coast some 1000km long. Farther into the Pacific were the elusive Solomon Islands found and lost by Mendaña, and, perhaps most significantly, Austrialia del Espíritu Santo, claimed in 1606 by Pedro Fernández de Quirós. By the early eighteenth century the evidence of Diego de Prado y Tovar and Luis Baéz de Torres that Espíritu Santo was an island was long forgotten, nor had the island been seen by Europeans since 1606. As a result, many geographers gave greater weight than they might otherwise have done to Quirós's passionate belief that it was part of a continent—a conviction he had maintained vigorously and unceasingly in years of argument before the king and councils of Spain. That continent, as he had promised his men, would bring its discoverers 'as much gold and silver as you can carry and such a quantity of pearls that you shall measure them by hatfuls'.[1] It was an unforgettable image. Perhaps, some thought, the South Land of centuries of belief and seeking still lay undiscovered somewhere to the east of New Holland.

On some maps these European discoveries in the Pacific were shown almost as part of Australia's unseen east coast. In 1714 the noted cartographer Guillaume de l'Isle published in Paris his *Hémisphère Méridional*, a map of the southern hemisphere based on an antarctic polar projection which shows only ocean at the bottom of the world. Nouvelle Hollande occupies Australia's west. To the south and east fragments of Tasmania, New Zealand, Vanuatu, the Solomons and New Guinea lie in an arc around a blank, borderless Terres Australes and, although no lines join them, one can hardly help thinking of them as connected. The illusion of unity is reinforced by the fact that Espíritu Santo, here labelled Terre Australis ou St Esprit, is drawn not as an island but as part of a mainland coast, complete with outsized renditions of Quirós's Jordan and San Salvador Rivers, and all but joined to the Solomons, some of which appear as jutting continental peninsulas, not islands. The result is the impression of a huge continent with Nouvelle Hollande in the west and these outlying areas possible sections of its distant east coast. The empty space between these sketched-in bits of coast still continued to stir visions of a magnificent land and indescribable riches. The De l'Isle map was very popular, reissued several times and in 1755 included in a French atlas.

In England the same intriguing concept was supported in a number of maps and writings from respected sources. A map engraved in 1744 by Emanuel Bowen also showed Hollandia Nova as merely the western portion of a much larger Terra Australis. One of its legends commented that 'the Country discovered by Fernando de Quiros lies according to his description on the East Side of this Continent',[2] adding that since there was a country where Quirós said he had found one, his descriptions of it, although 'very unjustly treated by some Critical Writers as a Fiction',[3] should be considered authentic. Bowen argued that as the new continent lay in the same latitudes as such rich lands as Sumatra, Java, the Moluccas, Peru and Chile, it too must 'overflow with' gems, ivory, precious metals and other valuable commodities.

Bowen's map was published in John Campbell's *Complete Collection of Voyages*, a tome intended to encourage English expansion and trade at a time of rising international rivalry on the oceans. Campbell was not alone in believing that the Dutch had concocted the grim view of a waterless New Holland, rimmed by forbidding rocks and reefs and inhabited by savage and backward people, to keep other nations from challenging their lucrative hold in the East Indies. The Dutch had not exploited their discovery, the thinking went, because they were prosperous enough in the Indies; they were keeping New Holland in reserve, an untapped resource to exploit at their leisure. Campbell saw Terra Australis in terms of his own time, an era of rising commercialism, yet it remained touched by something of the golden myth that had shaped European thinking about the South Land for centuries.

There were others for whom the Great South Land remained a utopian dream. Jean Pierre Purrij or Purry, the Swiss who had approached Dutch authorities in 1718 with a proposal to colonise Pieter Nuytsland, was a former VOC employee who believed that the best climates on earth existed at latitudes 35° north and south of the equator. After the Dutch rejected his scheme, he sought interest from the French and then the English. No one was prepared to back this uncertain, expensive project, but Purrij's enthusiasm made its mark. Bowen's 1744 map includes a brief comment written across Pieter Nuytsland: 'This is the country seated according to Coll: Purry in the best climate in the world.'[4] As Pieter Nuytsland extended along Australia's saltbush-studded Nullarbor Plain, where the average annual rainfall is less than 250mm, Purrij's information was indeed confused.

PURSUING THE LEGEND

For most mapmakers and geographers the realistic delineation of Australia, although incomplete, was dispelling at last the legend of the Unknown South Land. What lay at the polar extremities of the earth, north or south, was yet to be discovered, but the consensus of scientific opinion accepted that there was no enormous southern land mass to reflect and balance the continents of the northern hemisphere. By the mid-seventeenth century some satirists openly ridiculed the idea.

Some still believed in it, however. An English treatise of 1682 discoursed upon the characteristics of enormous countries extending from the South Pole through cold, temperate and tropical climates, and equalling in size Europe and Africa together. Terra Australis Incognita was also discussed in the 1692 geography of the Dutchman Joannis Luyts, and in 1698 William Dampier urged the First Lord of the Admiralty in London to focus attention on the southern continent before exploring any other part of the globe. Some geographers arrived at the conclusion that there were two southern continents. One was the increasingly well-defined territory of New Holland, which reached from the Indian Ocean to Van Diemen's Land to Espíritu Santo on its northeastern shoulder. The other lay farther out in the South Pacific, undiscovered and unexplored except possibly for a western promontory of which New Zealand was part. In his *Histoire des Navigations aux Terres Australes*, a compilation of Pacific explorations published in 1756, the French intellectual Charles de Brosses repeated the theory that a large southern continent was necessary to keep the rotating globe in equilibrium, and raised the fascinating prospect of finding new and different people, plants and animals for science as well as opportunities for profit. The eminent mathematician and naturalist George-Louis Leclerc, comte de Buffon, in his 1749 *Histoire et Théories de la Terre*, described a southern continent as large as Europe, Asia and Africa combined.[5] The phantasm of a Great South Land remained.

The search for new lands, begun by the Spanish, the Portuguese and the Dutch, was increasingly taken up by Europe's new powers, France and England. By the eighteenth century these nations had overcome their internal conflicts and, on the verge of industrialisation, were looking across the oceans with their own dreams of wealth and power—and scientific knowledge. This was the Age of Enlightenment, when a new spirit of reason and humanistic inquiry stirred widespread interest and eager investigation into every aspect of science—mathematics, anatomy, astronomy, anthropology, chemistry and physics, geology and geography. Learning more about the shape and size of the world, its land masses and oceans, its people, plants and animals, became one of the principal goals of exploration. Few expeditions were not accompanied by naturalists and other scientists, artists and draughtsmen, with their measuring instruments, preserving jars, drawing materials and textbooks. The reigning confidence in human beings' capacity to learn all there was to know about the world and its workings found itself faced with a most unsettling question mark: what did lie in the unexplored vastness of the southern seas? This enduring mystery of over 2000 years, this unsolved riddle on the face of a globe being inexorably measured, plotted and understood, had to be solved.

Jacob Roggeveen was the first of the new breed to search for the far southern continent. In 1676 his father had received from the Netherlands States General an unusual charter entitling him to organise a private expedition to discover the Great South Land. Unable to raise the necessary funds, Arent Roggeveen had died with his ambition unfulfilled. In 1721 Jacob, a wealthy man of 62, took up the charter and with the assistance of his brother, a well-to-do businessman and interested geologist, set about turning their father's dream into reality.

The Dutch West India Company, the VOC's lesser sister, prepared three ships for Roggeveen. The *Arend*, on which he was to travel, was approximately 36.5m long, carrying 32 cannons and 110 men. Somewhat smaller were the *Tienhoven* with 80 men and 24 cannons and the *Afrikanse Galei* with a company of 33 and fourteen cannons.

Provisions for more than two years were loaded, and on 26 July the squadron sailed for the South Pacific.

Like the unauthorised expedition financed by Isaac Lemaire's company in 1615, it rounded Cape Horn, and in April 1722 discovered Easter Island and its silent monoliths. In the vastness of the ocean beyond, the ships came upon scattered islands of the Tuamotu, Society and Samoan groups. Losing the *Afrikanse Galei* on a reef, the remaining two ships now steered for New Zealand, apparently with the intention of reprovisioning and then doubling back to Cape Horn as they searched, but sickness and lack of food incapacitated the ships and they turned instead to the north coast of New Guinea and on to Batavia.

Roggeveen's reception was very much like that of the Lemaire expedition. The governor-general accused him of violating the VOC monopoly, seized the ships, sold the cargo and sent the crews home. Assisted by the Dutch West India Company, Roggeveen eventually received compensation for his losses, but made no further attempts at exploration. Disappointingly, his voyage had discovered very little. Even his exact route was not known and so became a matter of dispute among geographers trying to prove or disprove the existence of a Great South Land.

In France the question received especially keen attention. In 1663 Jean Paulmier Courtonne, a churchman who was a descendant of the native 'prince' Essomericq who had been brought to France by de Gonneville in 1505, published a book asserting that the land of his ancestors had been Terra Australis and urging French authorities to find and christianise its people. Gonneville's description of the people he had encountered and their way of life in no way matched Dutch accounts of the New Holland Aborigines, and many Frenchmen now became convinced that he had visited an entirely different, uncharted Terra Australis. Courtonne became a popular figure, and speculation on the Great South Land flourished. Gonneville's landing, it was thought, had taken place either in the Atlantic or the Pacific in about 45°S latitude, where the climate was assumed to be pleasantly similar to that of southern France, lying at the same latitude in the northern hemisphere. That weather patterns differed north and south of the equator was not yet understood.

Savants and encyclopaedists, led by Charles de Brosses and the mathematician-astronomer Pierre-Louis Moreau de Maupertuis, contributed strongly to the impetus for a French search. For them it seemed imperative that Gonneville's South Land be found, studied and its contents incorporated into the sum of the world's knowledge. Their zeal coincided with the French government's desire for a convenient temperate-climate way station for French ships on the route to India, as well as for expanded trade opportunities, especially in spices.

Jean-Baptiste-Charles Bouvet de Lozier, son of a barrister, joined the the French East India Company fleet in 1731 and afterwards began submitting proposals for an expedition to locate Gonneville's lost continent. His ideas received support and in July 1738 he sailed from Lorient with two ships, the *Aigle* and the *Marie*, 160 men, ample provisions and trade goods and three launches for inshore work. His orders were to survey in the 40°S latitudes of the Atlantic and to take possession of any useful land he discovered.

Searching the cold and empty reaches of the South Atlantic Ocean between 40°S and 55°S, Bouvet encountered fog, snow and sea ice, which were believed to indicate nearby land. On 1 January 1739 he saw the icy cliffs of a jutting point of land, which he named Cape Circumcision and, although prevented by heavy weather from coming closer, immediately took to be part of the southern continent. On the 1740 edition of Guillaume de l'Isle's south polar projection map, this appeared as a disconnected bit of shoreline. Legends in Dutch and French described the discovery and a small corner map provided details of a detached peninsula. In 1755 Philippe Buaché's *Atlas* depicted the 'cape' as part of a great southern continent. Actually, it is a high, rocky little island now called Bouvetøya or Bouvet Island, some 2400km southwest of the Cape of Good Hope. Bouvet found no more land, but there was no shortage of others to take up the quest.

Charles de Brosses's widely read *Histoire des Navigations aux Terres Australes* reminded the French that a strategically located base in the South Pacific could not only be useful in time of war, but serve as a take-off point for securing the Great South Land, a magnificent prize that would compensate for France's recent loss of Canada to Britain. In 1766 the French government commissioned the nobleman Louis-Antoine de Bougainville, an army officer, to circle the earth on a journey of exploration. Bougainville entered the Pacific with two ships. He visited Tahiti and reached Vanuatu, where he confirmed that Espíritu Santo was an island and nowhere near any continent. He continued almost due east and in early July 1768 approached the Great Barrier Reef. Bougainville spent two days seeking a safe passage through the deceptively beautiful, seemingly endless white and blue-green line of breakers and barely submerged coral, and finally set a course to the north and around the top of New Guinea. Barred by the 2000km-long reef, he had failed to find the east coast of the Australian continent, which he might otherwise have encountered somewhere north of today's Cooktown.

In 1769 he completed the first French circumnavigation of the globe, having initiated French claims to empire in the Pacific but found no trace of the legendary continent. His book *Voyage autour du Monde* was widely read, painted a vivid picture of life in the South Seas, and helped popularise a notion current in Europe at the time: that in their natural state, without the laws, requirements or trappings of civilisation, human beings were virtuous and noble, living simply, harmoniously and happily. This was the idea of the 'natural man' or 'noble savage', developed by the philosopher Jean-Jacques Rousseau, which for many years to come gave Europeans a romanticised view of primitive peoples.

Enthusiasm for the search for the Great South Land did not abate. By late 1771 two rival French expeditions were at Mauritius, then occupied by France, both rapidly preparing to find the elusive southern continent. One was headed by Marc-Joseph Marion Dufresne, a prominent resident of Mauritius. Dufresne had served in the French navy and in the East, and his obsession now was to explore the immensity of uncharted ocean south of Mauritius. Three years earlier, when Bougainville returned to France, he had brought with him a Tahitian, Ahu-toru or Aotourou. This man was now on his way back to Tahiti and, having come as far as Mauritius, was waiting for a ship that would take him the rest of the way. Dufresne had proposed an expedition which would take Ahu-toru to Tahiti and search the southern oceans for the new continent on the way. By using Tasman's route south of Van Diemen's Land, he would find out for the French government if it would be suitable for mercantile traffic to the South Pacific. The exploration-minded local governor approved the plan, funds were raised and on 18 October 1771 Dufresne sailed from Port Louis with two ships.

Difficulties beset the expedition. Ahu-toru died of smallpox and Dufresne's first search, for two nonexistent islands that on certain charts appeared south of Africa, was abandoned in fierce winds. Continuing eastward through the southern Indian Ocean, the French encountered the Prince Edward Islands, 1900km southeast of Africa, and as the two ships moved in to investigate more closely, they collided. Temporary repairs took several days, and the sailing performance of each vessel was permanently impaired. Nevertheless, the expedition continued. Following the 46th parallel towards the east, the French came upon the tiny midocean Crozet Islands. These they found to be cold, barren and inhabited only by seals and birds, but they explored, named and claimed them for France. Dufresne believed that he was now not far from the Great South Land allegedly seen by Bouvet 33 years earlier, but rough weather and the ships' poor condition dissuaded him from pushing farther south. Still sailing east, on 1 February 1772 the vessels passed just north of the Kerguélen Islands, which would be discovered twelve days later by the rival expedition of Yves-Joseph de Kerguélen-Trémarec.

Following Tasman's track, Dufresne continued to Tasmania. There the French encountered Aborigines who initially accepted gifts, but then attacked, wounding Dufresne and others. The ships went on to New Zealand, where Dufresne and many others were killed and some were eaten by Maori. The survivors made it back to Mauritius in March 1773.

Kerguélen-Trémarec was a nobleman, ship designer and naval officer who had fought in the Seven Years War against Britain and earned distinction with his extensive surveys and oceanographic research. Fired with ambition to find Gonneville's lost continent, he used his connections at court and in intellectual circles to gain backing for an expedition. In late 1771 he found himself in Mauritius with two ships, the *Fortune*, with 24 guns and 200 officers and crew, and the *Gros Ventre*, with sixteen guns, 120 men and as captain, François Alesno de Sainte-Allouarn. Kerguélen-Trémarec was known to be an experienced seaman, and expectations of his quest were high. His instructions on reaching the Great South Land were to develop friendly relations with the natives and to establish a base with good timber resources for France's India-bound ships. On 16 January 1772 he sailed from Mauritius's Port Louis to solve the ancient riddle.

On 13 February the ships sighted the pinnacles of the island later named for the explorer. In rising winds and rough seas boats from both ships fought their way into a small bay and landed to claim the territory for France with a raised flag, musket volley and cheers. Kerguélen, aboard the *Fortune* and at some distance from land, decided that his ship was in danger, and in worsening weather, abruptly steered west. Picking up both boat crews, the *Gros Ventre* headed after the *Fortune*, which was now out of sight. When the wind abated, Sainte-Allouarn took his ship back to the island to search for the *Fortune*, but found no sign of the vessel. Following his orders, he proceeded with the hunt for Terra Australis, travelling eastward at about 45°S latitude. Sightings of birds, seals and sea lions convinced the ship's company that the elusive land mass was near, but bitter cold and heavy weather persuaded Sainte-Allouarn to abandon further search. He steered north for New Holland and on 17 March 1772 the *Gros Ventre* found shelter in today's Flinders Bay, just east of the Cape Leeuwin promontory. The ship then continued north to Shark Bay, and Sainte-Allouarn, too ill to go himself, sent a party ashore to take possession in the name of King Louis XV of France. A bottle containing a parchment record of the event was buried beside a tree together with two French coins. The Frenchmen then surveyed the area, fished, and buried the body of a sailor who had died of scurvy. They had no idea that two years before and thousands of kilometres away James Cook had claimed the same land for King George III of England.

The *Gros Ventre* left Australia at Melville Island, half the ship's company ill with scurvy. She arrived at Mauritius in September 1772. Sainte-Allouarn died three weeks later, aged 35.

On parting from the *Gros Ventre*, Kerguélen had returned to Mauritius and subsequently to France, claiming triumphantly that he had reached the Great South Land and found it a large, temperate region, cultivated and rich in resources. Such claims for the barren subantarctic

Kerguélen Island are difficult to understand, unless the explorer assumed that glaciers indicated rivers—a common belief at the time—and that the low, green vegetation he had seen from his ship was the result of cultivation. His controversial claims were soon denounced as fraudulent, and for reasons possibly related to this scandal, Sainte-Allouarn's claims of Australian soil for France remained unacknowledged by the government. Kerguélen-Trémarec made one more brief visit to his discovery but was afterwards court-martialled and imprisoned on various charges, including failure to carry out his mission. Released during the French Revolution, he attempted yet another expedition, but this was almost immediately captured by the British. In the political and social upheaval of the Revolution, the French dream of finding the Great South Land faltered. French scientific explorations continued into the early nineteenth century, but by then English explorers had already solved the enduring mystery.

11.

The English Quest—an End and a Beginning

England emerged relatively late as a maritime power. In the fifteenth and early sixteenth centuries, when Portugal and Spain were establishing themselves in the Americas and the East, England was plunged in domestic and foreign wars. The reign of Elizabeth I, however, sent a wave of Englishmen to sea in war, exploration, and privateering— licensed piracy against a wartime enemy. In 1580 the privateer-explorer Francis Drake became the first Englishman to circumnavigate the world, on the way having raided Spanish ships and settlements on the Pacific coast of South America with spectacular success. For the most part, however, English sea ventures stuck to the Atlantic, leaving the East to the Spanish and Portuguese.

In the later sixteenth century English interest in Terra Australis Incognita grew. Ortelius's great world map had come out in 1570, followed by those of Mercator, Wytfliet and others, and the huge expanse of land shown across the bottom of each could not be ignored. The distinguished alchemist, mathematician and geographer John Dee envisaged an empire based on English colonies in the South Land, and in his 1576 work, *The Great Volume of Famous and Rich Discoveries*, he urged that 'this land of Beach' should be 'come unto, [and] possessed'.[1] In 1574 the navigator Richard Grenville and his partners proposed a voyage to discover Terra Australis. They consulted Dee and received a royal permit, but the licence was cancelled for fear of Spanish reprisals. Drake, who probably had a copy of the popular Ortelius map on his voyage, is not known to have received any instructions to seek the South Land, but no one knows what was said in a personal conversation he maintained he had with Queen Elizabeth I, who for political reasons would not acknowledge any connection with the privately financed expedition. As it turned out, Drake's journey weakened the idea of a Great South Land. He followed Magellan's route through the strait between Tierra del Fuego and the South American mainland. As he emerged into the Pacific he was driven south by wild northwesterly gales. How far south he went is not known, but he saw no land. Edward Wright, on his map of 1600, commented that 'By the discoverie of Sr Francis Drake made in the year 1577 the streights of Magellane . . . seeme to be nothing els but broken land and Ilands,'[2] and showed no land to the south. In the East, however, south of Java, a small unnamed shoreline may have represented the southern continent. Wright's map was sufficiently well known for William Shakespeare to refer to it in his play *Twelfth Night*: 'He does smile his face into more lines than is in the new map with the augmentation of the Indies,' says Maria.[3]

Some writers mocked the idea of Terra Australis Incognita. Bishop Joseph Hall, author of the satirical *Mundus Alter et Idem*, asked why a place known to be a continent, and known to be a southern continent, should be considered unknown.[4] With his book, he included his own map of the missing continent, covered with absurd place names. In the 1657 edition of his *Cosmosgraphy*, Peter Heylin declared that he intended to 'make a search into this Terra Australis'[5] to find such places as Fairy Land, the Lands of Chivalry and the ridiculous country described in Hall's *Mundus Alter et Idem*.

By the middle of the seventeenth century there had been a few English sightings of the Australian coast. In 1622 the English East India Company ship *Trial* had been wrecked near the Monte Bello Islands, and about 60 years later the *London* came within view of the northern Wallabi group in the Houtman Abrolhos. Another sighting by English mariners was Cloates or Cloots Island, actually a headland near Ningaloo, Western Australia, and now called Cloates Point. Such incidents and observations brought little response from the few who read of them. Reports of Dutch encounters with New Holland that reached England portrayed an arid, inhospitable and thoroughly unpromising country which the English were content to leave alone. There had been at least one exception. In 1625 William Courteen, an extremely rich merchant and shipowner, applied to King James I for rights to 'all the lands in ye South parts of ye world called Terra Australis incognita'.[6] Within four years, however, Courteen had suffered heavy financial losses, and he did not pursue his South Land project. It was not until William Dampier published the narrative of his travels in 1687 that popular interest in the southern continent caught fire.

WILLIAM DAMPIER: PIRATE, EXPLORER, WRITER

William Dampier, in many ways an exceedingly private man, wrote little about his origins. The son of a tenant farmer, he was baptised in 1651 in the village of East Coker in rural Somerset and while a child lost both parents. As a teenager entranced by the sea, he persuaded his guardians to take him from school and apprentice him to a ship's master at Weymouth. Ocean voyages followed—to France, Newfoundland, the Dutch East Indies and the Caribbean—and in 1672–73 Dampier served with the English navy against the Dutch. Later he tried the life of a plantation manager in the West Indies, but the routine bored him and he soon returned to the sea. In 1675, aged about 24, he came upon something much more exciting.

The shores of Mexico's Campeche Bay on the Yucatán Peninsula were the haunt of English logwood-cutters, many of them ex-buccaneers, tough, violent men living a brutal existence in suffocatingly hot, semi-flooded forest camps, virtually at war with the Spanish authorities, who regarded their activities as illegal. Here Dampier threw himself into the wrenching labour of felling, cutting up and carrying away in logs the massive trees, valuable for their red heartwood which was used in dyeing. The logs were sold by the ton to trader-captains from Jamaica, who brought their vessels close to the shore. In the midst of this wild, crude, hard-drinking company Dampier managed not only to stay sober but to write vivid descriptions of his surroundings and of events. Dampier was a highly unusual mix of boldness, curiosity and scientific detachment. In his portrait wavy, uncut brown hair frames a thin, deeply tanned face with dark brows, a rather long nose and an obstinate lower lip. The eyes are deep-set and thoughtful, almost sad.

When after a few months a hurricane destroyed the camp, Dampier briefly joined some buccaneers, then in 1678 went back to England and married. Returning to the West Indies, he encountered in Jamaica a fleet of English and French buccaneers preparing to attack Spanish Porto Bello on the Panamanian coast. Here was a prospect for wealth and adventure, but also a new experience and new surroundings to write about, something this self-contained and highly observant man could not resist. Porto Bello surrendered, but an attempt at the city of Panama failed and there followed a brief piratical visit to the African coast and a series of land and sea battles along the western coasts of South America and Mexico. Dampier then joined the ship *Cygnet* and crossed the Pacific to the Philippines, where he became involved in seizing the ship and leaving the captain ashore. One John Read assumed command, and after some raiding among the islands and on the coasts of China and Taiwan, the *Cygnet* sailed for the East Indies.

On 17 December 1687 the ship was off the island of Timor in rain and gales that made any course except to the south difficult. So, Dampier wrote, 'we stood off South, intending to touch at New Holland, a part of Terra Australis Incognita, to see what that Country would afford us.'[7] Dampier understood New Holland to be 'a very large Tract of Land. It is not yet determined whether it is an Island or a main Continent; but I am certain that it joyns neither to Asia, Africa, nor America.'[8] He appears not to have any knowledge of Tasman's voyages.

Given the dismal reports then circulating about New

Holland, it seems unlikely that Dampier, Captain Read or any of the 50 or so seamen on board would have had any great expectations of what 'that country would afford'. Possibly the ship's company were simply seeking quieter waters after their round of plundering in the China Sea. They had with them at least some charts of the Australian coast—Dampier does not say which ones—and the wind was with them.

On 1 January 1688 they passed either Scott Reef or the shoals of the Ashmores, low coral islets on the northwestern edge of the continental shelf. Dampier found a reef wrongly placed on his map, but got around it. 'Then we trimmed sharp and stood to the Southward.'

> The 4th day of January, 1688, we fell in with the Land of New Holland in the Lat. of 16 d. 50 m . . . then came to a Point of Land, from whence the Land trends East and Southerly . . . About 3 Leagues to the Eastward of this Point, there is a pretty deep Bay, with abundance of Islands in it . . . we anchored January the 5th, 1688.

Dampier's landfall on the rugged Kimberley coast could have been at either Collier Bay or King Sound, and the 'abundance of Islands' was possibly the 200-odd reefs and islands of the Buccaneer Archipelago.

The *Cygnet* seems to have remained on the New Holland coast for two months. Taking advantage of the huge local tide variations—up to 10.5m—the men brought the ship into a small cove where low tide left her aground long enough for them to clean the bottom. A tent was set up, sails were mended, and turtle and dugong were captured for food. The encampment represented the longest known stay yet by Europeans on the Australian continent.

Dampier examined their surroundings with character-istic care. The land was low and level with rocky points to seaward, the soil dry, sandy and without surface water, the woods were sparse, and the trees varied but small and with-out fruit or berries. He saw few birds and no land animals, except on one occasion large paw prints which looked like those of a big mastiff. The flies were plague-like. His descriptions were factual, often detailed, infused with irre-pressible curiosity, yet almost scientifically objective. Always there was an undercurrent of simple delight in the newness of what he was seeing.

The Englishmen's encounters with the Aborigines were more or less peaceable, although threats were traded from time to time. Dampier observed the strangers carefully, noting their appearance and their lack of clothing, houses, boats, cultivated food or any other amenity. Their lives appeared to consist of nothing but sleeping on the ground and feeding themselves on fish caught in coves and inlets. The 'miserablest People in the world',[9] he called them, although he recognised that their surroundings offered few resources and no easy living.

After an unsuccessful attempt to exchange old clothing for help in carrying barrels of well water to a boat, Dampier commented, 'I did not perceive that they had any great liking to them [the clothing] at first, neither did they seem to admire any thing that we had.'[10] This impression was confirmed when the English took four men on board the ship and gave them boiled rice with boiled turtle and dugong. 'They did greedily devour what we gave them, but took no notice of the Ship, or any thing in it, and when they were set on land again, they ran away as fast as they could.'[11]

The *Cygnet* left New Holland on 12 March and headed for the Indian Ocean. For some time Dampier had wanted to leave the evidently poorly run *Cygnet* and its 'mad Crew' for an English trading post. While off the coast of New Holland, as he later wrote, 'I did endeavour to persuade our Men to go to some English Factory, but was threatened to be turned ashore, and left . . . This made me desist, and patiently wait for some more convenient place and opportunity to leave them, than here.'[12] Captain Read had no intention of losing any of his men, but in the Nicobar Islands Dampier and a few others escaped. Their native canoe overturned and on a lonely beach they built a fire to dry out the few belongings they had saved. 'I had nothing of value but my Journal,' Dampier wrote, 'which I much prized.'[13] Finally, in a remarkable feat of strength and navigation, he reached Sumatra, some 200km across open sea, by native canoe.

What sort of man was he, this pirate, writer and adventurer? In the crowded, ill-smelling space of a small, rolling and pitching ship, surrounded by loud, rude, often brawling seamen, he sat apart, undisturbed, writing. On strange shores he would wander away from the others, viewing his surroundings with endless pleasure and curiosity, studying and sketching plants, collecting shells, regarding the local people with steady, quiet interest—and then write it all down. Dampier's education had ended in his early teens, but he wrote easily in a straightforward, unassuming style, unconsciously eloquent and remarkably individual. As a member of the ship's company he held his own, at times with a flaring temper, and the prospect of great wealth lured him as strongly as it did any of his associates, but his overriding concern was his journal. He swam with it sealed with wax in a bamboo tube, took it with him—leaving everything else—in an escape, and on the Nicobar beach carefully dried its pages before an open fire. He intended to share its contents, and in time he did, having edited out all but the barest personal references to himself.

A New Voyage Round the World was published in London in 1697. It became a runaway best seller, in such demand that three new editions came out within months and others followed. Dampier's adventures and the strange world he so vividly described entranced not only the general public but also the country's most eminent literary men. The author and diarist John Evelyn noted:

> 6th August. I dined with Mr. [Samuel] Pepys, where was Captain Dampier, who had been a famous buccaneer . . . He seemed a more modest man than one would imagine by the relation of the crew he had assorted with. He brought with him a map of his observations.[14]

Men of science wanted to meet him—Charles Montague, President of the Royal Society; Sir Robert Southwell, a former president of the society; and the eminent physician and naturalist Sir Hans Sloane. He was asked to speak before the Council of Trade and Plantations. Montague was also Chancellor of the Exchequer, and he and the Earl of Orford, First Lord of the Admiralty, were most interested in the ramifications of further exploration for the

English East India Company, in which both were involved. Politicians, too, were galvanised by Dampier's book into reconsidering New Holland, not only for profit, which must surely be found in so vast a region, but also for naval purposes. Dampier had mentioned coastal features fit to shelter ships and to be fortified.

Dampier's limited exploration had left him uncertain whether New Holland was 'an Island or a main Continent', but maps by Herman Moll accompanying his book showed an area of continental size labelled 'New Holland or Terra Australis Incognita'. By now, Tasman's explorations too were known in Britain, and interest in what might lie on the unexplored east coast was undergoing a strong revival. Dampier himself wanted to see the Pacific side of Terra Australis, which would be most easily reached, he said, by the Cape Horn route.

The British Admiralty, buoyed by such widespread interest, began to lay plans for a naval expedition of discovery to Terra Australis, New Guinea and the surrounding archipelagos. No one but Dampier seems to have been considered for its command, and he exchanged letters on routes and arrangements with the First Lord. Initially, Dampier proposed to reach the South Land by sailing through Magellan's Strait or around Cape Horn into the Pacific, 'that I might have begun my Discoveries upon the Eastern and least known side of Terra Australis'.[15]

Such a voyage would have pre-empted the discoveries of James Cook by some 70 years. However, Dampier also said he could approach from the west, sailing from Africa to northwestern New Holland, then east towards New Guinea, looking for unexploited spice islands on the way, and coasting New Guinea before turning south into uncharted waters to find the Great South Land's mysterious east coast. Dampier added, 'and so [I] thought to come round by the South of Terra Australis on my Return back'.[16] It was a bold plan, anticipating the close circumnavigation of Australia by over a century.

After some discussion as to the choice of ship, HMS *Roebuck* was selected and Dampier began supervising its refitting at Deptford. At 290 tonnes, the ship was just under 30m in length and armed with twelve guns. There was a crew of 50, the usual naval officers including a clerk and a surgeon, and provisions for 20 months. In the autumn of 1698 Dampier was commissioned as an officer in the Royal Navy and officially joined the *Roebuck* as captain. In the midst of all these preparations, he had put together a second volume of his book, which was still with the printer when he left England.

Various delays and the problem of arriving at Cape Horn in the stormy southern winter finally sent the expedition to New Holland by the South African route. The *Roebuck* sailed on 14 January 1699. Just over six months later it was in Australian waters. On 6 August, with its boat taking soundings ahead, the *Roebuck* entered a bay edged with long white beaches. In the clear blue-green water Dampier saw 'chiefly Sharks. There are Abundance of them in this particular Sound, and I therefore give it the Name of Shark's Bay.'[17]

Dampier had entered the large shallow inlet south of Carnarvon seen 83 years before by Dirck Hartogs, and just eighteen months before by Willem de Vlamingh. Unknown to the English seamen, De Vlamingh's pewter plate hung fixed to its pole at the north end of one of the islands enclosing the bay.

The English badly needed fresh water. They searched the area for several kilometres around with no result, although low trees were plentiful and they chopped a supply of firewood. After eight days, having failed to find water, the expedition sailed north. There was a scary night encounter with a large number of whales, and they stopped at several islands where they saw no people but found burnt brushwood. Dampier was now using Tasman's map of the coast, and concluded from its errors that the Dutch explorer had remained a considerable distance from the shore. For a few days the coast was out of sight, but on 30 August the Englishmen made land again, saw smoke rising from numerous places near the shore, and anchored. During the night there was an eclipse of the moon.

On land the next morning a number of Aborigines appeared, shouting threateningly at the sailors who dug for water. Dampier tried to indicate peace as a preliminary to asking for help in getting fresh water. Failing, he set off along the beach with two men to capture one of the natives and try to get the information from him. When ten or twelve Aborigines appeared among the sand hills, one young sailor ran towards the nearest group. They fled, then turned and charged him, stabbing with spears as he slashed with his cutlass. Dampier fired a warning shot, then, as the Aborigines charged again, shot and wounded one man. The sailor broke away, speared in the face, while the Aborigines carried off their injured companion. 'I return'd back with my Men,' Dampier wrote later, 'being very sorry for what had happened.'[18] Some brackish water was found, suitable only to boil the men's oatmeal.

Early in September the *Roebuck* and its company left the coast of New Holland, and a little before sunset on 14 September 1699 they saw with great joy the high mountaintops of Timor rising out of the clouds.

During the first months of 1700 Dampier took his ship around the north of New Guinea, discovering the island of New Britain, then put in at Batavia for provisions and urgently needed repairs to the badly deteriorating ship. It had been a troubled journey, with antagonism verging on mutiny between Dampier, the former buccaneer, and his Royal Navy crew. This and the ruinous condition of the ship precluded further exploration. In October they sailed for England, but at Ascension Island in the mid-Atlantic the disastrously leaking *Roebuck* sank. The men were saved and picked up a little over a month later by passing English warships. Many of Dampier's papers, however, were lost. In June 1702 he was back in England, where he was court-martialled on charges that included cruelty to the *Roebuck*'s lieutenant, whom he had put ashore at a South American port. Dampier was fined his pay and declared not fit to command a king's ship.

By this time war had broken out with Spain. Dampier received command of a privateer and spent the next seven years raiding Spanish ships and towns up and down the South American coasts. In 1703 and 1709 in London he published in two parts his *Voyage to New Holland*, relating the *Roebuck* journey to Australia and beyond. A few years later, the accounts of his adventures appeared in Dutch.

Dampier had seen much the same country as several

Dutch explorers before him, but his reports of it had a very different effect. His fresh, vivid descriptions, drawings and maps gave new shape and vitality to the idea of New Holland, leading Englishmen to see it as a real, fascinating place charged with possibilities. As the first English explorer to deliberately seek out and describe Australia, he offered a rising nation a new arena—uncontested by other powers—in which to prove itself both strategically and scientifically.

Exciting shreds of information about places few Europeans would ever see inspired other English authors to weave them into fiction. Henry Neville's *The Isle of Pines: Or a late discovery of a fourth Island, in Terra Australis Incognita*, published in 1688, told of George Pine, who is shipwrecked on an idyllic island in the South Atlantic, where he takes four wives and has 47 children and, by the time of his death, 1789 descendants. Daniel Defoe based his *Robinson Crusoe* on the real-life experience of Alexander Selkirk, who was marooned at his own request on Juan Fernández Island off South America and in whose rescue Dampier had participated. Defoe borrowed the title of his *A New Voyage Round the World* directly from Dampier. In *Gulliver's Travels* Jonathan Swift has his hero, Lemuel Gulliver, refer to advice he gave to 'my Cousin Dampier' and to 'my worthy friend Mr. Herman Moll', Dampier's cartographer, while maps accompanying the story make free if jumbled use of such far-off lands as Japan and New Holland. Lilliput is an island in the Indian Ocean southwest of Sumatra, but also west of a peninsula labelled Diemens Land. The account of Gulliver's visit to the Land of the Houyhnhnms includes a map which places this imaginary island in the northeastern corner of the Great Australian Bight. The surrounding areas are labelled Edel's Land, Lewin's Land and Nuyt's Land, the island of St Peter is roughly in place in the Nuyts Archipelago, but the island of St Francis is displaced by Houyhnhnms Land. Somewhat on the lines of *Robinson Crusoe* but set in a South Land utopia was a Dutch tale, *Description of the mighty Kingdom of Kinke Kesmes*, published in 1708 by Hendrik Smeeks.

Terra Australis was also the setting of the 1766 novel *L'Histoire des Sévarambes*, by Denis Varaisse d'Alais. In it a Parisian traveller, Sevarais, and a learned Venetian found a utopian country from which pride, avarice and laziness have been eliminated, and where there is neither crime nor disorder, private property nor inequality. In this moneyless society, all citizens work for the state, producing useful goods which, together with education and culture, are distributed equally.

Scientists and scholars, meanwhile, were writing serious compilations of Pacific voyages, many still strongly supporting the existence of a vast southern continent that, when discovered, would supply enormous opportunities for wealth.

THE VOYAGE OF JAMES COOK

In the seventeenth and eighteenth centuries, New Holland was appearing on English charts with the considerable detail provided by Dutch discoveries. Some of John Seller's maps were actually reprints of Dutch work, sometimes with English titles simply replacing the Dutch. Herman Moll, originally from the Netherlands, produced 'A Map of the East Indies' in 1697 and 'A New Map of the Whole World' 30 years later, both featuring New Holland prominently, although with few labels. Samuel Thornton's 1740 'A Draught of the Coast of New Holland' included an inset showing Shark Bay as drawn by Dampier. The land's east coast was still either blank or suggested by an imaginary line, and the southern oceans were for the most part shown as waiting to be explored.

In the 1760s, the European wars having subsided, Britain began sending out official expeditions of discovery. The shadowy image of the Great South Land intrigued the British Admiralty, and in 1764 it sent John Byron, grandfather of the poet, on a voyage of exploration. His orders stated that there was reason to believe that 'Lands and Islands of great extent hitherto unvisited by any European Power may be found in the Atlantick Ocean between the Cape of Good Hope and the Magellanick Streight within Latitudes convenient for Navigation'.[19] As it turned out, Byron explored the Pacific, not the Atlantic, in 1764–65. He found more of the Tuamotu and Gilbert Islands, but was thwarted by contrary winds from going farther south. A year later Samuel Wallis and Philip Carteret followed, with official instructions from the Admiralty to search 'in the Southern Hemisphere between Cape Horn and New Zeeland'[20] for lands of great extent. When their ships became separated, Wallis discovered Tahiti and additional Tuamotu and Society islands, while Carteret found Pitcairn Island, rediscovered Mendaña's Santa Cruz group and went on to New Britain and the Bismarck Archipelago north of New Guinea. New Holland was not included in these navigators' directives. Carteret went farther to the south in mid-ocean than most previous mariners and in so doing pushed the unseen Great South Land deeper into the southern latitudes where the force of the legend continued to hover. Among European scientists and geographers, meanwhile, vehement speculations on a large southern land mass flowed fervently on.

Alexander Dalrymple, hydrographer for the British Admiralty and later a member of the Royal Society, was a powerful proponent of the Great South Land. In 1767 he published *An Account of the Discoveries made in the South Pacifick Ocean, previous to 1764*, which was based on his intensive study and analysis of all the information on the South Seas accumulated in two centuries of exploration. The book included tables comparing the areas of land and water at various latitudes north and south of the equator. Dalrymple pointed out that in the north the ratio of land to water at high latitudes was nearly equal, but that in the south known land masses accounted for less than an eighth of the area necessary to produce the same ratio. 'This is a strong presumption,' he wrote, 'that there are in the southern hemisphere, hitherto totally undiscovered, valuable and extensive countries, in that climate best adapted for the conveniency of man.'[21]

Dalrymple repeated the theory that the stability of the rotating earth required a 'counterpoize' in the south to balance the land mass of the north. Therefore, he concluded, the unexplored space 'in the Pacifick Ocean, from the Tropick to 50 degrees S. must be nearly all land'.[22] This theory was confirmed, he went on, by the wind directions noted at different times of the year by various navigators.

Dalrymple claimed that some mariners had actually seen the missing continent, among them the Spaniard Juan Fernández. He quoted the early seventeenth century scholar Juan Luis Arias de Loyola, who described Fernández's reputed voyage: 'he saw on the coast the mouths of very large rivers . . . The country is very fertile and agreeable . . . It was inhabited by white people, of our stature, very well disposed, and cloathed with very fine cloths.'[23]

Dalrymple also cited rumoured sightings by Dutch vessels of a snowy, mountainous country to the far south and the actual, similar report of Willem Schouten and Jacob Lemaire, as well as signs of continental land allegedly seen at the relevant latitudes by Quirós and Roggeveen. Finally he reverted to the old Spanish-Peruvian legend of a country to the west of Peru from which the Inca civilisation had come. The Southern Continent, he maintained, must have a population of tens of millions and stretch 8000km or more across the southern Pacific. He repeated his assertions in his two-volume *Historical Collection of the Several Voyages and Discoveries in the South Pacific Ocean*, published in 1770 and 1771. As the views of a highly respected British geographer, Dalrymple's arguments were a compelling incentive to finally settle the question of a 'great southern continent', and the British Admiralty resolved to find out whether the claims were true or not. Their decision happened to coincide with the desire of a number of astronomers to observe the transit of the planet Venus across the sun, due to occur in 1769. By observing the event closely from several widely dispersed locations on earth, astronomers hoped to determine more accurately than previously possible both the diameter of the sun and its distance from the earth. Ideally, one observation point should be in the central Pacific. Approached by the Royal Society, King George III promised to send out a ship of the Royal Navy, and Dalrymple, who was knowledgeable in astronomy and had gained experience in marine surveying during service in the East, was selected as the key observer. A search for the Great South Land would almost inevitably be part of such a voyage, and Dalrymple saw himself as its discoverer.

However, as it became clear that Dalrymple would also command the ship, the Admiralty flatly vetoed the choice. Command of a Royal Navy vessel and its company could not be given to anyone who was not a naval seaman. After some discussion, a Navy ship master, James Cook, was chosen as commander. This was unusual. A master was trained and qualified to handle the ship itself, but not to navigate or command, as was a captain, and crossing over from one line of expertise to another was rarely done in the Royal Navy. The exceptional abilities and personal qualities of James Cook seem to have been recognised as justifying the exception.

The Admiralty's instructions to Cook set out its directives on the observation of Venus, then outlined a projected search for the Great South Land. They emphasised the national prestige as well as the strategic and commercial advantages that the discovery of so-far unknown countries would bring to Britain. Cook's instructions read:

> whereas there is reason to imagine that a Continent or Land of great extent may be found to the Southward of

Instructions for the Endeavour's *voyage under James Cook included a search
for the Great South Land. Instead, by charting the east coast of the
Australian continent, Cook closed the book on a myth that had
prevailed for two millennia.*

the Track lately made by Captn Wallis in His Majs Ship
the Dolphin . . . You are to proceed to the Southward in
order to make discovery of the Continent above mentioned until you arrive in the Latde of 40 degrees, unless
you sooner fall in with it.[24]

Cook was to diligently survey and chart this continent, to
detail the appearance of its coast and its navigational features, and to explore it and describe its soil, animals,

minerals, precious stones and population. The Admiralty clearly differentiated between New Holland, about which Cook received no orders, and a hitherto undiscovered southern continent. Failing to find such a continent, Cook was to continue to New Zealand, which he would thoroughly investigate. His return route to England, whether by way of the Cape of Good Hope or back across the Pacific and around Cape Horn, was left to his judgment.

Thus in 1768 James Cook, aged 40, found himself commissioned as lieutenant, given command of a ship and charged with conveying the gentlemen of the Royal Society halfway around the world to Tahiti on an important scientific mission. It was a remarkable promotion, and Cook was to aquit himself with exceptional skill, judgment, perseverance and courage.

On 26 August 1768 the bark *Endeavour* put to sea from Plymouth. She rounded Cape Horn and reached Tahiti on 13 April 1769, then, the astronomical observations complete, steered as directed south to 40°, where the mirage of the great continent remained.

Standing out to sea on this strange voyage, seeking a country believed in but never confronted in more than 2000 years, what did Cook himself think of the possibility of a Great South Land? In March 1770, a year and seven months after sailing from Plymouth, he wrote in his journal,

> as to a Southern Continent, I do not believe any such thing exists, unless in a high Latitude, but as the contrary opinion hath for many years prevail'd, and may yet

prevail, it is necessary I should say something in support of mine.[25]

There was indeed a very large unexplored space in the Pacific Ocean, he wrote, 'room enough for the North Cape of the Southern Continent to extend to the Northward, even to a pretty low Latitude. But what foundation have we for such a supposition? None that I know of.'[26] He went on with a discussion of Quirós, who, more than any man, Cook thought, had had discoveries at heart. Cook disagreed with the belief of Quirós's officers that dense clouds on the horizon meant land. He had himself seen many proofs to the contrary, and if Quirós had thought his officers were right, he would certainly have stood to the south.

As to the claims made for Roggeveen, Cook went on, that navigator's route was not known, so no firm conclusions could be drawn from his reports. Cook's own exploration, he believed, would show that there was little chance of a large continent lying north of 40°S, although 'what may lie to the Southward of that Latitude I know not'.[27]

Cook was also well acquainted with the location and partial contours of New Zealand and Van Diemen's Land; indeed, he made a point of stating that he was not using common 'printed charts', but an extract copy from Tasman's own journal.

Cook knew, of course, of New Holland. It was clear from Dutch explorations that this was a territory of continental proportions, and as there was a west coast, so must there be an east coast. Yet, like Byron, Carteret and Wallis before him, Cook had no instructions to investigate New

Holland. He had with him two important maps, Gilles Robert de Vaugondy's 1753 'Carte Réduite de l'Australasie', which indicated New Holland's east coast with a long wavy line, and Dalrymple's, from his book on discoveries, on which the tracks of Torres's and Tasman's voyages were traced. Both maps show a strait separating New Holland from New Guinea.

On 6 October 1769 New Zealand was sighted, its ranges of hills rising into high mountains. Excitement swept through the ship. Was this part of the Southern Continent, as Tasman had believed? From a landfall on the east coast, Cook rounded the top of North Island, and on 30 January 1770, on an islet in Queen Charlotte's Sound at the northern end of South Island, he hoisted the British flag and took formal possession of the land for King George III. He then steered east through the present Cook Strait. At this point the notion spread among the ship's officers that North Island was not an island but extended away to the southeast from a section of coast they had not yet seen. Hopes of finally encountering the Southern Continent rose again, but were dispelled after two days of sailing along the east coast. The *Endeavour* now circled South Island. Tasman's Staten Landt was clearly no more than two large islands.

Six months were spent exploring and charting the New Zealand coasts with impressive thoroughness and accuracy. Gales and tides repeatedly brought the *Endeavour* to near disaster, and encounters with the Maori were both peaceable and violent. The ship was careened, the hull cleaned and repairs made. A 126-year-old theory was demolished, but the Southern Continent, if indeed it existed, was yet to be found.

Cook now considered the voyage home. He could double back across the Pacific to Cape Horn or he could continue westward, either by a more direct southern route or towards the north and through the East Indies—in either case eventually to round the Cape of Good Hope. Cook conferred with his officers and wrote, 'To return by the way of Cape Horn was what I most wished, because by this rout we should have been able to prove the Existance or Non-Existance of a Southern Continent, which yet remains Doubtfull.'[28]

On that route, however, the sea-worn *Endeavour* would have to face the storms of the southern winter in sub-antarctic latitudes. Cook continued:

> For the same reason [the southern winter] the thoughts of proceeding directly to the Cape of Good Hope was [sic] laid aside, especially as no discovery of any Moment could be hoped for in that rout. It was therefore resolved to return by way of the E. Indies by the following route: upon Leaving this Coast to steer to the Westward until we fall in with the E. Coast of New Holland, and to follow the direction of that Coast to the Northward, or what other direction it might take us, until we arrive at its Northern Extremity.[29]

This journey, together with necessary reprovisioning in Batavia and a crossing of the Indian Ocean, would place him at the Cape of Good Hope in summer.

On 30 March 1770 the *Endeavour* lay at anchor in a

jagged-sided inlet which Cook called Admiralty Bay, at the northwest corner of South Island. Preparations for departure were under way—the carpenter and his crew were ashore cutting wood, and the longboat shuttled between ship and beach with the water casks. On board, the men made repairs, checked rigging and other gear, and secured equipment against possible rough seas.

At daylight the next morning, in fine weather and a fresh wind, the *Endeavour* spread its sails, slipped out of Admiralty Bay and crossed the wide opening of today's Tasman Bay. In the evening twilight of 1 April 1770 it passed a high, forested headland lying to the south, a grey outline in the rain and darkening mist. Cook named it Cape Farewell and logged its position 'in the Latitude of 40°30'S. and Long. 185°58'W. from Greenwich'.[30] Behind them, he now knew, lay no vast Southern Continent. Ahead lay the eastern edge of New Holland, its much smaller but still marvellously strange replacement, which Cook would call New South Wales. Within 50 years this ancient island would surrender its entire coastline to the mapmakers and be known by the single name of Australia. On this April night, however, it lay beyond the horizon, still waiting to reveal, at last, its hidden face.

Epilogue

Between 1772 and 1775, as a result of James Cook's second voyage, the Great South Land, Magallanica, Terra Australis Incognita, contracted finally southward where, behind a rim of ice, it became the last continent, Antarctica. Founded in ancient times on misunderstandings of the nature of the globe, enhanced by centuries of error and imagination, it had completed its part in leading the adventurous and the aquisitive, the brave and the curious, through the veils of distance to bring before the world the realities of the southern hemisphere.

Notes

CHAPTER 1

1 Telephone conversation with Dr Pat Quilty, Chief Scientist, Australian Antarctic Division, Hobart, Tasmania, 18 August 1997.

CHAPTER 2

1 Juan Luis Arias de Loyola, 'Memorial to Philip III' in R. H. Major, ed., *Early Voyages to Terra Australis, now called Australia*, Hakluyt, London, 1859, p. 15.
2 T. M. Perry, *The Discovery of Australia*, Nelson, Melbourne, 1982, p. 20.
3 *ibid.*, pp. 21–22.
4 Cornelius de Jode 1593, 'Novae Gvineae Forma & Situs', *Speculum Orbis Terrae*, in Henry N. Stevens, 1930 and 1967, *New Light on the Discovery of Australia as Revealed by the Journal of Captain Don Diego de Prado y Tovar*, Hakluyt, London, p. 18.
5 Cornelius Wytfliet, 1597, *Descriptionis Ptolemaicae Augmentum*, p. 101, in *ibid.*, p. 20.
6 Duke of Sesa y de Vaena, 'Letter to Philip III of Spain, 1602', in Celsus Kelly, trans. and ed., *La Austrialia del Espíritu Santo*, Vol. II, Hakluyt Society, Cambridge, 1966, p. 302.
7 Jan Huyghen van Linschoten, *The Voyage of John Huyghen van Linschoten to the East Indies from the Old English Translation of 1598*, Arthur C. Burnell, ed., Burt Franklin, New York, 1970, p. 111.
8 Gerardus Mercator, *Weltkarte* (Duisburg, 1569) in Josephine

Waters Bennett 1954, *The Rediscovery of Sir John Mandeville*, The Modern Language Association of America, New York, note 37, p. 231.

9 Abraham Ortelius, *Theatrum Orbis Terrarum* (1572), in *ibid.*, note 38, p. 231.

10 *The Holy Bible, New International Version*, 1973, 1978, 1984, Hodder and Stoughton, Sydney, p. 348.

11 Pedro Fernández de Quirós, 'Eighth Memorial submitted to His Majesty', in *The Voyages of Pedro Fernãndez de Quirõs 1595 to 1606*, Clements Markham, ed., 1904 and 1967, Hakluyt Society, London, p. 478.

12 Willem C. Schouten 1619, *A Wonderful Voiage round about the World*, Da Capo Press and Theatrum Orbis Terrarum, Amsterdam and New York, 1968, p. A.

13 Augustine, *The City of God*, Book XVI, Ch. 9, trans. Marcus Dods in *The Great Books*, vol. 18, Encyclopaedia Britannica, Inc., Chicago, 1952, p. 428.

14 M. C. Seymour, ed, *Mandeville's Travels*, Clarendon Press, Oxford, 1967, p. 134.

15 Duke of Sesa y de Vaena, 'Letter', in Kelly, *op. cit.*, p. 302.

16 Quirós, *op. cit.*, p. 479.

17 Abel Janszoon Tasman, *Abel Janszoon Tasman's Journal of his discovery of Van Diemens Land and New Zealand in 1642 with documents relating to his exploration of Australia in 1644, being photo-lithographic facsimiles of the original manuscript in the colonial archives at the Hague with an English translation and facsimiles of original maps to which are added Life and Labours of Abel Janszoon Tasman by J. E. Heeres, LL.D. Professor at the Dutch Colonial Institute Delft and observations made with the compass on Tasman's voyage by Dr. W. van Bemmelen, assistant Director of the Royal Meteorological Institute Utrecht*, N. A. Kovach, Los Angeles, 1965, Appendix E, p. 132.

18 *Encyclopaedia Britannica*, Macropaedia vol. 11, Encyclopaedia Britannica, Inc., Chicago, 1974, p. 473.

19 Antonio Pigafetta, *Magellan's Voyage—A Narrative Account of the First Navigation*, trans. R. A. Skelton, Yale University, New Haven, Connecticut, 1969, p. 56.

20 J. E. Heeres, *The Part Borne by the Dutch in the Discovery of Australia 1606–1765*, Luzac & Co., London, 1899, p. 4.

21 Ton Vermeulen, 'The Dutch Entry into the East Indies' in John Hardy and Alan Frost, eds, *European Voyage toward Australia*,

Australian Academy of the Humanities and Highland Press, Canberra 1990, p. 39.

22 Christopher Columbus, *Journal* as retold by Bartolomé de Las Casas, in Björn Landström, *Columbus*, Macmillan, New York, 1966, p. 61.

23 Duke of Sesa y de Vaena, 'Letter', in Kelly, *op. cit.*, pp. 302–303.

24 Luis Vaz de Camõens, *The Lusiads*, trans. William C. Atkinson, Penguin, Harmondsworth, 1952, p. 247.

CHAPTER 3

1 Antonio de Morga, *Sucesos de las Islas Filipinas*, trans. and ed. J. S. Cummins, Hakluyt, Cambridge, 1971, p. 52.

CHAPTER 4

1 C. C. Macknight, *The Voyage to Marege*, Melbourne University Press, Melbourne, 1976, p. 81.

2 *ibid.* p. 98 and Notes 23 and 24, p. 162. (Tests, ANU-1295).

3 Chau Ju-Kua, *Chau Ju-Kua: His Work on the Chinese and Arab Trade in the twelfth and thirteenth Centuries, entitled Chu-fan-chï*, eds and trans F. Hirth and W. W. Rockhill, Paragon, New York, 1966, p. 210.

4 Brett Hilder, *The Voyage of Torres*, University of Queensland Press, St Lucia, 1980, Fig. 49, p. 110 and p. 116.

5 Luis Baéz de Torres, 'The Letter of Torres' in *New Light on the Discovery of Australia as Revealed by the Journal of Captain Don Diego de Prado y Tovar*, ed. H. M. Stevens and trans. George F. Barwick, Hakluyt Society, Nedeln/Liechtenstein, 1930, 1967, p. 233.

6 Diego de Prado y Tovar, 'Relación' in *ibid.* p. 173.

7 *ibid.* p. 179.

8 G. P. S. Freeman-Grenville, 'A Beach Find in the Northern Territory, Australia' in Victor T. King and A. V. M. Horton, eds, *From Buckfast to Borneo*, University of Hull, England 1995, pp. 536–540.

CHAPTER 5

1 Tomé Pires and Francisco Rodrígues, *The Suma Oriental of Tomé Pires and The Book of Francisco Rodrígues*, vol. 1, trans. Armando Cortesão, Hakluyt Society, London, 1944, p. 209.

2 *ibid.*, Introduction, p. xxv.

3 *ibid.*, p. 204.

4 *ibid.*, p. 136.

5 *ibid.*, pp. 164–165.

6 *ibid.*, p. 161.

7 *ibid.*

8 *ibid.*, p. 180.

9 Marco Polo, *The Travels of Marco Polo*, Ronald Latham, ed., Penguin, Harmondsworth, 1958, p. 251.

10 Jeremy Green, 'New Information on Southest Asia Gun Technology from Two Guns found on Carronade Island, in the North of Australia', *Ordnance Society Journal*, vol. 3, 1990, p. 54.

11 *ibid.*

12 Jeremy Green, 'Remote Sensing in Shipwreck Archaeology: Locating the Mahogany Ship' in *The Mahogany Ship—Relic or Legend?* ed. Bill Potter, The Mahogany Ship Committee and Warrnambool Institute Press, Warrnambool, Victoria, 1987, p. 110.

13 John Stanley, 'The Search for the "Mahogany Ship"—a Challenge for High Definition Geophysics' in the University of New England Research Report 1992, University of New England, Armidale, NSW, 1992, pp. 51–55.

14 Mike Pearson, 'The Bittangabee Ruin—Who Built It?', National Parks and Wildlife Service of New South Wales, Sydney, 1980, p. 1.

CHAPTER 6

1 Marco Polo, *op. cit.*, p. 251.

2 William A. R. Richardson, 'The Portuguese Discovery of Australia: Fact or Fiction?', National Library of Australia, Canberra, 1989.

3 Kenneth G. McIntyre, *The Secret Discovery of Australia—*

Portuguese Ventures 200 Years Before Captain Cook, Souvenir Press, Menindee, SA, 1977, p. 252 and Fig. 18.1, p. 249.

4 Lawrence FitzGerald, *Java La Grande—the Portuguese Discovery of Australia*, The Publishers, Hobart, 1984, p. 108.

5 François Rabelais, *The Complete Works of François Rabelais*, trans. Donald M. Frame, University of California Press, Berkeley, 1991, p. 437.

6 Jean Parmentier, trans. David Beers Quinn in Helen Wallis, 'Java La Grande: the Enigma of the Dieppe Maps', in Glyndwr Williams and Alan Frost, eds, *Terra Australis to Australia*, Oxford University Press, Melbourne, 1988, p. 77.

7 R. H. Major, ed. 1859, *Early Voyages to Terra Australis, now called Australia: A collection of documents, and extracts from early manuscript maps, illustrative of the history of discovery on the coasts of that vast island, from the beginning of the sixteenth entury to the time of Captain Cook*, Hakluyt Society, London, 1859, Introduction, p. v.

8 Cornelis Wytfliet, legend on his world map *Discriptionis Ptolemaicae Augmentum* in *ibid.*, Introduction, p. lxix.

CHAPTER 7

1 Pigafetta, *op. cit.*, p. 57.

2 Andrés de Urdaneta, 'Colección de documentos inéditos relativos al descubrimiento, conquista y organización de las antiguas posesiones españolas de ultramar, Secunda Serie, Madrid, 1864–1932, II, 109–110' in Nicholas P. Cushner, *Spain in the Philippines from Conquest to Revolution*, Ateneo de Manila University, Quezon City, 1971, p. 40.

3 Andrés de Urdaneta, 'Urdaneta's Report' in *The Christianization of the Philippines.*, trans. Rafael Lopez, OSA, and Alfonso Felix, Jr., Historical Conservation Society, University of San Agustin, Manila, 1965, pp. 311–312.

4 Juan de Silva, Memorial to Urban VIII, 'The Franciscan Missionary Plan' in Kelly, *op. cit.*, p. 368.

5 *ibid.*

6 Juan Luis Arias de Loyola, Memorial in R. H. Major, ed., *op. cit.*, pp. 27–28.

7 Andrés de Urdaneta in *The Philippine Islands—1493–1898*, eds E. H. Blair and J. A. Robertson, Clark, Cleveland, 1903–1909, p. 34.

8 Juan Luis Arias de Loyola, *op. cit.*, p. 20.

9 *ibid.*, p. 3.

10 Robert Langdon, *The Lost Caravel*, Pacific Publications, Sydney, 1975.

11 Roger Hervé in Jorge Berguño, 'The South and Mid-Pacific Voyages' in Hardy and Frost, eds, *European Voyaging*, p. 27.

12 Robin J. Watt, Cultural and Forensic Specialist, Wellington, NZ, in correspondence with the author 8 May 1995.

13 Robin J. Watt, 'The Myth of New Zealand's So-Called "Spanish Helmet"', *National Museum of New Zealand Records*, vol. 2, no. 11, 19 August 1983, pp. 133–136.

14 Juan de Iturbe, 'Sumario breve' in Celsus Kelly, OFM, ed., *La Austrialia del Espiritu Santo—the Journal of Fray Martín de Munilla, O.F.M. and other documents relating to the Voyage of Pedro Fernández de Quirós to the South Sea (1605–1606) and the Franciscan Missionary Plan (1617–1627)*, vol. 2, Hakluyt Society, Cambridge University Press, Cambridge, 1966, p. 276.

15 Pedro Fernández de Quirós, First Memorial to the King, in *ibid.*, p. 307.

16 Diego de Prado y Tovar, *op. cit.*, p. 165.

17 Luis Baéz de Torres, 'The Letter of Torres' in H. M. Stevens, ed., *New Light*, p. 231.

CHAPTER 8

1 Günter Schilder, 'From Secret to Common Knowledge: The Dutch Discoveries', *Studies from Terra Australis to Australia*, eds John Hardy and Alan Frost, Highland Press and the Australian Academy of the Humanities, Canberra, 1989, p. 72.

2 J. E. Heeres, *The Part Borne by the Dutch in the Discovery of Australia 1606–1765*, The Royal Dutch Geographical Society, London 1899, p. 4.

3 *ibid.*

4 *ibid.*, p. v.

5 *ibid.*, p. 7.

6 Willem C. Schouten, *op. cit.*, p. A.

7 J. P. Sigmond and L. H. Zuiderbaan, *Dutch Discoveries of Australia*, Rigby Ltd, Sydney, 1976, p. 32.

8 *ibid.*, p. 36.

9 Heeres, *op. cit.*, p. 11.

10 *ibid.*

11   Simon Dewez, 'Is This The First Printed Record Of The Dutch Discovery of Australia?', in *The Australian Antique Collector*, November 1996–April 1997, pp. 147–149.

12   Henricus Hondius 'India quae Orientalis dicitur, et Insulae Adiacentes', reproduced in T. M. Perry, *The Discovery of Australia—The Charts and Maps of the Navigators and Explorers*, Plate 11, Nelson, Melbourne, 1982, pp. 28–29.

13   Frederik de Houtman, letter to Prince Maurice in J. E. Heeres, *op. cit.*, p. 14.

14   *ibid.*

15   Jacob Dedel, letter in J. E. Heeres, *op, cit.*, p. 16.

16   Andrew Sharp, *The Discovery of Australia*, Clarendon Press, Oxford, 1963, p. 37.

17   Heeres, *op. cit.*, p. 13.

18   E. S. De Klerck, *History of the Netherlands East Indies*, vol. 1, W. L. & J. Brusse, Rotterdam, 1938, p. 226.

19   Heeres, *op. cit.*, p. 19.

20   Algemeen Rijksarchief, the Hague, VOC 850, ff.26–27v, in Schilder, 'From Secret to Common Knowledge', Hardy and Frost, eds, *Studies*, pp. 75–76.

21   Heeres, *op. cit.*, p. 20.

22   *ibid.* p. 34.

23   *ibid.*

24   *ibid.*, p. 23.

25   *ibid.*, p. 36.

26   *ibid.*

27   *ibid.*, p. 37.

28   *ibid.*, p. 41.

29   *ibid.*, p. 38.

30   Jan Carstensz, 'Journal', in *ibid.* p. 38.

31   *ibid.*

32   *ibid.*

33   Heeres, *op. cit.*, pp. 52–53.

34   *ibid.*, p. 52.

35   ARAKA 771, Batavias Brieff Boek lopende van 15 Januarij tot 29 November Anno 1644, No. 2, fol. 40 in Günter Schilder, *Australia Unveiled—The share of the Dutch navigators in the discovry of Australia*, trans. Olaf Richter, Theatrum Orbis Terrarum Ltd, Amsterdam 1976, p. 106.

36   Abel Janszoon Tasman, *Abel Janszoon Tasman's journal of his discovery of Van Diemens Land and New Zealand in 1642, with an*

English translation and facsimiles of original maps to which are added Life and Labours of Abel Janszoon Tasman by J. E. Heeres, Frederick Muller, Amsterdam, 1898, p. 106.

37 Estimate by Myra Stanbury, Curator, Marine Archaeology, Western Australian Maritime Museum, based on current value of silver and calculations of S. J. Wilson, *Doits to Ducatons, The Coins of the Dutch East India Company Ship* Batavia *Lost on the Western Australian Coast 1629*, Western Australian Museum, Perth, 1989.

38 Francisco Pelsaert, 'Journal' in Henrietta Drake-Brockman, *op. cit.*, p. 122.

39 *ibid.*, pp. 128–129.

40 *ibid.*, p. 129.

41 *ibid.*, p. 130.

42 *ibid.*

43 Gijsbert Bastiensz, 'Letter to his brethren', in Philippe Godard, *The First and Last Voyage of the* Batavia, Abrolhos Publishing, Perth, 1993, in Appendixes, p. 40.

44 David Blair, 'The First Imaginary Voyage to Australia', *Victorian Review*, 1 December 1882, vol. vii, no. 38, p. 199.

45 Willem Jansz, 'Letter to the Managers of the Amsterdam Chamber', in T. D. Mutch, *op. cit.*, p. 341.

46 *ibid.*

CHAPTER 9

1 Abel Janszoon Tasman, *Abel Janszoon Tasman's Journal*, Kovach, Los Angeles, 1965, Appendix E, p. 132.

2 *ibid.*, p. 134.

3 *ibid.*, p. 106.

4 *ibid.*, p. 12.

5 *ibid.*, p. 15.

6 Algemeen Rijksarchief, VOC 1142, ff. 7v. in Schilder, 'From Secret to Common Knowledge', Hardy and Frost, eds., *Studies*, p. 80.

7 Mutch, *op. cit.*, Note on p. 323.

8 *ibid.*, pp. 322–323.

9 *ibid.*, p. 322.

10 Algemeen Rijksarchief, VOC 1054, ff. 36–37 in Schilder, 'From Secret to Common Knowledge', Hardy and Frost, eds, *Studies*, p. 81.

11 Glyndwr Williams, 'New Holland to New South Wales: the English Approaches', Williams and Frost, eds, *op. cit.*, p. 117.

12 John Ogilby, *America*, London, 1671, p. 654, in *ibid.*, p. 119.

13 Samuel Volkerts, 'Journal' in J. E. Heeres, *Het Aandeel der Nederlanders in de Ontdekking van Australië 1606–1765* , Leyden, 1899, p. 76–80, in Sharp, *op. cit.*, p. 94.

14 Heeres, *op. cit.*, p. 81.

15 *ibid.*, p. 84.

16 *ibid.*

17 *ibid.*, p. 94.

18 *ibid.*

CHAPTER 10

1 Diego de Prado y Tovar, *op. cit.*, p. 101.

2 Perry, *op. cit.*, Plate 29, p. 63.

3 *ibid.*

4 *ibid.*, p. 62.

5 George-Louis Leclerc, Comte de Buffon, *Histoire et Théories de la Terre*, Paris, 1749, Art. VI, pp. 98–9, in Glyndwr Williams and Alan Frost, '*Terra Australis:* Theory and Speculation', Williams and Frost, eds, *op. cit.*, p. 28.

CHAPTER 11

1 John Dee, *The Great Volume of Famous and Rich Discoveries*, 1576, in Williams and Frost, '*Terra Australis:* Theory and Speculation', Williams and Frost, eds, *op. cit.*, p. 12.

2 O. H. K. Spate, *The Pacific since Magellan*, vol. I, *The Spanish Lake*, Australian National University Press, Canberra, 1979, p. 249.

3 William Shakespeare, *Twelfth Night* in *Shakespeare*, Hardin Craig. ed., Scott Foresman, Chicago, 1931, p. 459.

4 Glyndwr Williams, 'New Holland—the English Approach', in Hardy and Frost, eds, *Studies*, 1989, p. 85.

5 Peter Heylyn, *Cosmographie*, London 1657, in Williams and Frost, 'Terra Australis—Theory and Speculation', Williams and Frost, eds, *op. cit.*, p. 22,

6 Williams and Frost, '*Terra Australis*: Theory and Speculation', Williams and Frost, eds, *op. cit.*, p. 19.

7 William Dampier, *Dampier's Voyages*, vol. 1, ed. John Masefield, E. Grant Richards, London, 1906, p. 450.

8 *ibid.*, p. 452.

9 *ibid.*, p. 453.

10 *ibid.*, p. 457.

11 *ibid.*

12 Dampier, *A New Voyage around the World*, vol. 1, James and John Knapton, 1729, p. 469.

13 *ibid.*, p. 447.

14 John Evelyn, *Diary and Correspondence of John Evelyn, F. R. S., to which is subjoined the Private Correspondence between King Charles I. and Sir Edward Nicholas, and between Sir Edward Hyde, afterwards Earl of Clarendon, and Sir Richard Browne.* ed. William Bray, vol. II, Henry G. Bohn, London, 1859, p. 363.

15 William Dampier, *A Voyage to New Holland*, ed. James Spencer, Allan Sutton, Gloucester, 1981, p. 148.

16 Dampier, *Dampier's Voyages*, p. 148.

17 Dampier, *A Voyage to New Holland*, p. 110.

18 *ibid.*, p. 122.

19 Glyndwr Williams, 'New Holland to New South Wales: the English Approaches' in Williams and Frost, eds, *op. cit.*, p. 140.

20 *ibid.*

21 Alexander Dalrymple, *An Account of the Discoveries made in the South Pacifick Ocean*, Australian National Maritime Museum and Horden House, Sydney, 1996, p. 91.

22 *ibid.*, p. 94.

23 *ibid.*, p. 101.

24 'Instructions to Captain Cook for His First Voyage, July 1768' in ed. M. Clark, *Sources of Australian History*, Oxford University Press, London, 1957, p. 38.

25 James Cook, *Captain Cook's Journal during his First Voyage round the World made in H. M. Bark "Endeavour" 1768–1771*, Elliot Stock, London, 1893, Facsimile Edition, 1968, ed. W. J. L. Wharton, p. 226.

26 *ibid.*

27 *ibid.*, p. 228.

28 Cook, *op. cit.*, p. 213.

29 *ibid.*

30 Cook, *Captain Cook in Australia*, ed. A.W. Reed, A.H. and A. W. Reed, Wellington, 1969, p. 29.

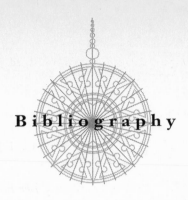

Bibliography

Augustine 1952, *The City of God*, trans Marcus Dods, Great Books of the Western World, vol. 18, Encyclopaedia Britannica, Chicago

Badger, Geoffrey 1988, *The Explorers of the Pacific*, Kangaroo Press, Sydney

Bagrow, Leo 1964, *History of Cartography*, rev. R. A. Skelton, C. A. Watts, London

Banks, Joseph 1962, *The Endeavour Journal of Joseph Banks, 1768–1771*, ed. J. C. Beaglehole, Trustees of the Library of New South Wales in association with Angus & Robertson, Sydney

Bassett, Jan, ed. 1995, *Great Southern Landings*, Oxford University Press, Melbourne

Blair, Emma Helen, and J. A. Robertson, eds. 1903–1909, *The Philippine Islands 1493–1803*, vol. 2, 1521–1569, Clark, Cleveland

Boxer, C. R. 1969, *The Portuguese Seaborne Empire 1415–1825*, Alfred A. Knopf, New York

Brissenden, Alan, and C. Higham, 1961, *They Came to Australia*, F. W. Cheshire, Melbourne

Camõens, Luis Vaz de 1952, *The Lusiads*, trans. William C. Atkinson, Penguin, Harmondsworth, UK

Cannon, Michael 1972, *The Exploration of Australia*, Reader's Digest, Sydney

Castlereagh, Duncan 1973, *The Great Age of Exploration, A History of Discovery and Exploration*, Aldus Books/Jupiter Books, London

Chau Ju-Kua 1966, *His Work on the Chinese and Arab Trade in the Twelfth and Thirteenth Centuries entitled Chu-fan-chi*, trans. Frederich Hirth and W. W. Rockhill Paragon Book Reprint Corp., New York

Clark, C. M. H. 1962, *A History of Australia I—From the Earliest Times to the Age of Macquarie*, Melbourne University Press, Melbourne

——ed. 1957, *Sources of Australian History*, Oxford University Press, London

Collingridge, George 1983, *The Discovery of Australia*, Facsimile Edition, Golden Press, Sydney

Cook, James 1968, *Captain Cook's Journal during his First Voyage Round the World made in H. M. Bark "Endeavour" 1768–1771*, Facsimile Edition, ed. W. J. L. Wharton, Eliot Stock, London, 1893

——1969, *Captain Cook in Australia*, ed. A. W. Reed, A. H. and A. W. Reed, Wellington

Crawford, I. M. 1968, *The Art of the Wandjina*, Oxford University Press, Melbourne

Crone, G. R. 1972 *The Discovery of the East*, Hamish Hamilton, London

Cushner, Nicholas P. 1971, *Spain in the Philippines—from Conquest to Revolution*, Ateneo de Manila University, Quezon City, Philippines

Dalrymple, Alexander 1770, *An Historical Collection of the Several Voyages and Discoveries in the South Pacifick Ocean*, Nourse, London

Dampier, William 1931, *A Voyage to New Holland*, ed. Clennell Wilkinson, Argonaut, London

——1981, *A Voyage to New Holland*, ed. James Spencer, Allan Sutton, Gloucester

——1906, *Dampier's Voyages*, vols. 1, 2, ed. John Masefield, E. Grant Richards, London

De Klerck, E. S. 1938, *History of the Netherlands East Indies*, vol. I, W. L. & J. Brusse, N. V., Rotterdam

Drake-Brockman, Henrietta 1965, *Voyage to Disaster: the Life of Francisco Pelsaert*, Angus & Robertson, Sydney

Duyker, Edward 1995, *An Officer of the Blue, Marc-Joseph Marion Dufresne, South Sea Explorer, 1724–1772*, Melbourne University Press, Melbourne

Emery, James 1973, *The Discovery of Australia*, Hamlyn Guides, Sydney

Evelyn, John 1859, *Diary and Correspondence of John Evelyn, F. R. S.* ed. William Brag, vol. II, Henry G. Bohn, London

FitzGerald, Lawrence 1984, *Java La Grande—The Portuguese Discovery of Australia*, The Publishers, Hobart

Flinders, Matthew 1966, *A Voyage to Terra Australis undertaken for the*

Purpose of completing the discovery of that vast country, and prosecuted in the years 1801, 1802, and 1803 in His Majesty's Ship The Investigator *and subsequently in the armed vessel* Porpoise *and* Cumberland *schooner with an account of the Shipwreck of the* Porpoise, *arrival of the* Cumberland *at Mauritius, and imprisonment of the commander during six years and a half in that island*, G. and W. Nicol, London 1814, vol. 2, Australiana Facsimile Editions No. 37, Libraries Board of Australia, Adelaide

Garran, Andrew, ed. 1886, *Picturesque Atlas of Australasia*, vols. 1, 2, 3, Picturesque Atlas Publishing Co., Melbourne

Gerritsen, Rupert 1994, *And Their Ghosts May Be Heard . . .*, Fremantle Arts Centre Press, Fremantle, WA

Gill, J. C. H. 1988, *The Missing Coast—Queensland Takes Shape*, Queensland Museum, Brisbane

Godard, Philippe 1993, *The First and Last Voyage of the* Batavia, Abrolhos Publishing, Perth

Grey, Sir George 1841, *Journals of Two Expeditions of Discovery in North-west and Western Australia During the Years 1837, 38 and 39*, vols. 1, 2, T. and W. Boone, London, Facsimile Edition, 1964

Hardy, John, and A. Frost, eds. 1990, *European Voyaging towards Australia*, Australian Academy of the Humanities, Canberra

——eds. 1980, *Studies from Terra Australis to Australia*, Australian Academy of the Humanities, Canberra

Heeres, Jan Ernst 1899, *The Part Borne by the Dutch in the Discovery of Australia 1606–1765*, Luzac & Co., London

Henderson, J. A. 1993, *Phantoms of the* Tryall—*Australia's First Shipwreck 1622*, St. George's Books, Perth

Hilder, Brett 1980, *The Voyage of Torres*, University of Queensland Press, Brisbane

Hyma, Albert 1953, *A History of the Dutch in the Far East*, George Wahr, Ann Arbor, Michigan

Jayne, K. G. 1910, *Vasco da Gama and His Successsors 1460–1590*, Methuen, London

Joy, William 1964, *The Explorers*, Shakespeare Head Press, Sydney

Kelly, Celsus 1965, *Calendar of Documents—Spanish Voyages in the South Pacific*, Franciscan Historical Studies, Madrid

——ed. 1966, *La Austrialia del Espíritu Santo—the Journal of Fray Martín de Munilla, O. F. M., and other documents relating to the voyage of Pedro Fernández de Quirós to the South Sea (1605–1606) and the Franciscan Missionary Plan (1617–1627)*, vol. 2, Hakluyt, Cambridge University Press, Cambridge

Kenny, John 1995, *Before the First Fleet, Europeans in Australia 1606–1777*, Kangaroo Press, Sydney

King, Voctor T. and A. V. M. Horton, *From Buckfast to Borneo—Essays presented to Father Robert Nicholl on the 85th Anniversary of his Birth 17 March 1995*, University of Hull, UK

Kippis, Andrew 1925, *Captain Cook's Voyages*, Alfred A. Knopf, New York

Langdon, Robert 1975, *The Lost Caravel*, Pacific Publications, Sydney

——1988, *The Lost Caravel Re-explored*, Brolga Press, Canberra

Laseron, Charles 1954, *Ancient Australia*, rev. R. O. Brunnschweiler 1984, Angus & Robertson, Melbourne

Lee, Ida 1925, *Early Explorers in Australia*, Methuen, London

Ley, C. D., ed. 1947, *Portuguese Voyages 1498–1663*, J. M. Dent, London

Linschoten, Jan Huyghen van 1970, *The Voyage of John Huyghen van Linschoten to the East Indies from the Old English Translation of 1598*, vol. I, Arthur Coke Burnell, ed., Burt Franklin, New York

Lloyd, Christopher 1966, *William Dampier*, Archon Books, Hamden, Connecticut

Loney, Jack 1981, *An Atlas History of Australian Shipwrecks*, A. H. & A. W. Reed, Sydney

Lopez, Rafael, and A. Felix, Jr, trans, 1965, *The Christianization of the Philippines*, Historical Conservation Society, University of San Augustín, Manila

Macknight, C. C., ed. 1969, *The Farthest Coast*, Melbourne University Press, Melbourne

——1976, *The Voyage to Marege*, Melbourne University Press, Melbourne

McIntyre, Kenneth G. 1977, *The Secret Discovery of Australia—Portuguese Ventures 200 Years before Captain Cook*, Souvenir Press, Medindie, SA

Major, R. H., ed. 1859, *Early Voyages to Terra Australis, now called Australia: A collection of documents from early manuscript maps, illustrative of the history of discovery on the coasts of that vast land, from the beginning of the sixteenth century to the time of Captain Cook*, Hakluyt Society, London

Marchant, Leslie R. 1982, *France Australe*, Artlook Books, Perth

Marques, A. H. de Oliveira 1972, *History of Portugal, vol. 1, From Lusitania to Empire*, Columbia University Press, New York

Martins, J. P. Oliveira 1914, *The Golden Age of Prince Henry the Navigator*, Chapman & Hall, London

Merrimen, Roger Bigelow 1962, *The Rise of the Spanish Empire in the Old World and in the New, vol. 3, The Emperor*, Cooper Square Publishers, New York

Morga, Antonio de 1971, *Sucesos de las Islas Filipinas*, trans. and ed., J. S. Cummins, Hakluyt, Cambridge

Morrison, Reg 1988, *Australia—the Four Billion Year Journey of a Continent*, Weldon, Sydney 1988; reprinted for Facts on File, Sydney, 1990.

Mulvaney, D. J. 1969, *The Prehistory of Australia*, London

Murdoch, Priscilla 1974, Duyfken *and the First Discoveries of Australia*, Antipodean Publishers, Sydney

Perry, T. M. 1982, *The Discovery of Australia*, Nelson, Melbourne

Petersen, Kai 1957, 1963, *Prehistoric Life on Earth*, Methuen, London

Pires, Tomé, and F. Rodrígues 1944, *The Suma Oriental of Tomé Pires and The Book of Francisco Rodrígues*, trans. Armando Cortesão, vol. 1, Hakluyt, London

Playford, Phillip 1996, *Carpet of Silver—The Wreck of the* Zuytdorp, University of Western Australia Press, Perth

Polo, Marco 1958, *The Travels of Marco Polo*, trans. Ronald Latham, Penguin, Harmondsworth, UK

Powell, Alan 1988, *Far Country—A Short History of the Northern Territory*, Melbourne University Press, Melbourne

Reader's Digest 1994, *Atlas of Australia*, Reader's Digest, Sydney

Reed, A. W., ed. 1969, *Captain Cook in Australia—Extracts from the journals of Captain James Cook, giving a full account in his own words of his adventures and discoveries in Australia*, A. H. & A. W. Reed, Auckland and Sydney

Rowan, Ellis 1898, *A Flower-hunter in Queensland and New Zealand*, Angus & Robertson, Sydney

Russell, W. Clark 1889, *William Dampier*, Macmillan, London

Saville-Kent, W. 1893, *The Great Barrier Reef of Australia: its products and potentialities*, W. H. Allen, London

Schilder, Günter 1976, *Australia Unveiled: The Share of the Dutch Navigators in the Discovery of Australia*, trans. O. Richter, Theatrum Orbis Terrarum, Amsterdam

Schurz, William Lytle 1959, *The Manila Galleons*, E. P. Dutton, New York

Scott, Ernest 1929, *A Short History of Australia*, Oxford University Press, London

Sharp, Andrew 1963, *The Discovery of Australia*, Clarendon Press, Oxford

Sigmond, J. P., and L. H. Zuiderbaan 1976, *Dutch Discoveries of Australia*, Rigby, Adelaide

Spate, O. H. K. 1983, *Monopolists and Freebooters, The Pacific since Magellan*, vol. II, Australian National University Press, Canberra

——1979, *The Spanish Lake, The Pacific since Magellan*, vol. I, Australian National University Press, Canberra

Stevens, H. M., ed. 1930, 1967, *New Light on the Discovery of Australia as Revealed by the Journal of Captain Don Diego de Prado y Tovar*, trans. George Barwick, Hakluyt, Nedeln/Liechtenstein

Stockdale, John Joseph 1812, *Sketches, civil and military, of the island of Java and its immediate dependencies: comprising interesting details of Batavia and authentic particulars of the celebrated poison tree*, 2nd edn, Stockdale, London

Subrahmanyam, Sanjay 1993, *The Portuguese Empire in Asia, 1500–1700: A Political and Economic History*, Longman, Harrow, Essex

Tasman, Abel Janszoon 1898, *Abel Janszoon Tasman's journal of his discovery of Van Diemens Land and New Zealand in 1642 with an English translation and facsimiles of original maps to which are added Life and Labours of Abel Janszoon Tasman by J. E. Heeres*, Frederik Muller & Co., Amsterdam

——1965, *Abel Janszoon Tasman's Journal of his Discovery of Van Diemen's Land and New Zealand in 1644, being photo-lithographic facsimile of the original maps to which are added Life and Labours of Abel Janszoon Tasman by J. E. Heeres, LL. D., Professor at the Dutch Colonial Institute Delft, and observations made with the compass on Tasman's voyage by Dr. W. van Bemmelen, Assistant Director of the Royal Meteorological Institute, Utrecht*, N. A. Kovach, Los Angeles

Thomson, J. Oliver 1965, *History of Ancient Geography*, Biblo and Tannen, New York

Thrower, Norman J. W., ed. 1984, *Sir Francis Drake and the Famous Voyage, 1577–1580, Essays commemorating the quadricentennial of Drake's circumnavigation of the Earth*, University of California Press, Berkeley

Tooley, Ronald Vere 1952, *Maps and Map-Makers*, Batsford, London

——1979, *Tooley's Dictionary of Mapmakers*, Map Collectors Publications, Tring, Hertfordshire, UK

Ure, John 1977, *Prince Henry the Navigator*, Constable, London

Vickers-Rich, Patricia, and T. Hewet-Rich 1993, *Wildlife of Gondwana*, Reed, Sydney

Vlekke, Bernard H. M. 1944, *Nusantara*, Harvard University Press, Cambridge

Ward, Russel 1992, *Concise History of Australia*, University of Queensland Press, Brisbane

Williams, Glyndwr, and A. Frost, eds. 1988, *Terra Australis to Australia*, Oxford University Press, Melbourne

Williams, Neville 1973, *Francis Drake*, Weidenfeld & Nicolson, London

Wilson, Derek 1989, *The Circumnavigators*, M. Evans & Co., New York

Wilson, S. J. 1989, *Doits to Ducatons—Coins of the Dutch East India Compny Ship* Batavia *Lost on the Western Australian Coast 1629*, Western Australian Museum, Perth

Wood, G. Arnold 1922, *The Discovery of Australia*, Macmillan, London

Wroth, Lawrence C. 1944, *The Early Cartography of the Pacific*, Papers of the Bibliographical Society of America, vol. 38, No. 2.

Yarrow, Stephen 1980, *We Discovered an Island*, Regency Print, Booragoon, WA

Zainu'ddin, Ailsa 1968 *A Short History of Indonesia*, Cassell Australia, Melbourne

RESEARCH REPORTS

Bickford, Anne, S. Blair, and P. Freeman 1988 'Ben Boyd National Park Bicentennial Project—Davidson Whaling Station—Boyd's Tower—Bittangabee Ruins', National Parks and Wildlife Service of NSW, Sydney, pp. 73–98.

Green, Jeremy 1977, 'Australia's Oldest Wreck: the Loss of the *Trial*, 1622', BAR Supplementary Series 27, British Archaeological Reports

Loney, Jack 1985, 'The Mahogany Ship', Neptune Press, Geelong

Pearson, Mike 1980, 'The Bittagabee Ruin—Who Built It?' National Parks and Wildlife Service of NSW, Sydney

Potter, Bill, ed. 1987, 'The Mahogany Ship—Relic or Legend?' Proceedings of the Second Australian Symposium on the Mahogany Ship. The Mahogany Ship Committee, Warrnambool, Vic.

Richardson, W. A. R. 1989, 'The Portuguese Discovery of Australia:

Fact or Fiction', Occasional Lecture Series, No. 3, National
Library of Australia, Canberra

Murray, Tim 1992, 'An Archaeological Perspective on the History of
Aboriginal Australia', Working Papers in Australian Studies,
Working Paper No. 80, University of London, London

Smith, Timothy, and W. Johnson 1993, 'Inspection of Possible
Maritime Related Relics Located near Milk Beach, Rose Bay',
Heritage Branch, NSW Department of Urban Affairs and
Planning, Sydney

Stanley, John 1992, 'The Search for the "Mahogany Ship"—a
Challenge for High Definition Geophysics', University of New
England, Armidale, NSW

JOURNALS

Blair, David, 1 Dec. 1882 'The First Imaginary Voyage to Australia',
Victorian Review, vol. VII, No. 38.

Boyd, W. E., et al. 1994 'The Suffolk Park Shipwreck, Northern
NSW: Pre-Cook Explorer or 19th Century Trader?' *Archaeology
in Oceania*, vol. 29, no. 2, pp. 91–4

Beaton, J. M. 1995, 'The Transition on the Coastal Fringe of Greater
Australia', 'Transitions' eds Jim Allen and James F. O'Connell,
Antiquity, vol. 69, Special number 265, pp. 799–806

Dewez, Simon 1997, 'Is This the First Printed Record of the Dutch
Discovery of Australia?', *The Australian Antique Collector*,
November 1996–April 1997, pp. 147–153.

Green, Jeremy 1990, 'New Information on South-east Asian Gun
Technology From Two Guns Found on Carronade Island, in the
North of Australia', *Ordnance Society Journal* , vol. 3, pp. 47–57

——1982, 'The Carronade Island Guns and Australia's Early Visitors',
*The Great Circle, Journal of the Australian Association for Maritime
History*, vol. 4, no. 2, pp. 73–83

Mira, W. J. 1993 'A Dutch and East African Coin "Find" from
Northern Australia', *The Journal of the Australian Numismatic
Society* 1993, pp. 50–58

Mutch, T. D. 1942 'The First Discovery of Australia', *Journal and
Proceedings of the Royal Australian Historical Society*, xviii, p. 308

Porch, Nick, and J. Allen 1995, 'Tasmania: Archaeological and
Palaeo-ecological Perspectives', 'Transitions', eds Jim Allen and

James F. O'Connell, *Antiquity*, vol. 69, Special number 265, pp. 714–732

Stokes, Evelyn 1970 'European Discovery of New Zealand before 1642', *New Zealand Journal of History*, vol. 4, no. 1, pp. 3–19

Wade, John 1977 'Shou Lao: A Chinese Figurine Excavated at Darwin in 1879' *Australian Society for Historical Archaeology Newsletter*, vol. 7, no. 2, pp. 15–16

Watt, Robin J. 1983 'The Myth of New Zealand's So-Called "Spanish Helmet"', *National Museum of New Zealand Records*, vol. 2, no. 11, pp. 131–137

Index

Index